KU-331-772

Perfect Pub Quiz

David Pickering, an English graduate of St Peter's College, Oxford, is an enthusiastic quiz team member as well as being an experienced reference book compiler, freelance since 1992. He has worked for many prestigious British and US reference publishers, contributing (often as sole author or chief editor) to around 200 books, most of them falling within the categories of general reference, English language, the arts, history, folklore, entertainment and popular interest. He has also broadcast many times on a variety of subjects on radio and television. He lives in Buckingham with his wife and two sons.

Other titles in the *Perfect* series

Perfect
Pub Quiz

David Pickering

BOOKS

Published by Random House Books 2007

12

Copyright © David Pickering 2007

David Pickering has asserted his right under the Copyright, Designs
and Patents Act 1988 to be identified as the author of this work

This book is sold subject to the condition that it shall not, by
way of trade or otherwise, be lent, resold, hired out, or otherwise
circulated without the publisher's prior consent in any form of
binding or cover other than that in which it is published and
without a similar condition, including this condition,
being imposed on the subsequent purchaser

First published in the United Kingdom in 2007 by
Random House Books

Random House Books
Random House, 20 Vauxhall Bridge Road,
London SW1V 2SA

www.randomhouse.co.uk

Addresses for companies within The Random House Group Limited
can be found at: www.randomhouse.co.uk/offices.htm

The Random House Group Limited Reg. No. 954009

A CIP catalogue record for this book
is available from the British Library

ISBN 9781905211692

Typeset by Palimpsest Book Production Limited, Grangemouth, Stirlingshire

Penguin Random House is committed to a sustainable future for
our business, our readers and our planet. This book is made from
Forest Stewardship Council® certified paper.

Printed and bound in Great Britain by Clays Ltd, St Ives plc

Contents

The author would like to acknowledge the help he has received from fellow members of the Periodicals quiz team, drawn from members of the Old Gaolers Drama Group, and to all others involved in the quizzes contested at the Whale Pub in Buckingham. He would also like to thank Sophie Lazar and Emily Rhodes at Random House Books for their patient assistance.

While every effort has been made to ensure that the information contained in this book is accurate, there must always remain the possibility of there being the odd inaccuracy, which the author humbly acknowledges as entirely his own fault.

Introduction

The pub quiz has become an established feature of modern social life. Thousands of people make a regular journey, rain or shine, to their local for the evening to pit their knowledge against their fellows while enjoying a drink or two in convivial surroundings. Added to these jolly but competitive gatherings are the countless family and other social occasions on which people of all ages pass an hour or two testing their individual or combined knowledge by attempting a quiz of some description, whether it be in the form of a board game or a list of questions in a magazine, newspaper or a book like this one.

The quizzes in this book include a huge variety of types of question, varying from straightforward tests of general knowledge to multiple choice and true-or-false posers. Each quiz begins and ends with a pot luck round covering a random selection of themes and is completed by two specialist rounds as well as by half-time teasers and jackpot questions. Subjects covered in the specialist rounds include all manner of topics, from current affairs, history, the arts and culture to science and nature, sport, entertainment, people and places. Easier questions are mixed in with harder ones, meaning that everyone has a chance of knowing an answer, regardless of age and ability. Later on in this section you will find suggestions for diverting interval rounds, and as well as the 100 general mixed quizzes there are a further 10 themed quizzes designed for use on special dates through the year.

How to use this book

This book is virtually unique in offering a complete quiz of 42 questions on each double-page spread. Quizmasters may choose to deliver the quizzes as presented, complete with half-time teaser and jackpot questions and perhaps with the addition of their own interval round, or else select rounds from different quizzes and compile their own combination of questions. Of course, there is absolutely no reason why enthusiastic quiz players should not use the book simply to test their own knowledge to their own satisfaction or to brush up their question-answering skills for future quizzes.

Half-time teasers

After the first two rounds, the teams are presented with a half-time teaser, which is designed to be used as a tie-breaker in the event that one or more teams finish with the same total. It will be noted that these questions generally have quantitative answers in which the winners are those who get closest to the solution (this makes the chance of an outright winner more likely).

Jackpot questions

The hardest questions are reserved for the jackpot round (though some are easier than others, and a question is only hard if you don't know the answer). There are various ways in which the jackpot question can be used. It can be employed to settle the final result of the quiz should the half-time teaser fail to produce a winner or, alternatively, it can be offered to the team that has won the basic quiz (as decided if necessary by the result of the half-time teaser): if the winning team gets the jackpot question right they win a pot of cash built up over the weeks or some other extra prize over and above what they win for the quiz itself. This system offers the exciting possibility of a fairly impressive sum being contested at the jackpot stage if no team has managed to answer the jackpot for several weeks.

Fascinating facts

Another unique feature of this book is the addition of a fascinating fact relating to one question in each quiz. Indicated by an asterisk (✳) after the question, such glosses are designed purely for the enjoyment and elucidation of quizmaster and contestants alike. If the sharing of such priceless information allows the quizmaster to look much cleverer and well informed than he or she really is, this is entirely intentional!✳

> ✳ Did you know, for instance, that the word 'quiz' came about as the result of a bet? When the eighteenth-century Irish theatre manager James Daly was wagered that he could not make a new word catch on in a single day, he travelled all over Dublin writing the mysterious word 'quiz' on walls – with the result that soon everyone was talking about it and the word itself entered the language.

Adding your own touches

The number of questions in the typical pub quiz varies. Most tend to comprise between 40 and 50 questions, which may take from around an hour to an hour and a half to go through, at a pleasantly relaxed pace. Quizzes in this book include 40 questions each, together with the extra half-time teasers and jackpot questions, so there remains ample opportunity for the quizmaster, if he or she wishes, to insert a round of their own devising, perhaps when the quiz reaches the halfway stage.

The interval round provides the quizmaster with the opportunity of expanding the range of questions for the evening by introducing a set of self-compiled questions that may have particular relevance to the locality or other context in which the quiz is taking place. Alternatively, these questions may deal with current affairs or topical issues that inevitably cannot be covered in a book such as this.

Points won during this round may be added to the overall total, or else treated separately and rewarded (at the quizmaster's discretion) with a special prize.

There are numerous alternatives for interval rounds, but the following pages suggest just a few ideas that might inspire quizmasters to think about adding a round or two of their own devising.

Current affairs quiz rounds

Although every effort has been made to introduce plenty of recent material in questions for this book, quiz teams are usually surprised and entertained to be asked questions about events that have taken place in the last few weeks, days or even hours. Ideas for possible questions on such diverse topics as politics, sport, gossip, television and the royal family quickly suggest themselves from a cursory read of the day's newspapers or through other branches of the media. Ten carefully chosen questions on current affairs arranged on the pattern of other rounds in this book are sure to go down well.

Local knowledge quiz rounds

Quiz teams always enjoy and appreciate questions that relate to the place where they live. Such questions are beyond the scope of this book, but may prove a very popular choice for interval rounds. Consider compiling a round of 10 questions that test the local knowledge of those present – but try not to get too bogged down in questions that focus primarily on local history: there are many other kinds of questions that may be asked about the typical town or village, as the following suggestions indicate.

What is the name of the river that flows through the town?
In which year did the town receive its charter?
What is the name of the current mayor?
Which school stands at [location]?
What would you buy at [name of local store]?
Which road connects [name of local landmark] and [name of local landmark]?
Whose statue stands in [location]?
What disaster befell the people of the town in [date]?
Which [animal, symbol, etc.] is featured on the town crest?
Which celebrity was born in [local place]?
What is the name of our twin town in [country]?

Which day of the week is market day?
Which family built [name of stately home, monument, etc.]?
Which king or queen stayed in the town in [date]?
Which pub is located in [name of street]?
How much is the hourly charge in [local car park]?
What colour strip does the town's football team play in?
Which king said of the town '[famous quote]'?
What is the number of the road leading to [neighbouring town]?
Which building in [name of street] is said to be haunted?
In which US state is there a town that shares the same name?
What might you do at [address of library, gym, swimming pool, etc.]?
Which of the following is nearer – [name of town] or [name of town]?
How far is it to the sea – [offer choice of three distances]?
How many banks have branches in the town?

Music quiz rounds

One of the most popular of optional interval rounds is the music quiz round. Indeed, many pubs host whole evenings devoted to music questions, which may vary from straightforward questions about music and musicians of all kinds to challenges to identify excerpts of particular songs or other musical works. One relatively easy option for the quizmaster wishing to do this would be to extract the musical questions in this book and reassemble them in an all-music quiz.

Perhaps the most entertaining way to organise an interval music round is to record the opening notes or bars of a piece of music and then challenge teams to identify the piece and the performers or composer (or even all three). Alternatively, vary the formula by asking for the year in which it was released, or reached number one, etc. In many cases it is possible to play the whole opening verse of a song before the chorus gives the game away. In others, a single note provides a sufficient clue (for instance, the opening chord of 'Hard day's night' by the Beatles). Preparing such a round may be fairly time-consuming, and organising something to play the clips on may be an issue, but the result usually makes the effort worth while.

Picture quiz rounds

Another great favourite is the picture quiz round, which can take a number of different forms. One that goes down particularly well is the challenge to identify pictures of celebrities of various kinds, disguised by showing only part of their face, showing the person in an out-of-character context or at an odd angle or even with a beard and moustache being drawn on the photograph. All the quizmaster needs to do is find suitable pictures of 10 or more well-known people, cut them out as desired and then paste them on to a piece of paper, number them, and photocopy the sheet for all the teams attending, who must match each number with the correct name. The process is even easier using a computer.

Alternative versions of the picture quiz round might involve teams identifying places (perhaps in the town where they live) from pictures of distinctive architectural details, etc. Particularly ambitious quizmasters may like to compile sets of three or four pictures and challenge teams to identify the link between them (for instance, pictures of a red squirrel, a football player wearing red, a Red Army flag and Mick Hucknall of the pop group Simply Red – 'red' being the link).

Atlas rounds

There are many imaginative optional rounds that a quizmaster can construct based on photocopied pages from an atlas (preferably one that presents just outlines of countries etc. and little written information). These may relate to the whole world, a continent or just a single country, such as the UK. The teams may then be challenged to identify marked countries, towns, islands, mountains, seaside resorts, rivers, or a host of other features. Alternatively, draw a line between two locations in different parts of the world and challenge the teams to identify all the countries, states or counties that a person would go through if flying directly between the two places (a line taking in the newer countries of south-east Europe or the states of the central USA would certainly test most teams).

Name the year rounds

'Name the Year' rounds are an alternative for interval rounds with which most quiz teams will be familiar. The usual option is to list three contrasting events of major or minor importance and challenge teams to guess the year. To make things a little easier, the quizmaster might offer leeway of a year either side.

Quotation rounds

Quotation rounds are a popular choice, especially if the quotations themselves are humorous or surprising in some way. There are various ways in which each question may be asked: teams may have to identify the person who said it, the work or context in which they said it – or even how the quotation ends. Here are some examples, with the answers in brackets.

Who said 'Some people think football is a matter of life and death – I can assure them it is much more serious than that'? (Bill Shankly)

What did Ronald Knox call 'A loud noise at one end and no sense of responsibility at the other'? (a baby)

Complete the musical quotation 'Prove to me that you're no fool –' ('– walk across my swimming-pool')

Of whom did Lyndon Johnson say 'He played too much football without a helmet'? (Gerald Ford)

Who said 'Work is the curse of the drinking classes'? (Oscar Wilde)

Which nation was summed up by Margaret Mahy as 'Americans with no Disneyland'? (Canadians)

Complete the quotation 'Never give a sucker –'? ('– an even break')

What did Samuel Johnson call 'The triumph of hope over experience'? (marriage)

Who did Lady Caroline Lamb call 'Mad, bad and dangerous to know'? (Lord Byron)

Who said 'I don't want to achieve immortality through my work – I want to achieve it through not dying'? (Woody Allen)

Matching pairs rounds

These rounds comprise two lists of items that teams have to match up correctly. The difficulty of such rounds is up to the quizmaster. Teams may find it relatively easy to match famous husbands and wives or inventions with inventors, for instance, but much harder to pair up car models with manufacturers or battles with the wars they occurred in. The possibilities are endless – teams may be asked to pair sports teams with their nicknames, football teams with their grounds, artists with masterpieces, singers with hit songs, comedians with their partners, film stars with films, detectives with their assistants, sailors with their ships, people with their animals, companies with their logos, etc. etc. etc.

Running a quiz

To run a successful pub quiz, more is required than just a set of questions and answers (as provided by this book). Having found a venue, the potential quizmaster should negotiate with the landlord or landlady how best to set things up, ensuring that there is sufficient space for everyone, an adequate sound system and agreement about any prizes on offer to the winning team. Big prizes are not essential, but they add to the attraction and most pubs offer a small cash prize to the winning team (perhaps the total raised from the modest entry fees paid by each person taking part). Alongside this main prize, many pubs – bearing in mind the extra custom a quiz can bring in on an otherwise quiet night of the week – are happy to contribute a small sum to act as a jackpot (which will build up steadily over the weeks until someone wins it).

Managing teams

It is advisable to restrict team numbers to five or six people, if only because it may be difficult to get more than this round one table. The teams themselves will need to be supplied with sheets upon which to write their answers, as well as with pens or pencils: a sample answer sheet suitable for photocopying may be found at the end of this book. Each team must choose a name and write this on their answer sheet. Quizmasters must make sure that all the teams understand the way the quiz will work. Contestants should be reminded that cheating is not allowed, and that the use of mobile phones during the quiz is frowned upon. Above all, everyone must understand that the decision of the quizmaster, right or wrong, is final.

Scoring

The easiest way to score is to reward each correct answer with one point, the total being calculated after all the answers are announced at the end of the evening. Quizmasters may, of course, elect to award double points for their own interval rounds if they so wish. One option is to tot up scores after each round, as this can increase the tension as teams see how they are faring against each other. This also works best if jokers are to be employed (a joker being the option of each team to choose one round in which every correct answer they give is rewarded with double points). When totting up points at the end, incidentally, it can be advisable to get teams to swap answer sheets and to double-check the winning sheet before announcing the final result.

Perfect
Pub Quiz

Quiz 1

....

Round 1: Pot Luck

1 Which is the longest river in the world?
2 What is the national emblem of Canada?
3 What is the correct collective noun for a group of crows?
4 Which one of the following is not the name of a town in the USA – Boring, Odd or Splatt?
5 What does the acronym 'nimby' stand for?
6 Which English town boasts a 600-year-old church steeple that is famously bent and twisted?
7 What do the initials 'BOLTOP' mean when written on the back of a love letter?
8 Which British football team play at the Stadium of Light?
9 What is a sequoia?
10 In cockney rhyming slang, what would you get if you ordered an 'Al Pacino'?

....

Round 2: Books

1 What were the first names of the three Brontë sisters?
2 Which crime writer created private detective Philip Marlowe?
3 What did the P. G. in the name of comic novelist P. G. Wodehouse stand for?
4 Who were Athos, Porthos and Aramis?
5 In the novel by James Fenimore Cooper, who was the last of the Mohicans?
6 Allan Quatermain appears as the central character in which classic Victorian adventure story?
7 Who was the author of *The Secret Garden*?
8 What was the real name of The Scarlet Pimpernel in the novel of the same name published by Baroness Orczy in 1905?
9 What was the name of the skipper of the whaling ship *Pequod* in Herman Melville's novel *Moby-Dick*?
10 Who wrote *Chitty-Chitty-Bang-Bang*?

....

Half-time teaser

Cambodian has the largest alphabet of all the world's languages – how many letters does it have?

....

Round 3: Pets

1 What was the name of Martin Crane's dog in the long-running US television comedy series *Frasier*?
2 John Lennon had a cat called Mozart – true or false?
3 Who invented the cat-flap?
4 When were hamsters first domesticated – 1730, 1830 or 1930?
5 Which of the following has never been kept as a pet by a president of the USA: an ostrich, a hyena or an alligator?✶
6 Who owned a parrot called Captain Flint?
7 Where were goldfish first bred?
8 What is a female ferret called?
9 What kind of animal was the subject of Michael Jackson's 1972 hit 'Ben'?
10 Owning a pet has been proved to raise a person's IQ – true or false?

Round 4: Pot Luck

1 Which is the largest island in the world?
2 If you are mad, what kind of animal do you have in your belfry?
3 With what weapon was Russian revolutionary Leon Trotsky assassinated in Mexico City in 1940?
4 Which Victorian architect designed the Houses of Parliament?
5 What is the name of the stone in Ireland that is said to confer gifts of speaking upon anyone who kisses it?
6 In Britain's pre-decimal coinage, which coin had the nickname 'half a dollar'?
7 By what other name is the mountain ash commonly known?
8 What is the correct spelling of 'rhythm'?
9 What do the initials SWAT in SWAT team stand for?
10 What was the name of the snail in *The Magic Roundabout*?

Jackpot

In American slang, what is a 'hoosegow'?

✶ Other pets kept by US presidents have included a pygmy hippo (Calvin Coolidge), an elephant (James Buchanan) and a cow (William Taft).

Quiz 2

Round 1: Pot Luck
1 Which is the world's largest living mammal?
2 By what name was the general reawakening of culture and the arts that took place in late-medieval Europe known?
3 Which country lies immediately to the east of the Czech Republic?
4 How did the mythological monster called the basilisk kill its victims?
5 To which official post was Jacqueline Wilson appointed in 2005?
6 On which island did the mutineers from the *Bounty* eventually settle?
7 In which city is Strangeways prison?
8 Is a Tasmanian devil a carnivorous marsupial, a whirlwind or a cocktail?
9 Who composed the New World Symphony?
10 Whose hits included 'Bootylicious', 'Lose my breath' and 'Say my name'?

Round 2: Creepy-crawlies
1 Which food colouring is made from dried, crushed insects?
2 What insect-related name is given to the notion in chaos theory that a small event in one part of a system can have a major effect elsewhere?
3 What is apiology the study of?
4 What is the name of the world's heaviest beetle?
5 A leatherjacket is the larval form of which insect?
6 Which crop is damaged by Colorado beetles?
7 Which kind of animal inspired Robert the Bruce to try again?
8 Does a grasshopper have two, five or twelve eyes?
9 Who composed the operas *Tosca* and *Madame Butterfly*?
10 Who was 'the Wasp of Twickenham'?

Half-time teaser
Up to and including George W. Bush, how many US presidents have been Republicans?

Round 3: London

1 By what name is the Millennium Wheel also known?
2 Which London bridge is the furthest downstream?
3 Which London postal area has the postcode W1? ✶
4 Which monumental structure stands where the Mall leads into Trafalgar Square?
5 Which London fish market closed in 1982 after 700 years, only to be reopened elsewhere three days later?
6 Where is the centre of London, from which distances to other places are measured?
7 Which is London's oldest football club?
8 On which London road do Madame Tussaud's and the Planetarium stand?
9 Where in London would you find St Stephen's Tower and the Victoria Tower?
10 Where did Dick Whittington turn on hearing the City of London's bells?

Round 4: Pot Luck

1 Which wartime German code was broken by British mathematicians at Bletchley Park?
2 Whose books included *The Old Devils* and *Jake's Thing*?
3 Where does UNESCO have its headquarters?
4 Which television soap opera is set in Capeside, Massachusetts?
5 In football, what name is given to the shot in which a player kicks the ball back over his head while facing away from the goal?
6 According to the proverb, what should you save your breath for?
7 Which member of the British royal family was informally known as Dickie?
8 Which Australian tennis player won nine Wimbledon Men's Doubles titles between 1993 and 2004?
9 Who wanted you to save your kisses for them in 1976?
10 By what name is Marshall Mathers better known?

Jackpot

Pete Sampras won the Men's Singles title at Wimbledon every year from 1993 to 2000, except for 1996, when it was won by whom?

✶ The first London postcodes were introduced by Sir Rowland Hill as early as the 1850s. The rest of Britain did not follow until the 1960s.

Quiz 3

Round 1: Pot Luck

1 Whose catchphrases include 'Eat my shorts'?
2 What did the abbreviation ANZAC stand for?
3 In which war was the Battle of Edgehill fought?
4 In which Shakespeare play does the stage direction 'Exit, pursued by a bear' appear?
5 Who is the patron saint of lost causes?
6 Which British soap opera was first broadcast on 19 February 1985?
7 What kind of animal is a spotted wobbegong?
8 In cockney rhyming slang, what is a 'country cousin'?
9 Which is the largest lake in the world?
10 Which two bodies of water are linked by the Straits of Magellan?

Round 2: Music

1 What was Frank Sinatra's middle name?
2 Who returned to the top of the charts after a 29-year-gap in 2006 with 'Thunder in my heart'?
3 What was Beethoven's only opera called?
4 Which pirate radio station first broadcast from a ship in the North Sea on 29 March 1964?
5 By what name is Harold Webb better known?
6 How did soul singer Otis Redding die?
7 Who topped the charts with 'Black coffee' in 2000?
8 What is the literal meaning of the Japanese word *karaoke*?
9 Who wrote the music for 'Onward, Christian soldiers'?
10 Who became Master of the Queen's Music in 2004?

Half-time teaser

The Andes, the longest mountain range in the world, extends for how many miles?

Round 3: Nicknames

1 Who acquired the nickname 'the Animated Meringue'?
2 Which football club have the nickname 'the Toffees'? ✳
3 Which US city has the nickname 'Motown'?
4 Who became known as 'the Comeback Kid'?
5 By what nickname did Iraqi General Ali Hassan al-Majid become widely known?
6 Which British political leader was sometimes referred to as 'Tina'?
7 What is the traditional nickname of *The Times* newspaper?
8 Which business tycoon was known as 'the Bouncing Czech'?
9 Who was attacked in the US press as 'Hanoi Jane'?
10 Who became known as 'Doctor Death'?

Round 4: Pot Luck

1 According to the Bible, how old was Noah when he died?
2 Where is the headquarters of Interpol?
3 Which of Tchaikovsky's symphonies is known as the *Pathétique*?
4 In 2000 Michael Caine won the Oscar for Best Actor for which film?
5 In which castle was Edward II murdered?
6 In cookery, what does the term *al forno* mean?
7 Who was the Greek hero who fell in love with his own reflection?
8 Which US state has among its nicknames Old Dominion and Mother of Presidents?
9 Which chemical takes its name from the island of Cyprus?
10 Upon whose life was the film *Citizen Kane* loosely based?

Jackpot

What do you call a curve formed by cutting a right circular cone with a plane parallel to the sloping side of the cone?

✳ The nickname referred to the toffees that were sold to early fans of the team from a nearby sweet shop by a woman known as Old Ma Bushell. Competition from the black-and-white striped mints made by the rival Mother Nobletts Toffee Shop encouraged Old Ma Bushell to seek permission to sell toffees inside the club's ground.

Quiz 4

Round 1: Pot Luck

1 How were George V and Kaiser Wilhelm II related?
2 When does the grouse shooting season begin?
3 How many lines are there in a sonnet?
4 During the war years, which London theatre boasted 'We never close'?
5 Where is the Tomb of the Unknown Soldier in Paris?
6 Who wrote *The Owl Service*?
7 Who was the Norse god of mischief?
8 By what other name is the yeti of the Himalayas known?
9 Whose hits included 'Hey Mamma', 'Shut up' and 'Where is the love'?
10 What colour is malachite?

Round 2: Mountains

1 What is the highest mountain in the Alps called?
2 In which country are the Sierra Madre mountain ranges?
3 High Willhays is the highest point of which moorland?
4 In which mountain range would you find Ben Nevis?
5 Which European mountain was first climbed by Edward Whymper in 1865?
6 Which mountains in south-western Syria were occupied by Israel in 1967?
7 What is the highest point of the Peak District called?
8 The Great Saint Bernard Pass connects which two countries?
9 Which mountain range begins in the Alps and ends in the Ukraine?
10 Annapurna is situated in which country?

Half-time teaser

For how many seconds did the first powered flight by the Wright Brothers last?

Round 3: Nursery Rhymes

1 Which nursery rhyme character went to Gloucester?
2 What did Georgie Porgie do when the boys came out to play?
3 Where was Little Boy Blue?
4 Which nursery rhyme character lost her pocket?
5 What was Jack Sprat's wife unable to eat?
6 Who pulled pussy out of the well?
7 On which day of the week was Solomon Grundy married?
8 Who killed Cock Robin?
9 Which nursery rhyme was supposedly inspired by the plague?
10 Where did Mary's little lamb follow her to?

Round 4: Pot Luck

1 Which historical event was depicted in the films *Saving Private Ryan* and *The Longest Day*?
2 Who did it his way in 1969?
3 Cars from which European country bear the letter S?
4 What kind of animal lives in a formicary?
5 What is the name of the Indian doctor who gets into trouble on a trip to the Marabar Caves in E. M. Forster's *A Passage to India*?
6 Which late medieval prophet is said to have prophesied such future events as the French Revolution and the rise of Adolf Hitler?
7 Who wrote *The Carpet People*, *Hogfather* and *Mort*?
8 What is Wardour Street in London a centre of?
9 By what name is Oswald Cobblepot known in the *Batman* stories and films?
10 Which war was recorded in photographs by Mathew Brady?

Jackpot

Only one person out of a population of 26,000 survived the volcanic explosion that destroyed St Pierre on Martinique in 1902 – where was he at the time?

✶ 'Yeh-the' means 'the thing' in the Sherpa language.

Quiz 5

Round 1: Pot Luck

1 Who, when asked why he wanted to climb Everest, answered 'Because it's there'?
2 Which side did Bulgaria, Hungary and Romania fight on in World War II?
3 How, in 1997, did the authorities in Kelantan, Malaysia, dissuade courting couples from kissing in cinemas?
4 What does the ancient Celtic word 'boggart' refer to?
5 Which slab of rock, now in the British Museum, proved the key to understanding Egyptian hieroglyphics?
6 Who returned to music after a 20-year break in 2005 with the album *Aerial*?
7 Which king lost his crown jewels in the Wash?
8 Who, at a UN party in 2004, shook hands with the controversial Robert Mugabe of Zimbabwe before realising who he was?
9 Of which organisation was Stella Rimington head?
10 Which masterpiece by Norwegian expressionist Edvard Munch was stolen by thieves in 1994?

Round 2: Sport and Leisure

1 Which football team has the nickname 'the Biscuitmen'?
2 What was remarkable about Olympic marathon winner Abebe Bikila?
3 Who won the Wimbledon singles title on his first and only attempt?
4 In which sports do participants compete for Doggett's Coat and Badge?
5 Who became the youngest world heavyweight champion?
6 In which sport is 'laundry' a technical term?
7 What number does the bingo call 'two fat ladies' refer to?
8 Which British driver finished third in his very first Formula One race in 2007?
9 Who, in 2006, emulated her mother by winning the BBC Sports Personality of the Year award?
10 What colour is the centre of the target in archery?

Half-time teaser

How long does it take light from the Sun to reach the Earth?

Round 3: Royalty

1 Who completely lost his head on 30 January 1649?
2 Who was the last ruler of Britain who could not speak English?
3 Who was beheaded at Fotheringay Castle in 1587?
4 By what name did Edward, Prince of Wales become known after his death in 1376?
5 What did the wives of Henry IV, William III and George V have in common?
6 How many times had Wallace Simpson been married before she became involved with Edward VIII?
7 According to Shakespeare, which English king offered his kingdom for a horse?
8 What was Queen Victoria's first name?
9 Who was the Sun King?
10 What unusual feature did the newly born Richard III, Napoleon Bonaparte and Julius Caesar have in common?

Round 4: Pot Luck

1 What is taught at the Slade School in London – art, engineering or rock music?
2 Which famous New York square is located at the intersection of Seventh Avenue, 42nd Street and Broadway?
3 What is a Bath Oliver?
4 Apart from Edward V and Lady Jane Grey, who was the only other English monarch never to have a coronation?
5 For what television programme was 'I'll be there for you' the theme tune?
6 Which coin disappeared from use in the UK in 1984?
7 Who flew Thunderbird 1?
8 Who was Dirk McQuickly in the Rutles?
9 What alcoholic drink is made from juniper berries?
10 'Edelweiss' is the national anthem of Austria – true or false?

Jackpot

Which Soviet leader was the first to visit Disneyland in California?

*The television cookery programme *Two Fat Ladies* borrowed its title from the bingo call. The two fat ladies who presented the programme even had a motorbike with the registration number TFL 88.

Quiz 6

Round 1: Pot Luck

1 Which city is sometimes nicknamed 'the Smoke'?
2 Which Polish opposition movement founded in 1980 was led by Lech Walesa?
3 Who invited you to come as you are in 1992?
4 What did the British government nationalise on New Year's Day 1948?
5 Who became the first footballer in England to be paid £100 a week?
6 What word describes a holy war waged by Muslims against unbelievers?
7 Who defeated Edward II at Bannockburn?
8 Where is the Scottish Grand National run?
9 After whom was the US state of Virginia named?
10 Who released an album called *Jagged Little Pill*?

Round 2: Money

1 Which type of animal comes in money, house and trapdoor varieties?
2 How many sides are there to a 20 pence coin?
3 Who released an album called *Billion Dollar Babies*?
4 Whose legs were allegedly insured for one million dollars?
5 John F. Kennedy does not feature on any dollar bill -- true or false?
6 Which millionaire did Leonardo DiCaprio play in *The Aviator*?
7 In which country is the bolivar the main unit of currency?
8 Which president appears on a US one dollar bill?
9 In which year (to within a year either side) was the one pound coin introduced in the UK?
10 In which country can you buy things with a dong?

Half-time teaser

What was the top speed on the first car speedometers?

Round 3: Indoor Games

1 How many counters does each player have in backgammon?
2 Boston, Michigan, Old Maid and Pope Joan are all names of what?
3 In bingo, which number may be announced as 'droopy drawers'?
4 Which chess player was the last to hold the world championship for the USA?
5 There are six weapons in Cluedo – a knife, a revolver, a lead pipe, a rope, a candlestick and what else?
6 How many tiles are there in a game of dominoes?
7 Which Chinese game involves the use of 144 tiles?
8 Which classic board game was invented by a heating engineer called Charles Darrow?
9 Which company makes Scrabble?
10 In what deck of cards would you find cups and swords?

Round 4: Pot Luck

1 In which Shakespeare play do Antonio, Gobbo and Portia appear?
2 Dalmatian dogs are born all black – true or false?
3 Scurvy is a consequence of a lack of which vitamin?
4 Which French word is used by English speakers to indicate a small amount or hint of something?
5 Who won the English Derby for two years running in 2003 and 2004?
6 What did Winston Churchill call his 'black dog'?
7 Who, in 1968, said he would get by with a little help from his friends?
8 In which Welsh county is the town of Mold?
9 Mark, Jason, Howard and Gary are all members of which pop group?
10 Whose plays included *Design for Living* and *Present Laughter*?

Jackpot

Tom Joad is a character in which classic novel?

✳ This compares with Fred Astaire's feet, which were insured for $650,000, and Jimmy Durante's nose, which was insured for $140,000.

Quiz 7

Round 1: Pot Luck

1 Which King Louis of France died on the guillotine during the French Revolution?
2 Which character made his screen début in the 1945 film *The Friendly Ghost*?
3 What IQ score indicates average intelligence?
4 Which Australian singer and actress was the granddaughter of a Nobel Prize-winning scientist?
5 What kind of salad includes such ingredients as olive oil, lemon juice, raw egg, Worcestershire sauce and croutons?
6 What were the code names given to the two Normandy beaches assigned to US troops on D-Day?
7 In which mountain range would you find K2?
8 What was the name of the character in *Neighbours* played by Kylie Minogue?
9 The Elizabethan artist Nicholas Hilliard became famous for what kind of paintings?
10 According to the rhyme, what is Friday's child?

Round 2: Science and Technology

1 Which is the only planet in the solar system not named after a classical god?
2 Which metal is produced by combining copper and tin?
3 What was the name of the lunar module from which Neil Armstrong made the first steps on the Moon?
4 Which English scientist discovered oxygen?
5 Television pictures are composed of just three colours, of which two are red and blue. What is the third?
6 Which video format launched in the 1970s was eventually eclipsed by the rival VHS system?
7 In the nuclear industry, what is water enriched with deuterium oxide called?
8 What did Hiram Stevens Maxim invent in 1883?
9 Krypton is not a real chemical element – true or false?
10 US patent number 174,465, registered in February 1876, is considered to be the most valuable ever recorded – what did it relate to?

Half-time teaser

In 1998 a US clothing company established a record when it placed a pizza order on behalf of its 40,160 employees – how many pizzas were ordered?

Round 3: Pirates

1 What is the popular name for the pirate flag?
2 Which English buccaneer won a royal pardon and became lieutenant governor of Jamaica?
3 Which part did actor Bill Nighy play in *The Pirates of the Caribbean: Dead Man's Chest*?
4 In Robert Louis Stevenson's *Treasure Island*, whose treasure map falls into the hands of Long John Silver?
5 What was the name of Captain Pugwash's ship?
6 By what name was Edward Teach better known?
7 In the pirate song, how many men were 'on a dead man's chest'?
8 Who captained the *Golden Hind*?
9 What was the name of the short sword used by pirates and other contemporary seafarers?
10 In J. M. Barrie's *Peter Pan*, how did Captain Hook lose his hand?

Round 4: Pot Luck

1 In Cluedo, what is the name of the person who has been found dead at the start of the game?
2 Which musical play by Bertolt Brecht was based on John Gay's *The Beggar's Opera*?
3 What was the name of the empire founded by Akbar, Sultan of Delhi in the late sixteenth century?
4 Who served as vice-president under John F. Kennedy?
5 Who had a number one hit in the UK in 2002 with 'The tide is high'?
6 Which fictional London club included Bertie Wooster among its members?
7 By what name is Barbara Millicent Roberts, whose career was launched at the American Toy Fair in New York in 1959, better known?
8 Which US president had the nickname Ike?
9 Which nursery rhyme character spilled her curds and whey?
10 Who demanded the head of John the Baptist?

Jackpot

In Greek mythology, who was the wife of Hephaestos?

✷ The first serious attempt to climb K2 was organised in 1902 by Oscar Eckenstein and Aleister Crowley, later to achieve notoriety as 'the wickedest man in the world': they failed and it was not until 1954 that the peak was successfully scaled.

Quiz 8

....

Round 1: Pot Luck

1 What does a cooper make?
2 What is a squirrel's home called?
3 In golf, where is the US Masters held?
4 What disease kills Gustav von Aschenbach in *Death in Venice*?
5 In which year was the MOT test introduced – 1950, 1960 or 1970?
6 What did Chris Chataway, Sebastian Coe and Lord Burghley all do after retiring from sport?
7 Which car manufacturer makes the Highlander, the Prius and the Tundra?
8 Who had hits with 'Girls on film', 'Hungry like the wolf' and 'Rio'?
9 Which sport is played on a pitch that is 300 yards by 200 yards in size?
10 Who was the first jockey to be knighted?

....

Round 2: Planet Earth

1 Where is the lowest point of Asia?
2 Which country in Africa boasts the continent's most northerly point?
3 In which country is the highest waterfall in the world?
4 Which country not actually landlocked has the shortest coastline?
5 In which continent is the driest place on earth?
6 In which country is the Qattara Depression?
7 What name is given to that part of the Earth between the core and the crust?
8 What are the Diablo, the Elephanta and the Fremantle Doctor?
9 Challenger Deep is the deepest point of which ocean?
10 Which sea borders on Egypt, Sudan, Eritrea, Ethiopia, Djibouti, Saudi Arabia and Yemen?

....

Half-time teaser

How many popes have been assassinated?

....

Round 3: Haute Cuisine

1 What shouldn't you eat when there is an R in the month?
2 What does 'al dente' mean?
3 What is the main ingredient of calamares?
4 From which country does goulash come?
5 What kind of fish do Germans use to make a rollmop?
6 Christmas Drumhead, January King and Spivoy are all types of what?
7 A brown egg is more nutritious than a white egg – true or false?
8 What foodstuff did Clifton Fadiman call 'milk's leap towards immortality'?
9 In which part of the British Isles may one be served a bannock?
10 What are oysters wrapped in bacon called?

Round 4: Pot Luck

1 After whom was the month of January named?
2 What is the main ingredient of hummus?
3 Who founded a famous academy in Athens in 387 BC?
4 Who became leader of the Conservative Party in 1965?
5 Who released an album called *Atom Heart Mother*?
6 Amethyst is the birthstone for which month?
7 Which mythological hero killed the Nemean lion?
8 In the Boat Race, Oxford's reserve boat is called *Isis* – what is the Cambridge reserve called?
9 In which war was napalm first used as a weapon?
10 In which popular US television series were Lieutenant Mitch Bucannon and C. J. Parker central characters?

Jackpot

Which film star had the real name Reginald Truscott-Jones?

✳ The Prius is one of a new generation of environmentally friendly 'hybrid' cars and thus much loathed by *Top Gear* host Jeremy Clarkson, who memorably arranged to have one shot to pieces and then destroyed by fire.

Quiz 9

Round 1: Pot Luck

1 Who played Woody Allen's love interest in the 1977 film *Annie Hall*?
2 What country did Germany annex in 1938 in the so-called 'Anschluss'?
3 By what name was Mark Feld better known?
4 Who designed the Morris Mini?
5 What dance was invented by Harry Fox in 1914?
6 Is a cheongsam a dress, a chopstick or a type of noodle?
7 In which sitcom did Ricky Tomlinson play Caroline Aherne's father?
8 Who wrote the opera *Carmen*?
9 Which famous architect designed the celebrated 'Barcelona chair'?
10 Albert de Salvo strangled 13 women in Massachusetts in the early 1960s – by what name was he better known?

Round 2: Novels

1 With whom did Lady Chatterley have an affair in D. H. Lawrence's novel?
2 In *The Lord of the Rings* what is the name of Gandalf's horse?
3 With which novel would one associate the concept of doublethink?
4 What is the name of Sharpe's sergeant and best friend in the *Sharpe* novels of Bernard Cornwell?
5 Which novel by C. S. Forester, set in Africa, became a hugely successful film starring Humphrey Bogart?
6 Who wrote the novel *Brideshead Revisited*?
7 In which 1924 novel do three brothers join the French Foreign Legion after falsely admitting to stealing a diamond in order to protect the reputation of their family?
8 In the crime novel by Raymond Chandler, what is 'the big sleep'?
9 Who drew on his own experiences of life in a borstal in the novel *Borstal Boy*?
10 On which Greek island was the 1994 novel *Captain Corelli's Mandolin* by Louis de Bernières set?

Half-time teaser

How many aeroplanes did Britain lose in combat during World War II?

Round 3: Soap Operas

1 Which popular television soap opera is set in Albert Square?
2 In *The Archers*, who became notorious for his black satin sheets?
3 Which British soap opera is set in the fictional village of Beckindale?
4 On which street do television's *Neighbours* live?
5 In which year was the first episode of *Coronation Street* broadcast?
6 Which BBC soap opera was cancelled in 1993 after just one year?
7 Which soap opera is set in the town of Summer Bay?
8 What was the name of the slow-witted handyman in *Crossroads*?
9 Who plays both Debbie Aldridge in *The Archers* and Doctor Caroline Todd in *Green Wing*?
10 Members of which rock band made appearances in *Coronation Street* in 2005?

Round 4: Pot Luck

1 How many people are there in a rugby league team?
2 Which is the world's highest volcano?
3 Who had a number one hit in the UK in 1997 with 'Blood on the dance floor'?
4 Where is the Sea of Tranquillity?
5 Which aircraft manufacturing company produced the Hurricane, Hunter and Harrier fighters?
6 Which work by Igor Stravinsky was greeted by a riot on its first performance?
7 Which members of the British armed forces are eligible for the Dickin Medal for gallantry?
8 What is vexillology the study of?
9 What is the state capital of Missouri?
10 What was the name of the White House intern with whom US President Bill Clinton finally admitted having an inappropriate relationship?

Jackpot

What is the smallest country in Africa?

* The pseudonym in question is variously suggested to have been inspired by the name of US singer Bob Dylan or else by that of his flatmate, one of the stars of the television series *The Likely Lads*.

Quiz 10

Round 1: Pot Luck

1 Where were Davy Crockett and Jim Bowie killed?
2 From which film comes the line 'Blessed are the cheesemakers!'?
3 In which country was the sauna introduced?
4 By what name was Sellafield nuclear power station formerly known?
5 In darts, what is a spider?
6 Whose hits included 'Breaking up is hard to do' and 'Daydreamer'?
7 What was football's Fairs Cup renamed as?
8 What type of plant is dead man's fingers?
9 Over whom did Atahualpa reign?
10 What is a drumlin?

Round 2: Science and Nature

1 Which element has an atomic number of one?
2 From the bark of which tree did aspirin originally come?
3 Which unit of energy amounts to 746 watts?
4 What is acetic acid commonly known as?
5 What is the chemical name for salt?
6 Which set of scientific siblings comprise Ed Simons and Tom Rowlands?
7 Which English chemist of the early 19th century listed among his discoveries potassium, sodium, barium, strontium, calcium, magnesium and laughing gas?
8 What would you measure with an odometer?
9 In which 2001 film did Russell Crowe play tormented mathematical genius John Nash?
10 Which layer of the Earth's atmosphere absorbs most of the incoming solar UV radiation?

Half-time teaser

How many strings does a harp have?

Round 3: High Days and Holidays

1 Which day of the year first became an official public holiday in 1974?
2 How many guns are fired at the Tower of London in salute to the Queen's birthday?
3 What is celebrated on the fourth Sunday in Lent?
4 Which English Quarter Day falls on 25 March?
5 When does the Mardi Gras festival take place?
6 On which date is Trafalgar Day celebrated?
7 To whom was Stevie Wonder's 1982 hit 'Happy birthday' addressed? *
8 What is 12 July celebrated as by Irish Protestants?
9 How many years are a couple married on their lace anniversary?
10 Why is Christmas particularly special for actress Sissy Spacek and singers Annie Lennox and Dido?

Round 4: Pot Luck

1 What does Anzac Day on 25 April commemorate?
2 François-Louis Cailler of Switzerland introduced the first solid form of what in 1819?
3 How was safety in horse racing improved in 1924?
4 Which television western series was set on the Shiloh Ranch?
5 Which cricket club was admitted to the County Championship in 1992?
6 What is the gemstone for September?
7 Which film became the first sequel to win a Best Picture Oscar?
8 Which was the first capital city to be bombed from the air?
9 By what name are the Sandwich Islands now known?
10 In which year did the Sydney Harbour Bridge open – 1932, 1952 or 1972?

Jackpot

Besides black, which other colour features on an Eton school tie?

* The tune of 'Happy birthday' was composed in 1893 by two US schoolteachers for their children to sing at the start of the day, the words originally starting 'Good morning to you'. The version known today was copyrighted in 1935: until 2030 every time it is sung royalties should, strictly speaking, be paid to the copyright owners, Warner Chappell.

Quiz 11

Round 1: Pot Luck

1 Who composed the music for the ballet *Swan Lake*?
2 What happened to Colombian footballer Andres Escobar after he scored an own goal in the 1994 World Cup?
3 What was the uneasy period of peace that followed the declaration of war in 1939 known as?
4 Who had a number one hit in the UK in 2005 with 'Dakota'?
5 From which stage show and film come the characters Dr Frank N. Furter and Riff Raff the butler?
6 Which city is known as the Big Easy?
7 Is a catafalque a sort of catapult, a hat or a platform on which a dead body is placed?
8 What did Danish chemist Søren Sørensen devise to measure acidity and alkalinity in 1909?
9 What is the meaning of the army slang term 'jankers'?
10 What were the names of the two houses who fought each other in the Wars of the Roses?

Round 2: Sport and Leisure

1 Where were the 2004 Summer Olympics held?
2 Which British Formula One champion also had a world-championship-winning father?
3 What internationally played board game was invented by Alfred Butts in 1921?
4 What was the name of the schoolboy who in 1823 invented rugby when he picked up the ball and ran with it?
5 Modern winners in the Olympic Games receive gold medals, but what did they receive in classical times?
6 Cricket has never been an Olympic sport – true or false?
7 Which modern sport was first marketed under the name Sphairistike?
8 Which major baseball star moved from the New York Yankees to the Boston Red Sox in 1921?
9 Who was the first black footballer to captain England?
10 What was unusual about the Austrian tennis player Hans Redl, who played at Wimbledon from 1947 to 1956?

Half-time teaser

The oldest caged bird ever recorded was a budgerigar called Joey – how old was he when he died?

Round 3: Advertising

1 Which lager 'refreshes the parts other beers cannot reach'?
2 Which company advertises its products with the slogan 'Finger lickin' good'?
3 Who are 'never knowingly undersold'?
4 Which make of car is advertised under the slogan 'Vorsprung durch technik'?
5 Which product 'does exactly what it says on the tin'?
6 Which product was advertised with the slogan 'Hello boys'?
7 Complete the slogan 'Happiness is a cigar called . . .'
8 What, according to the advertisers, 'prevents that sinking feeling'?
9 Which product considers itself 'the right one'?
10 What was born in 1820 and is still going strong?

Round 4: Pot Luck

1 What name is given to the greenish surface glow of a statue or other ornament that comes with age?
2 Who earned the nickname 'El Bandito' after England knocked Argentina out of the 1966 World Cup?
3 Which organisation had its headquarters in Transport House in Smith Square until 1980?
4 Who was the television detective played by Peter Falk in a shabby raincoat in the 1970s?
5 Which predecessor of the United Nations held its last meeting in April 1946?
6 Whose admired paintings included *The Night Watch*?
7 Which product manufactured by the Swedish Gas Accumulator Company has long been a desired feature of country homes throughout middle-class Britain?
8 What was the name of the chief engineer on the starship *Enterprise*?
9 What is the name of the dog owned by the Simpson family in *The Simpsons*?
10 What colour is topaz?

Jackpot

Which is the oldest letter in the English alphabet?

✳ This Greek title was selected when the game in question was reorganised in 1874, but was later replaced by the current name on the suggestion of the British prime minister Arthur Balfour.

Quiz 12

Round 1: Pot Luck

1 How many squares are there on one side of a Rubik's cube?
2 Who was 'the Divine Sarah'?
3 Who preceded John F. Kennedy as US president?
4 Who, in Tolkien's books, was the Lord of the Rings?
5 After which two places was the World War II machine-gun called the Bren gun named?
6 Charles Dickens and Jane Austen were both born in which county?
7 Which footballer played his 700th game for Manchester United early in 2007?
8 Whose hits included 'Call me', 'Maria' and 'Picture this'?
9 In the opera *Tosca*, how does Tosca herself die?
10 What is the nationality of tennis player Roger Federer?

Round 2: Fashion

1 Which snake has given its name to a frivolous fashion garment worn round the neck?
2 What is Manolo Blahnik famous for?
3 What is a bumfreezer?
4 What name is given to a pad or frame worn to puff out a woman's skirt at the rear?
5 Who designed the wedding dress worn by Diana, Princess of Wales?
6 Who markets the Obsession, Eternity, Escape and CK One fragrances?
7 What kind of goods does the Louis Vuitton company specialise in?
8 With which colour was Italian fashion designer Elsa Schiaparelli particularly associated?
9 In a Harvey Nichols poll conducted in 2005, what emerged as Britain's favourite fashion item ever?
10 Which 1960s model was known as 'the Shrimp'?

Half-time teaser

How heavy, in kilograms, was the average rider in the 2005 Tour de France cycle race?

Round 3: Islands

1 What is Lindisfarne otherwise known as?
2 Fair Isle is part of which island group?
3 Which medal was awarded to the island of Malta for its heroic defence during World War II?
4 Which Caribbean island is shared by the Dominican Republic and Haiti?
5 On which island would you find Pearl Harbor?
6 On which island was Nelson Mandela imprisoned for many years?
7 On which island is the volcano Mount Etna?
8 On which island might you view the Blue Grotto?
9 What is the name of the island on which the Statue of Liberty stands?
10 What animals were the Canary Islands named after?

Round 4: Pot Luck

1 What is the nationality of rock group AC/DC? *
2 What colour is argent?
3 Of which country is Nuuk the capital?
4 Which tennis star did actress Brooke Shields marry in 1997?
5 How many times has Italy won football's World Cup?
6 Which 1925 film included a classic sequence filmed on the Odessa Steps?
7 Vincent Van Gogh did not sell a single painting during his lifetime – true or false?
8 By what name did Charles Dodgson become better known?
9 Which part of the body is the patella?
10 Who was the last emperor of India?

Jackpot

What is the highest number on a European roulette wheel?

*The story goes that brothers Angus and Malcolm Young settled on the name after noticing it on the back of their sister Margaret's sewing-machine.

Quiz 13

....

Round 1: Pot Luck

1 Who made an album entitled *Swing When You Are Winning*?
2 Which London street is renowned for its many doctors?
3 Which US president held office for just 1,000 days?
4 What is the name given to a grotesque carving on a church or other building, often serving as a gutter for rainwater?
5 In which book does Rikki Tikki Tavi appear?
6 Where do the British Open Horse Trials take place?
7 Who founded the British Union of Fascists?
8 What were members of the British Expeditionary Force to France in 1914 known as?
9 How many carats does pure gold have?
10 Who was sacked as a spokesman for the Green Party in 1991 after claiming to be the son of God?

....

Round 2: A Round of Drinks

1 Which nation drinks the most beer per head of population?
2 Which popular fizzy drink is sold under a brand name that is an anagram of 'episcopal'?
3 Which Australian animal has a name that means 'no drink' in the Aboriginal language?
4 Which strong alcoholic drink contains wormwood?
5 What type of drink includes such brand names as Red Square, Two Dogs and White Mountain Cooler?
6 What kind of drink is Canada Dry?
7 What carbonated drink was invented by US chemist John S. Pemberton in 1886?
8 Which organisation founded in 1972 promotes the drinking of cask-conditioned beer?
9 What brand of beer do John Mills and his companions look forward to drinking in the 1958 film *Ice Cold in Alex*?
10 Which product is advertised with the slogan 'Reassuringly expensive'?

....

Half-time teaser

To the nearest thousand, how many Allied troops were rescued at Dunkirk in May 1940?

....

Round 3: Last Words

1 Whose last words were 'I've had eighteen straight whiskies, I think that's the record'?

2 Whose last words were 'I am just going outside and may be some time'?

3 Whose last words are variously reported to have been 'How is the empire?' or 'Bugger Bognor!'? ✶

4 Who died with the words 'I realise that patriotism is not enough. I must have no hatred or bitterness towards anyone'?

5 Whose last words were 'I shall hear in heaven'?

6 Which fictional character died with the words 'the rest is silence'?

7 Who said on his deathbed 'Let not poor Nelly starve'?

8 Which English queen died with the line 'All my possessions for a moment of time'?

9 What were the last words of Horatio Nelson at Trafalgar?

10 Whose last words on the scaffold were 'So the heart be right, it is no matter which way the head lieth'?

Round 4: Pot Luck

1 Which famous outlaw was shot by Pat Garrett in 1881?

2 Who, in 1966, encouraged everyone to 'turn on, tune in, drop out'?

3 In 2001 the Police Service of Northern Ireland replaced what former police force?

4 What was the name of the family ranch in television's *Dallas*?

5 Which senior member of Tony Blair's government was criticised after opposing the official policy on Iraq while still remaining a member of the cabinet?

6 Who played Alfie in the original film version of Bill Naughton's play of the same name?

7 Which dynasty succeeded the House of Bruce as rulers of Scotland?

8 Which US river has the nickname 'Old Man River'?

9 Who sang about an 'American idiot' in 2004?

10 Which great military leader is said to have died of a nosebleed on his wedding night?

Jackpot

Who is the patron saint of television?

✶ The latter quotation was the person in question's response to a suggestion that he would soon be well enough to visit Bognor Regis.

Quiz 14

Round 1: Pot Luck

1 What is the longest reef in the world called?
2 From which tree does turpentine come?
3 What was added to the British coinage in 1986?
4 How many times must horses jump to complete the Grand National course?
5 Which new county was formed in 1974 from parts of Durham and Yorkshire?
6 Which band made an album entitled *The Lamb Lies Down on Broadway*?
7 Who wrote the plays *Forty Years On* and *The History Boys*?
8 Which newspaper used to be called the *Daily Herald*?
9 Which sport did Edward IV ban in 1477?
10 Who went down Devil Gate Drive in 1974?

Round 2: Shipwrecks

1 Which vessel, lost in 1545, was recovered in 1982 and is now preserved in Portsmouth?
2 The SS *Carpathia* rescued survivors from which ship in 1912?
3 What was the name of the dredger involved in the *Marchioness* disaster of 1989?
4 Who famously rescued people from the stricken steamer *Forfarshire* in 1838?
5 Which former transatlantic liner was destroyed by fire in Hong Kong in 1972?
6 Which US battleship is said to have been the first sunk at Pearl Harbor in 1941?
7 Which British car ferry sank off Zeebrugge in 1987 with the loss of 193 lives?
8 Which German pocket battleship was scuttled off Montevideo in 1939?
9 Which oil tanker ran aground off Milford Haven in 1996, spilling thousands of tons of oil?
10 How many funnels did the *Titanic* have – three, four or five?

Half-time teaser

What is the record number for dimples on a golf ball?

Round 3: Down Under

1 What name do Australian aboriginals give to the period when the Earth and all living things were created?
2 Is a billabong a small furry animal, a kind of boomerang or a pool?
3 Which Australian song features a Jolly Swagman? *
4 Sydney is the capital of which Australian state?
5 What colour shirts are worn by Australia's rugby union team?
6 On which vessel did Captain Cook explore Australia and New Zealand?
7 What is the name of Sydney's famous surfing beach?
8 What is the state capital of Queensland?
9 Which political party does Australian prime minister John Howard represent?
10 Which sea lies between Australia and New Zealand?

Round 4: Pot Luck

1 Who was the first cricketer to score six sixes in a single over of first-class cricket?
2 On which river does the Hoover Dam stand?
3 Who, in the 1960s, was dubbed 'the best prime minister we never had'?
4 Which children's novel follows three children sent to live with relatives after their parents are killed in a fire?
5 What colour light is placed on the starboard side of a vessel?
6 Who adopted 'La mer' as his signature tune?
7 Which is the longest book in the Bible?
8 Who is the man behind housewife-superstar Dame Edna Everage?
9 Which country is serviced by Crossair Airline?
10 Which US organisation has its headquarters at Langley, Virginia?

Jackpot

Ulan Bator is the capital of which country?

*A swagman was an itinerant worker, who wandered from place to place in search of employment carrying all his belongings (his 'swag') in a roll on his back.

Quiz 15

Round 1: Pot Luck

1 On which date did World War I end?
2 Which sport did one wag dismiss as 'competitive housework'?
3 'The urban spaceman' was the only chart hit for which eccentric British band?
4 By what name is Brazilian footballer Ronaldo de Assis Moreira better known?
5 What was Spike Milligan's real first name?
6 Which song has been a number one hit in the UK charts in versions by Norman Greenbaum, Doctor and the Medics and Gareth Gates?
7 In November 2005 *Sun* editor Rebekah Wade was arrested for assaulting which well-known actor?
8 Which film was advertised with the line 'In space no one can hear you scream'?
9 Who was the first woman to win a Nobel Prize?
10 Who was J. R. Ewing's first wife in the US television series *Dallas*?

Round 2: Catchphrases

1 In which film did John Wayne say 'A man's gotta do what a man's gotta do'?
2 Which Catherine Tate character isn't 'bovvered'?
3 Which classic British comedy television series linked sketches with the catchphrase 'And now for something completely different'?
4 Which character delivered the catchphrase 'Don't panic!' in the television comedy series *Dad's Army*?
5 Whose catchphrases included 'It's turned out nice again'?
6 With whom was the catchphrase 'I want to be alone' associated?
7 Which character had as his catchphrase 'To infinity and beyond'?
8 Which television character has the catchphrase 'yeah but no but yeah but'?
9 As well as being their catchphrase, *Another Fine Mess* was the title of a 1930 film starring Laurel and Hardy – true or false?
10 Which antiques expert has the catchphrase 'As cheap as chips'?

Half-time teaser

How long (in feet and inches) was the longest beard ever recorded?

Round 3: History

1 Which king of England signed the Magna Carta?
2 At which battle were cannon first used?
3 In World War II, what was the code name given to the Allied invasion of Normandy in 1944?
4 What is the emperor Nero said to have done while Rome burned in AD 64?
5 Which military conflict contributed to the English language the word 'yomp'?
6 Which World War II general was known for the pair of ivory-handled pistols he carried?
7 With which country did Britain fight the so-called War of Jenkins' Ear? ✶
8 Which barbarian king was known as 'the Scourge of God'?
9 At what military action did British troops win a record 11 Victoria Crosses?
10 During World War I, who did the Germans call the 'Ladies from Hell'?

Round 4: Pot Luck

1 What is the slang term for £500 or $500?
2 Which British poet wrote the words for the hymn 'Jerusalem'?
3 What kind of animal did Glenn Close pop in a cooking pot in *Fatal Attraction*?
4 In which television comedy series did Craig Charles play crewman David Lister?
5 Which is the highest mountain in England?
6 In films of which Terence Rattigan play did Michael Redrave star in 1951 and Albert Finney in 1994?
7 What was the name of the venue in Liverpool that became particularly associated with the Beatles in their early years?
8 Which Italian hero had a biscuit named after him?
9 Which popular television series set in a fictional Irish village in County Kerry ended in 2001?
10 Where is the Ideal Home Show held each year?

Jackpot

In 1891 Frenchman Sylvain Dornon walked from Paris to Moscow on stilts – how far did he travel?

✶ The war was triggered by an assault upon an English sea captain, Robert Jenkins, during which he lost an ear. Jenkins subsequently brought his severed, pickled ear before an outraged House of Commons, leading to the declaration of war.

Quiz 16

Round 1: Pot Luck

1 In Greek mythology, what was the name of the three-headed dog that guarded the entrance to Hades?
2 How many people are there in a baseball team?
3 Who sang about 'Grandad' in 1970?
4 What is the name of the wine bar frequented by fictional barrister Horace Rumpole?
5 The British Museum is the oldest museum in Britain – true or false?
6 What is an akousticophobic afraid of?
7 In which year did Britain recognise American independence – 1776, 1783 or 1812?
8 What is the name of the long-running court case in *Bleak House* by Charles Dickens?
9 In fencing, which is the heaviest – a foil, an épée or a sabre?
10 Which British athlete broke three world records in 41 days in 1979?

Round 2: Deep Waters

1 In which sea did the Battle of Jutland take place?
2 Which is the largest lake in England?
3 In which sea is Martinique situated?
4 Which seaweed-strewn sea lies south of Bermuda?
5 Alongside Huron, Ontario, Michigan and Erie, which is the other Great Lake?
6 What do the initials SCUBA stand for?
7 Who set stories in the town of Lake Wobegon?
8 In which continent would you find Lake Volta?
9 Whereabouts is St George's Channel?
10 What was the sea area Fitzroy called until 2002?

Half-time teaser

How many islands are there in Indonesia?

Round 3: Famous Families

1 Which film actor's daughter is actress Angelina Jolie?
2 Which *Star Wars* actress is the daughter of Debbie Reynolds?
3 Indira Gandhi was the daughter of Mahatma Gandhi – true or false?
4 How are Tippi Hedren and Melanie Griffith related?
5 How was Franz Liszt related to Richard Wagner?
6 Who is singer Norah Jones's famous father?
7 How are Margaret Drabble and A. S. Byatt related?
8 Who is the mother of British actress Joely Richardson?
9 Which actress is the daughter of actress Maureen O'Sullivan?
10 Which famous couple had a daughter called Horatia?

Round 4: Pot Luck

1 What title was bestowed upon the eldest son of a French king?
2 Which instrument did Glenn Miller play?
3 Operation Dynamo involved the evacuation of Allied troops from where?
4 What would you keep in a binnacle?
5 What is the maximum number of clubs a golfer is allowed?
6 Who wrote 'I'm a believer'?
7 What name was given by US troops to the woman who made Japanese propaganda broadcasts in English during World War II?
8 Where does the Scottish Grand National take place?
9 Which organisation was founded by the Reverend Chad Varah in 1953?
10 What is a black bottom, a cakewalk or a hay?

Jackpot

What name is given to the circular target area in curling?

∗ The 'Lake Wobegon effect' describes the tendency of ordinary people to overestimate their achievements and capabilities. An example of the effect may be seen in the 1981 survey which revealed that 80 per cent of drivers believed they were in the top 30 per cent of drivers.

Quiz 17

Round 1: Pot Luck

1 Of which African country is Nairobi the capital city?
2 What is the name of the fashion-obsessed villainess in *101 Dalmations*?
3 Which great jazz saxophonist who died in 1955 had the nickname 'Bird'?
4 Which English poet had the second name Bysshe?
5 In which role did Jane Fonda star as a blonde space voyager in 1967?
6 Which Rodgers and Hammerstein musical was dismissed in 1943 with the words 'No legs, no jokes, no chance'?
7 Who designed the Lloyd's building in London?
8 Where did Bow Wow Wow go wild in 1982?
9 On which island near Harrisburg, Pennsylvania, did a serious nuclear accident take place on 28 March 1979?
10 What is the popular name for a fruit machine operated by the pulling of an arm or lever?

Round 2: Horses

1 What was the name of Alexander the Great's horse?
2 Who rode to York on a horse called Black Bess?
3 What was the name of the horse ridden by the Duke of Wellington at Waterloo?
4 Which British artist born in 1724 was especially admired for his paintings of horses?
5 Who played Colin 'Trigger' Ball in the television sitcom *Only Fools and Horses*?
6 What was the name of the racehorse that won the Cheltenham Gold Cup three years in a row in the years 1964 to 1966?
7 What was the name of the horse ridden by Don Quixote?
8 What was the name of the Lone Ranger's horse?
9 Who had a 'horse with no name' in 1972?
10 What kind of animal is a devil's coach-horse?

Half-time teaser
What is the height (in feet) of the Angel Falls in Venezuela?

Round 3: Movies
1 Who starred in the films *Easy Street* and *The Kid*?
2 Who directed *Lawrence of Arabia*?
3 Which 1969 film revolves around a Chicago dance marathon with a $1,500 cash prize?
4 For which film did Anton Karas write the 'Harry Lime theme'?
5 Who played the lead role in the 1977 film *Jesus of Nazareth*?
6 Who made his final appearance in *The Shootist*?
7 Whose Hollywood screen test contained the memorable remarks 'can't act, slightly bald . . . can dance a little'? ✷
8 In which film did Russell Crowe play Royal Navy captain Jack Aubrey?
9 Who is the only person to have won a posthumous Best Actor Oscar?
10 Which film starring Kris Kristofferson entered movie legend in 1980 for losing more than any other film ever made?

Round 4: Pot Luck
1 Which aeroplane that came into service in 1976 flew its last flight in 2003?
2 In which museum can you see the *Mona Lisa*?
3 At what gathering in AD 664 was the dating of Easter finally settled in the English church?
4 What is the secret identity of Billy Batson?
5 Which US comedienne starred in the long-running sitcom *Roseanne*?
6 Which Scottish footballer has won the most caps playing for his country?
7 Which of the following is an island – Liberia, Madagascar or Sierra Leone?
8 What was the name of the *Doctor Who* assistant played by Billie Piper?
9 Winston Churchill's mother was one-eighth Chinese – true or false?
10 In text messaging, what do the initials GAL stand for?

Jackpot
What was the first synthetic polymer, introduced in 1909, called?

✷ Not dissimilar to the verdict on Ava Gardner's screen test, which had the director observing happily, 'She can't talk! She can't act! She's sensational!'

Quiz 18

Round 1: Pot Luck

1 Which mythological hero was spared by a lion after he had taken a thorn out of its paw?
2 Of which country is Colombo the capital?
3 What did Harriet Tubman campaign against?
4 Which part of a rabbit is its scut?
5 Which bibulous Glaswegian was played on television from the late 1980s by Gregor Fisher?
6 Phil Lynott was lead singer with which band?
7 Who, in 1991, became the first President of the Russian Federation?
8 How many bottles are there in a magnum?
9 How many gates does the Thames Barrier have – six, eight or ten?
10 What is the southernmost tip of South America called?

Round 2: Worship Around the World

1 In which religion is the Tibetan Book of the Dead a revered text?
2 What is the name of the holy book of Islam?
3 Shiva is the destroyer and creator of life in which religion?
4 What signals the election of a new pope?
5 The I Ching is a sacred text in which religion?
6 What is the name given to Islamic law?
7 Which religious organisation was founded in Boston by Mary Baker Eddy in 1879?
8 Which is the motto of the Salvation Army – 'God and grace', 'Blood and fire' or 'Jam and Jerusalem'?
9 In which religion is the Torah a sacred text?
10 Which religious organisation was founded by Sun Myung Moon in 1954?

Half-time teaser

How many inches were there in a biblical cubit?

Round 3: Whiffy Wonders

1 Which small black-and-white mammal defends itself by emitting an unbearable smell? ✳

2 Birds have a better sense of smell than most mammals – true or false?

3 In 1858 the smell coming from sewage in the River Thames led to that year being labelled The Year of the Great – what?

4 Which perfume house makes perfumes called Opium, Paris and Rive Gauche?

5 What kind of plant is a stinkhorn?

6 Which perfume was first made in 1768 in response to a Russian count's challenge to recreate the smell of old leather?

7 What does hydrogen sulphide smell like?

8 What, according to Shakespeare's Juliet, would smell as sweet by any other name?

9 The titan arum is said to be the world's smelliest plant – what does it smell of?

10 Which song title did Cliff Richard use for the name of his first perfume?

Round 4: Pot Luck

1 The modern A5 follows the route of which Roman road?

2 Which author wrote such books as *Jolly Super*, *Jolly Marsupial* and *Riders*?

3 Which active volcano overlooks the city of Naples in Italy?

4 What name was given to the boundary between the former slave states of the southern USA and the northern states?

5 Who played the suburban witch Samantha Stephens in the 1960s US sitcom *Bewitched*?

6 What kind of animal was Beatrix Potter's Mrs Tiggywinkle?

7 Which football team plays at the Bernabeu Stadium?

8 Who won an Oscar in 1997 for her performance in *Fargo*?

9 What distinction did Jim Clark and Jochen Rindt share as Formula One world champions?

10 Which is the shortest of Shakespeare's plays?

Jackpot

What was the name of Joanna Lumley's character in *Absolutely Fabulous*?

✳ The chemical causing the smell is butyl seleno-mercaptan. Bad though it is, modern scientists have created even worse stinks. Examples include 'Who-Me', a chemical that smelt of rotting carcasses: it was created during World War II and used by the French Resistance to smear on their German occupiers, thus humiliating them.

Quiz 19

Round 1: Pot Luck

1 Which of the four Beatles was the youngest?
2 Where is Camp X-Ray?
3 Who became leader of the Labour Party in 1980?
4 Where might you find the Great Red Spot?
5 How many feet are there in a fathom?
6 Which sport did James I of Scotland ban in 1424, finding it too 'rough and violent'?
7 Which oceans are linked by the Panama Canal?
8 To which country did the Hebrides belong until 1266?
9 Which former leader of the Irgun military organisation later became prime minister of Israel?
10 Which US president chose politics over a career in American football playing for the Detroit Lions and the Green Bay Packers?

Round 2: Space

1 Which planet in the solar system is nearest to the Sun?
2 What was the name of the world's first artificial satellite?
3 Which planetary body officially lost planetary status in 2006?
4 Which British space probe came to grief landing on Mars on 25 December 2003?
5 Which book about the origins of the universe proved an unexpected bestseller in 1988?
6 What is the name of the malfunctioning computer in the 1968 film *2001: A Space Odyssey*?
7 Which spacecraft suffered a major malfunction on its way to the moon in 1970?
8 What was the name of the dog that in 1957 became the first mammal in space?
9 Which US space shuttle exploded on 28 January 1986?
10 Around which planet do Deimos and Phobos revolve?

Half-time Teaser
How deep (in feet) is the Marianas Trench in the Pacific Ocean?

Round 3: Pop Music

1 Who was 'alone again (naturally)' in 1972?
2 Which one of the Bee Gees died in 2003?
3 With which hit did the Verve enter the UK charts at number two in 1997?
4 Who had a brand new piece of agricultural equipment in 1976?
5 Who wanted you to stand a little further away in 1980?
6 Who was writing 'love letters in the sand' in 1957?
7 In 1980, the Undertones had a hit with a song about a close relation – was it 'my perfect sister', 'my perfect cousin' or 'my perfect brother'?
8 Who had hits with 'Really saying something', 'Robert De Niro's waiting' and 'Shy boy'?
9 Who released an album called *Blondes Have More Fun*? ✳
10 What nationality are the pop group Franz Ferdinand?

Round 4: Pot Luck

1 Apart from Bolivia, which is the only country in South America with no coastline?
2 Who was the last wife of Henry VIII?
3 What was Gavin Maxwell's 1960 novel about the lives of two otters on the west coast of Scotland?
4 Who was dubbed 'the thinking man's crumpet' in the 1960s?
5 What is the chemical name for rust?
6 What connects Saratoga, Brandywine and Yorktown?
7 Which apostle was a collector of taxes?
8 How many players are there in a Gaelic football team?
9 Which part of Britain was the first to give women the vote?
10 In which year were pound notes replaced with pound coins?

Jackpot

In which city was the world's first pizzeria opened in 1830?

✳ According to some scientists, blondes are more likely to be left-handed and are also more susceptible to learning disabilities (though they hesitated to suggest this lent credence to the notion of the 'dumb blonde').

Quiz 20

Round 1: Pot Luck

1 On which day are hot cross buns supposed to be eaten?
2 What is the state capital of Arizona?
3 Who among the disciples was the brother of Peter?
4 What word meaning 'separateness' characterised the internal policies of the South African government from 1948 to 1991?
5 What kind of milk is used in Roquefort cheese?
6 Robert Muldoon, Geoffrey Palmer and Jim Bolger have all served as prime minister of which Commonwealth country?
7 What nationality are the Cheeky Girls?
8 In which Dickens novel do Abel Magwitch and Joe Gargery appear?
9 Where did Fiddler's Dram go on a day trip in 1979?
10 What is the English equivalent of an American 'davenport'?

Round 2: Bad Behaviour

1 Which boxer was bitten on the ear by Mike Tyson during a fight?
2 Who stole fire from Mount Olympus?
3 On whom did Michael Fagin make a surprise visit in 1982?
4 Who was stabbed in the arras by Hamlet?
5 Who was murdered in Canterbury Cathedral in 1170?
6 In the *Stars Wars* saga, which character was transformed into the evil Darth Vader?
7 Who was spied on by Peeping Tom in 1040?
8 What name was given to disgruntled workers who set about destroying industrial machinery in the early nineteenth century?
9 Who did John Hinckley Junior take a pot shot at?
10 In 2006 which squash legend found himself facing a possible death sentence on charges of assault?

Half-time teaser

How long, in metres, is the course over which the Oxford and Cambridge Boat Race is competed?

Round 3: Signs and Symbols

1 Which mathematical symbol describes the ratio of a circle's circumference to its diameter?
2 In which hand does the Statue of Liberty hold her flaming torch?
3 Which animal features on the club crests of both Coventry and Dumbarton football clubs?
4 What is the sign of the zodiac for Capricorn?
5 What first appeared on roads in Slough in 1956?
6 Which city has a silver hallmark comprising a harp and crown?
7 What is the symbol of the Democratic Party in the USA?
8 Cars from which country are represented by the letters IRL?
9 Which sign of the zodiac is represented by a pair of scales?
10 In Morse code, which letter is represented by a single dot?

Round 4: Pot Luck

1 In which London park is Speaker's Corner?
2 In which sport might competitors perform a 'lutz' or a 'salchow'?
3 By what name were the Home Guard known because of their advanced average age?
4 What is dry ice made of?
5 Where is the Unknown Warrior's Tomb in London?
6 In which year did Brazil win the Jules Rimet Trophy outright after winning the World Cup competition for the third time?
7 Who took over Baron von Richthofen's squadron when he was killed in 1918?
8 Who played Boromir in the film version of *The Lord of the Rings*?
9 From which album did the Michael Jackson chart-topping single 'Billie Jean' come?
10 In the mystery novel by Wilkie Collins, what is the Moonstone?

Jackpot

What name is given to the silver mascot on most Rolls-Royce models?

✳ All their songs were written by their mother. In a Channel Four survey of 2004 'The Cheeky song (Touch my bum)' was voted the worst pop record of all time.

Quiz 21

Round 1: Pot Luck

1 Which celebrated character made his first appearance in the 1934 Disney cartoon *The Wise Little Hen*?

2 Which word connects 'family', 'marines' and 'jelly'?

3 Which two animals appear on the Australian coat of arms?

4 From which ship were 299 British prisoners of war rescued by HMS *Cossack* in 1940?

5 In which city is Aston University located?

6 What was the name of Blackadder's slow-witted, slovenly servant?

7 Who wrote the soundtrack for the 1981 film *Chariots of Fire*?

8 Who starred in the 1955 film *Rebel Without a Cause*?

9 What is the name of the house at Hogwarts in which Harry Potter is enrolled in the novels of J. K. Rowling?

10 Which Trojan prophetess was granted the ability to foretell the future but was also fated never to be believed?

Round 2: Animals

1 Many kinds of shark will drown if they stop swimming – true or false?

2 Gorillas have the loudest snore in the animal kingdom – true or false?

3 What kind of fish does the fisherman in Ernest Hemingway's *The Old Man and the Sea* manage to catch?

4 The chough belongs to which family of birds?

5 Pandas are not bears – true or false?

6 A 'spat' is a baby what?

7 What does the Ancient Mariner kill in Samuel Taylor Coleridge's poem 'The Rime of the Ancient Mariner'?

8 Which insects do you have in your pants if you are restless or jittery?

9 Is the bongo a species of snake, lizard or antelope?

10 What is the offspring of a male ass and a mare called?

Half-time teaser

How many times does the word 'and' appear in the Bible?

Round 3: Weird Words

1 What is xenophobia?
2 Which Italian city gave its name to jeans?
3 What is the English equivalent of the US 'bobby pin'?
4 If a person is 'hippophobic' what is he or she afraid of?
5 What is a campanologist interested in?
6 According to a survey conducted in London in 2000, what is the British nation's favourite word – mellifluous, onomatopoeia, serendipity or football?✳
7 In his famous dictionary, what did Dr Samuel Johnson define as 'anything reticulated or decussated at equal distances, with interstices between the intersections'?
8 What is a hostelaphilist interested in?
9 In the expression 'sweet Fanny Adams', who was Fanny Adams?
10 Which metal was named after the island of Cyprus?

Round 4: Pot Luck

1 Which two Scottish football teams are known as 'The Old Firm'?
2 In business jargon, what do the initials BOGOF mean?
3 Who painted *The Haywain*?
4 Which 1970s rock band was named after the eighteenth-century inventor of the seed drill?
5 What innovation was introduced in the February 1954 issue of *Playboy* magazine?
6 Which celebrated flyer died when her plane ditched in the Thames estuary in 1941?
7 Who played detective Paul Temple on television in the early 1970s?
8 What is the chief ingredient of scampi?
9 Which country lies to the south of Afghanistan?
10 From whom did Demi Moore separate in 1998?

Jackpot

Who saw a 'bad moon rising' in 1969?

✳ According to US wit Dorothy Parker, the two most beautiful words in the English language are 'check enclosed'.

Quiz 22

Round 1: Pot Luck

1 Benidorm is a resort in which country?
2 Which Shakespeare play includes characters called Peaseblossom and Mustardseed?
3 In the film *The Sound of Music*, how many Von Trapp children were there?
4 The Duke of Monmouth, leader of the Monmouth Rebellion of 1685, was a son of which English king?
5 What is a kitchen on a ship known as?
6 Who said 'Hit me with your rhythm stick' in 1978?
7 On which subject is Oz Clarke an acknowledged expert?
8 Which was the world's first iron-hulled battleship?
9 Which sea area includes the Inner Hebrides?
10 At which racecourse is the St Leger run each year?

Round 2: Love and Marriage

1 For which television programme was 'Whole lotta love' the theme tune for many years?
2 How many of Henry VIII's wives survived him?
3 Who wrote the line 'Stop all the clocks, cut off the telephone', as featured in the film *Four Weddings and a Funeral*?
4 Which anniversary does a married couple celebrate when they have been married for 45 years?
5 Which director's last film starred husband-and-wife team Tom Cruise and Nicole Kidman?
6 What was Basil Fawlty's wife's name in *Fawlty Towers*?
7 Whose marriage to Elizabeth Throckmorton incurred the wrath of Elizabeth I?
8 Businessman Angus Ogilvy married which British royal in 1963?
9 To whom is film director Blake Edwards married?
10 Which was the only one of the Brontë children to marry?

Half-time teaser

How many miles does light travel in one second?

Round 3: History

1 Which trade did William Wilberforce help to end?
2 What were banned from village greens by the Puritans in 1644 as a 'heathenish vanity'?
3 How did Mata Hari die?
4 What did the Duke of Wellington dismiss as 'the scum of the earth'?
5 With which English hero was Emma Hamilton associated?
6 Which is the ancestral home of the dukes of Devonshire?
7 Which British monarch refused to allow his queen to attend her own coronation?
8 Which English king had the philosopher Thomas More beheaded?
9 Who was crowned king of Scotland on New Year's Day 1651?
10 Who designed the Bouncing Bomb?

Round 4: Pot Luck

1 By what name is the Gravelly Hill Interchange in Birmingham better known?
2 In which novel do children called Peter, Phyllis and Roberta play central roles?
3 What do baseball players call a complete miss of the ball?
4 Across which ocean does El Niño travel?
5 Which religious movement was founded by John Wesley in 1738?
6 What is an archaeological excavation commonly known as?
7 What may be decorated in the Doric, Ionic or Corinthian manner?
8 To win which sporting title must competitors complete the Farmer's Walk and the Carry and Drag among other events?
9 What was the name of the royal council in Anglo-Saxon times?
10 Which musical instrument features in the royal arms?

Jackpot

What kind of animal is a drongo?

⚹ The husband in question was later executed, after which Bess Throckmorton carried his embalmed head around with her for the rest of her life. After her death, the head passed to their son and was eventually buried with him.

Quiz 23

Round 1: Pot Luck

1 Which item of clothing was named after an atoll in the Pacific Ocean?
2 Bel Paese (meaning 'beautiful country') is a variety of which of the following – cheese, wine or sausage?
3 Under what name did Marcella Detroit and Siobhan Fahey enjoy chart success?
4 Which 1912 disaster was re-enacted in the 1958 film *A Night to Remember*?
5 Which children's television programme included a fire chief called Captain Flack?
6 What was W. G. Grace's occupation off the cricket pitch?
7 Who partnered Jack Lemmon in *Grumpy Old Men* and other films?
8 In which part of Los Angeles have numerous Hollywood stars bought homes since the 1920s?
9 Who sang about a laughing gnome in 1967?
10 What is Harry Ramsden famous for selling?

Round 2: Aliases

1 By what name is Vincent Damon Furnier better known?
2 Under what pseudonym did Charles Dickens write some of his earlier stories?
3 By what name did audiences know William Henry Pratt?
4 Under what pseudonym did Hector Hugh Munro publish volumes of celebrated short stories in the early twentieth century?
5 What name did Frances Ethel Gumm choose when she became famous?
6 From what did Samuel Langhorn Clemens take the alias 'Mark Twain'?
7 Lord Greystoke became better known by what name?
8 By what name is the prehistoric smilodon better known?
9 What is the formal name of the Dog Star?
10 In 1988 what famous site in central Australia reverted to its aboriginal name Uluru?

Half-time teaser

How many miles has the average housewife been calculated to walk as she goes about her duties in a single year?

Round 3: Food

1 According to a recent poll, which flavour of crisps is most popular among British children?
2 Which food provides Popeye with his superhuman strength?
3 In 1992 it became illegal to import what foodstuff into Singapore because of the mess it made?
4 What invention was introduced in 1795 to make it easier to feed French armies on campaign?
5 The Birdseye food company was founded by a fur trapper named Clarence Birdseye – true or false?
6 What food from heaven kept the Israelites from dying of starvation in the desert?
7 Food rationing was still in force in the UK in 1956 – true or false?
8 After whom did the French chef Escoffier name the peach melba?
9 Who painted *The Potato Eaters*?
10 Which nation eats more ice-cream than any other?

Round 4: Pot Luck

1 How did the Greek philosopher Socrates commit suicide?
2 What significant number would you reach if you added up all the numbers on a roulette wheel?
3 Which is the largest part in a Shakespeare play?
4 What was the name given to a group of lively young Hollywood stars, including Tom Cruise, Emilio Estevez and Patrick Swayze, in the mid-1980s?
5 Which Beatles album includes the tracks 'Can't buy me love', 'Tell me why' and 'And I love her'?
6 Is a baobab a type of monkey, a tree or a chocolate and banana pudding?
7 Which sport is controlled from the Hurlingham Club in London?
8 In which satirical show did Alan Bennett, Dudley Moore, Peter Cook and Jonathan Miller have their first big success in 1960?
9 Apart from being a film title and an album by the Grateful Dead, what is an American Beauty?
10 Which underground publication of the 1960s ended up in court after presenting among other subjects the sex life of Rupert Bear?

Jackpot

Who made a solo trek on foot to the South Pole in 1996?

✳ The *Voyager 2* spacecraft, launched in 1977, is expected to reach the Dog Star in just 250,000 years' time.

Quiz 24

Round 1: Pot Luck

1 What is the infield area called in baseball?
2 What is an alternative name for belladonna?
3 In which equestrian sport was Ann Moore a well-known figure?
4 Who released an album called *Electric Warrior*?
5 In which year was the first British census held – 1801, 1821 or 1851?
6 What is the source of ermine?
7 Which two cities are connected by the M11?
8 What does the medical term strabismus refer to?
9 In Shakespeare's *Romeo and Juliet*, who is killed in a sword fight with Tybalt?
10 What nationality were the pop group Catatonia?

Round 2: Parks and Gardens

1 In which park might you find Yogi Bear and Booboo?
2 Who said that all he needed to make a film was park, a policeman and a pretty girl?
3 What was the destination of Operation Market Garden?
4 Whose statue was placed in Kensington Gardens in 1912?
5 Which is the largest national park in Britain?
6 In which part of Britain is Parkhurst prison?
7 Who wrote *Barefoot in the Park*?
8 Which member of the British royal family lives at Gatcombe Park?
9 Which comedian, as gardening expert Arthur Fallowfield, advised, 'I think the answer lies in the soil'?
10 Which character in *South Park* is killed in each episode?

Half-time teaser

How many hours would it take the average reader to read the whole Bible?

Round 3: Music

1 The Three Choirs Festival involves choirs from which three cities?
2 Which British television comedy had 'Liberty Bell' as its theme tune?
3 Who was 'born to make you happy' in 2000?
4 In which city is the Hallé Orchestra based?
5 From which show does the song 'Another suitcase in another hall' come?
6 A trumpet voluntary is usually played on which instrument?
7 Which Mussorgsky work was inspired by an art show?
8 What instrument do Vanessa Mae and Anne-Sophie Mutter play?
9 Whose number one hits have included 'Careless whisper', 'Don't let the sun go down on me' and 'A different corner'?
10 Where did the Thompson Twins get their name from?

Round 4: Pot Luck

1 What does a vintner sell?
2 In which country is the world's longest railway tunnel?
3 Which British city has the telephone dialling code 0121?
4 Which Roman emperor is said to have made his horse Incitatus a consul of Rome?
5 Who is the fourth archangel, alongside Gabriel, Raphael and Uriel?
6 What was the original name of the Commonwealth Games?
7 Who was propaganda minister under Adolf Hitler?
8 What is Mount Godwin-Austen in the Himalayas usually referred to as?
9 Which is the only continent upon which strawberries are not grown?
10 Which novel by Margaret Atwood was filmed in 1990 with Natasha Richardson as Offred?

Jackpot

What is the name of the fearsome beast that Winnie-the-Pooh attempts to trap in *The House at Pooh Corner*?

⚹ In 1997 the Mars Pathfinder rover examined a large rock on the surface of Mars: because it resembled in shape the head of a bear, scientists christened it Yogi Rock.

Quiz 25

Round 1: Pot Luck

1 In what natural disaster did 36,000 people die on 27 August 1883?
2 To what group of artists did Degas, Manet, Monet and Renoir belong?
3 Which part of the human body is technically known as the niddick?
4 In which country was the 1952 film *The Quiet Man* set?
5 What was the battle-cry of Japanese soldiers in the World War II?
6 Who played drums with The Who until his death in 1978?
7 Who was sacked from the Conservative shadow cabinet after making a speech in which he prophesied 'rivers of blood'?
8 Who made a racket without a racket at Wimbledon in 1996?
9 Who became manager of the Ireland football team in 1986?
10 Which footballer remains unique in scoring a hat trick in a World Cup final?

Round 2: Detectives

1 Who created the archetypal fictional detective Sergeant Richard Cuff in his novel *The Moonstone*?
2 What was the name of Sherlock Holmes's landlady?
3 What was the name of the fictional detective created by G. K. Chesterton?
4 Who created the police detective Roderick Alleyn?
5 Which San Francisco detective was played for many years by Raymond Burr?
6 Which medieval detective appears in stories by Ellis Peters?
7 What, in a 1997 episode of *Inspector Morse*, turned out to be the detective's first name?
8 Which famous private detective was played on the big screen in 1990 by Warren Beatty?
9 Which fictional detective was created by Margery Allingham?
10 Which television detective operated in the Channel Islands?

Half-time teaser

How big, in feet and inches, was the world's biggest bra, made by Triumph International in 1990?

Round 3: Inventions

1 For what invention is Christopher Cockerell remembered?
2 The saxophone was named after its inventor – true or false?
3 Which English novelist invented the pillar box for posting letters? *
4 Who introduced the miniskirt to Britain?
5 Which rock star was backed by the Mothers of Invention?
6 What did Isaac Singer invent?
7 Who invented the 'wall of sound' technique in pop music?
8 Which author invented the word 'chortle'?
9 Who invented the bouncing bomb?
10 What did John McAdam invent?

Round 4: Pot Luck

1 Who wrote the short story filmed by Alfred Hitchcock as *The Birds*?
2 Which word connects 'circle' and 'Sid'?
3 Whose plays included *You Never Can Tell*, *The Devil's Disciple* and *Man and Superman*?
4 Which Palestinian terrorist group assassinated 11 Israeli athletes at the 1972 Olympic Games?
5 Who played the drums in the Lennon and McCartney band the Quarrymen?
6 What was the name of the regional manager played by Ricky Gervais in the television sitcom *The Office*?
7 Which pop group took its name from that of a medieval torture instrument?
8 What was the name of the official news agency of the former Soviet Union?
9 Which British politician was nicknamed Tarzan?
10 In which Jane Austen novel did Mr Darcy provide the love interest?

Jackpot

Which cartoon character has the middle name Fauntleroy?

* This novelist rose to a relatively senior position in the Post Office. When he was stuck for an idea, he is said to have based plots on letters that the Post Office had been unable to deliver and left to gather dust in their 'lost-letter' box.

Quiz 26

....

Round 1: Pot Luck

1 Who was 'the Pelvis'?

2 Which plant does saffron come from?

3 Which is the 'bluegrass state'?

4 In which sport was Henry Segrave a well-known figure?

5 Who opposed John F. Kennedy in the presidential election of 1960?

6 What were the young men conscripted to work in Britain's coal mines during World War II called?

7 Who wrestled naked with Alan Bates in the 1969 film *Women in Love*?

8 Julian Bream and John Williams are associated with which instrument?

9 What kind of transport would you be taking if you were travelling in a Pendolino?

10 In *Alice in Wonderland*, what are used as mallets in croquet?

....

Round 2: Babes and Sucklings

1 Which chromosome dictates that a baby will be male – X or Y?

2 What was the baby in the 1938 film *Bringing Up Baby*?

3 In Oscar Wilde's *The Importance of Being Earnest*, what was the infant Jack Worthing found in?

4 What medical first was recorded by Louise Brown in 1978?

5 Which 2001 film concerned the attempts of a robot child to find his mother?

6 What is the name of the injured bear used to promote BBC Children in Need events?

7 What informal name is commonly given to the generation born immediately after World War II?

8 According to the proverb, what is Friday's child?

9 The Spice Girls comprised Baby, Ginger, Posh, Scary – and who else?

10 In 2005, for which film did Hilary Swank, Clint Eastwood and Morgan Freeman all win Oscars?

....

Half-time teaser

The list of named cast at the end of the 1987 film *Little Dorrit* is the longest of any British film – how many names does it include?

....

Round 3: British Radio and TV Comedy

1 Benny Hill worked as a milkman before becoming famous as a comedian – true or false?

2 Which contemporary British comedian was previously known as Dr Matthew Hall?

3 What was the name of the character played by Michael Crawford in *Some Mothers do 'ave 'em*?

4 In which city did comedian Tony Hancock die in 1968?

5 Which comedian has published the books *Gridlock*, *Popcorn* and *Stark*?

6 To whom is comedienne Dawn French married?

7 Which catchphrase from *Little Britain* was voted Best Comedy Catchphrase Ever in a 2005 poll?

8 Which controversial television comedy series is set on the inner-city Chatsworth Estate?

9 Alan Partridge and Paul Calf were creations of which comedian?

10 From which popular radio sitcom did the catchphrase 'Left hand down a bit' come?

Round 4: Pot Luck

1 Which city was the capital of the USA before Washington?

2 What does the musical term 'diminuendo' mean?

3 What is 11.50 p.m. on a 24-hour clock?

4 In which sport do teams contest the Pura Cup (formerly known as the Sheffield Shield)?

5 Which type of animal comes in edible, robber and spider varieties?

6 Which RAF squadron carried out the Dambusters raid in World War II?

7 What does the word 'bible' mean?

8 In what guise did the god Zeus seduce Leda?

9 The Chicago Bulls are a leading side in which sport?

10 Which actor has won the most Oscars?

Jackpot

Which unit is used to measure radiation activity?

⁎ *Bringing Up Baby* is thought to have been the first film in which the word 'gay' was used to refer to matters homosexual.

Quiz 27

Round 1: Pot Luck

1 Who was the Roman god of war?
2 Which novel by Erich Maria Remarque remains a classic of literature about World War I?
3 From which album came the Beatles single 'Can't buy me love'?
4 How many teeth do most adult humans have?
5 On what river does the royal residence Balmoral stand?
6 In which 1980s television series were Denis, Neville and Bomber leading characters?
7 What was the name of the royal fortress stormed by the Paris mob during the French Revolution of 1789?
8 Which area east of Florida has a notorious reputation for the ships and aircraft that have disappeared there?
9 Which football club got to number five in the UK charts in 1981 with 'Ossie's dream'?
10 Which golfing trophy was first contested by teams representing Britain and the USA in 1927?

Round 2: Names

1 Which animal has a name that in ancient Greek meant 'pebble-worm'?
2 Which Ford car was named after the Greek god of the wind?
3 What was the name of Nelson's flagship at the Battle of Trafalgar?
4 Which film actor had the real name Archie Leach?
5 What was the original name of New York?
6 Cigarette, Euthanasia and Vaselina have all been registered as girls' names in recent years – true or false?
7 What is the Argentinian name for the Falkland Islands?
8 Which insulting nickname evokes the memory of sixteenth-century Archbishop of Canterbury Matthew Parker?
9 What was Bonnie Prince Charlie's surname?
10 Which Norwegian politician's name became a byword for a traitor?

Half-time teaser

Bangladesh is the most crowded country on earth – on average, how many people does it have per square mile?

Round 3: Transport

1 Which great passenger liner is now preserved at Long Beach, California?
2 How fast were the first motorists in Britain allowed to drive, providing they were preceded by a man carrying a red flag?
3 In what aeroplane did Charles Lindbergh complete a solo crossing of the Atlantic in 1927?
4 Why did a US ferry reduce its capacity from 250 seats to 230 in 1998?
5 What is the US equivalent of a British ring road?
6 Which 1971 Spielberg film starred Dennis Weaver as a motorist menaced by a huge tanker truck?
7 Who starred as the time-traveller Doctor Who when the series was revived in 2005?
8 What is the name of the ferryman who in Greek mythology rows the dead across the Styx?
9 In which film does a Miss Froy do a disappearing act while on a train?
10 Which tennis player was nicknamed the Chattanooga Express?

Round 4: Pot Luck

1 Which London museum based in Covent Garden closed in January 2007 due to lack of funds?
2 Which folk rock group named itself after an island off the north-east coast of England?
3 Of which African country is Kigali the capital?
4 What tax did William Pitt introduce in 1799 as a temporary measure to finance the Napoleonic Wars?
5 Who had a number one hit in the UK in 2002 with 'Round round'?
6 Which cathedral appears on the back of the £20 note (as first issued in 1999)?
7 Who was the only man to become Vice-President and President of the USA without being elected to either post?
8 What change was made to the ballboys at Wimbledon in 1985?
9 Which English king died a prisoner in Pontefract Castle?
10 For what television programme was 'I could be so good for you' the theme tune?

Jackpot

On which island was the last living dodo recorded?

⋇ If so, they take their place alongside Antique, Tequila, Ultraviolet and Syphilis.

Quiz 28

Round 1: Pot Luck
1 Which plant grows the fastest?
2 Which Minister of Transport introduced the breathalyser?
3 What was introduced to the British coinage in 1982?
4 What is electrical resistance measured in?
5 In which field did Sir Leonard Woolley become a prominent figure?
6 In cockney rhyming slang, what is a 'Cain and Abel'?
7 With which song did Elton John and RuPaul enter the Top Ten in 1994?
8 Which kind of bird comes in mute, trumpeter and whooper varieties?
9 A lime tree and a linden tree are alternative names for the same thing – true or false?
10 In which literary work does Captain Cat appear?

Round 2: International Bodies
1 Which international movement has the motto 'Faster, higher, stronger'?
2 Ban Ki-moon succeeded Kofi Annan as secretary-general of which organisation on 1 January 2007?
3 Who to date has been the only Briton to serve as president of the European Commission?
4 In which country does football's FIFA have its headquarters?
5 Which international religious organisation was founded by George Fox in 1650?
6 What is the emblem of the World Wide Fund for Nature?
7 Which international criminal organisation provided the villains in the *Man from Uncle* series?
8 Austria became a member of the European Union at the same time as the UK – true or false?
9 Which international humanitarian organisation was founded in Geneva in 1863?
10 Which international religious organisation was founded by Charles Taze Russell in 1881?

Half-time teaser
Under manager Alf Ramsey England played 113 games – how many did they win?

Round 3: Wales

1 Which Welsh city became capital of Wales in 1955?
2 Who designed the building occupied by the Welsh Assembly in 2006?
3 What two main ingredients are needed to make Welsh rarebit?
4 Which vegetable is a national emblem of Wales? *
5 Which Welsh actor, born Richard Walter Jenkins, received seven Best Actor Oscar nominations?
6 Which Welsh designer died after falling downstairs in 1985?
7 Where is the Welsh Grand National run?
8 Which Welsh playwright wrote the play *The Corn is Green*?
9 In which field is Welshman Jeff Banks a prominent name?
10 Which famous singer was born in Tiger Bay, Cardiff in 1937?

Round 4: Pot Luck

1 In which city is the Prado gallery?
2 What was the name of the ship in which Sir Francis Drake sailed against the Armada?
3 From which city does Parmesan cheese get its name?
4 In which war was the Battle of Antietam fought?
5 What is the name of the one college of Dublin University?
6 In which play by Richard Brinsley Sheridan does Mrs Malaprop appear?
7 Which group started out with a line-up comprising Louise Clarke, Flick Colby, Babs Lord, Ruth Pearson, Andi Rutherford and Dee Dee Wilde?
8 Who is the senior Roman Catholic prelate in England and Wales?
9 Which religion was founded by Guru Nanak?
10 Is shiatsu a form of massage, a Japanese hat or a breed of dog?

Jackpot

Which figure from French history was known as the 'Sea-Green Incorruptible'?

* The vegetable in question was supposedly worn by Welsh soldiers fighting under King Cadwallader to distinguish them from their Saxon enemies.

Quiz 29

Round 1: Pot Luck

1 What was the name of Elvis Presley's home in Memphis?
2 In which US television series are Bree, Gabrielle and Susan central characters?
3 The memoir *As I Walked Out One Midsummer Morning* by Laurie Lee was a sequel to which better-known work?
4 Who had hits with 'Lamplight', 'Rock on' and 'Stardust'?
5 What, in US army slang, is a 'jarhead'?
6 What object displayed as a work of art in 1915 was in 2005 voted the most influential work of art of the twentieth century?
7 Where on the body might one find a whorl?
8 Who wore a fur bikini in the 1966 film *One Million Years B.C.*?
9 What is the state crop of the US state of Georgia?
10 During the Napoleonic Wars, what were the 95th Rifles better known as?

Round 2: Saints

1 Which saint is credited with ridding Ireland of its snakes?
2 Who is the patron saint of Scotland and Russia?
3 Pope John Paul II created more saints during his reign than had been created in the previous 500 years – true or false?
4 Which of the early martyrs of the Church was, at his own request, crucified head downwards?
5 Who is the patron saint of mountaineers and skiers?
6 Who was patron saint of England before the adoption of St George?
7 After which saint is Newcastle United's ground named?
8 As what pop group did Natalie Appleton, Nicole Appleton, Melanie Blatt and Shaznay Lewis become well known?
9 Which university did Prince William attend?
10 How did St Paul originally make his living?

Half-time teaser

Lewis Carroll was a prolific letter-writer – over the last 37 years of his life, how many letters did he write?

Round 3: Television

1 Who played Robin Hood in the classic 1950s series *The Adventures of Robin Hood*?
2 Which long-running US series had a theme tune that was turned into a chart hit with the title 'Suicide is painless'?
3 Which series followed the long-running romance of Jean and Lionel?
4 What was the subject of the UK's first television advertisement?
5 What is the name of the city in which the medical drama series *Casualty* is set?
6 Who was the Polish-born scientist who presented *The Ascent of Man* in 1973?
7 Who hosts the television archaeology series *Time Team*?
8 In which television sitcom is Patsy Stone a character?
9 Which part did former child star Jackie Coogan play in television's *Addams Family*?
10 With whom did Andy Pandy share a basket in *Watch with Mother*?

Round 4: Pot Luck

1 What name did the press give the Venezuelan assassin Illich Ramirez Sanchez, otherwise known as Carlos?
2 The first pound note was introduced in which year – 1854, 1894 or 1914?
3 To which piece of music did Jayne Torvill and Christopher Dean skate to Olympic gold in 1984?
4 To which order of fishes do plaice belong?
5 Which band has included in its line-up Dan Felder, Glenn Frey, Don Henley, Timothy B. Schmit and Joe Walsh?
6 In which British city can you go aboard Scott's ship *Discovery*?
7 What do the initials SAD stand for?
8 Who said 'It's not that I'm afraid to die. I just don't want to be there when it happens'?
9 What style of art dating from the 1960s incorporates patterns and optical illusions that dazzle the viewer?
10 What is the name given to a pedestrian crossing light comprising an amber-coloured globe mounted on a black-and-white banded pole?

Jackpot

Who had a number one hit in 1972 with 'Mouldy Old Dough'? ✳

✳ Interestingly enough, the ragtime piano that thumped out the tune was played by Hilda Woodward, mother of the band's frontman.

Quiz 30

Round 1: Pot Luck
1 Which biblical character had a coat of many colours?
2 With which band does 'The Edge' play guitar?
3 Who, in March 1942, promised to return?
4 According to the proverb, what is the road to hell paved with?
5 Who wrote the plays *The Chairs* and *The Bald Prima Donna*?
6 What kind of garment is a montero?
7 Which constituency did Margaret Thatcher represent?
8 What does the word pope mean?
9 Who has won golf's World Matchplay Championship six times since 1993?
10 What do the initials P&O stand for?

Round 2: Computers
1 In computer jargon, what does the acronym 'wysiwyg' stand for?
2 On a computer keyboard, which is the only vowel not on the top row?
3 What do the initials CGI stand for?
4 Which keyboard symbol is variously known as the little snail, monkey tail or elephant's trunk?
5 Which computer company makes the iMac?
6 What does the internet chat abbreviation KISS stand for?
7 Which early computer pioneer is credited with designing the first programmable computing machine in 1837?
8 In computer jargon, what do the initials FAQ stand for?
9 What is a CPU?
10 What does the internet chat abbreviation ROFL stand for?

Half-time teaser
How many litres are there in 50 gallons?

Round 3: Premature ends

1 Which suffragette threw herself under the king's horse during the 1913 Epsom Derby? *

2 In which river did Virginia Woolf drown herself in 1941?

3 With which band was John Bonham drummer until his death from alcoholic poisoning?

4 How did Otis Redding die at the age of 25 in 1967?

5 Which fashion designer was murdered outside his Miami home in 1997?

6 Which composer was shot dead by a US military policeman while out during curfew – Gershwin, Webern or Debussy?

7 Which Wild West legend died with the words 'That picture is crooked'?

8 To whom was film actress Carole Lombard married at the time of her death in a plane crash?

9 Which Swedish prime minister was assassinated in Stockholm in 1986?

10 Which film was Oliver Reed making when he died?

Round 4: Pot Luck

1 What is the Thursday before Easter called?

2 What was Malcolm Campbell's record-breaking car called?

3 Which rock group had a Top Ten hit with 'Cigarettes and alcohol'?

4 In which part of the USA is *The Shipping News* set?

5 What term was given to the alliance of Fascist powers in World War II?

6 In which film did the central character find himself living the same day over and over again?

7 Where did Scottish novelist Robert Louis Stevenson spend his final years?

8 What was baseball legend 'Babe' Ruth's first name?

9 Which British battleship of 1906 gave its name to a whole class of similar warships?

10 Which European city is served by the port of Piraeus?

Jackpot

How many Brandenburg Concertos are there?

* It is uncertain whether the lady in question intended to throw herself under the king's horse, or merely to stop the race. The fact that she had bought a return rail ticket that morning suggests to some that she fully intended returning home.

Quiz 31

Round 1: Pot Luck
1 What do the initials 'SWALK' mean when written on the back of a love letter?
2 Which vegetable has the Latin name *capsicum annuum*?
3 Which band's line-up included Bert Jansch, Jacqui McShee, John Renbourn and Danny Thompson?
4 Which television programme had a theme tune based on Khachaturian's *Spartacus*?
5 Which king of England was known by such nicknames as Tum-Tum, Edward the Caresser and Uncle of Europe?
6 Which television quiz was presented by Bamber Gascoigne from 1962 to 1987?
7 What make and model of car was Herbie?
8 Which country has the largest number of prisons and other penal establishments?
9 The Colossus of Rhodes was a huge bronze statue of which Greek god?
10 By what name is novelist David John Moore Cornwell better known?

Round 2: Crime
1 Who, in the Sherlock Holmes stories, was called 'the Napoleon of crime'?
2 What does the acronym 'twoc' stand for?
3 Why was Colonel Thomas Blood arrested in London in 1671?
4 What is the International Criminal Police Organisation otherwise known as?
5 Which television programme about real crime was presented for many years by Shaw Taylor?
6 Who was the special agent who put an end to scores of criminal enterprises with the help of his assistants Snowey White and Jock Anderson between 1946 and 1951?
7 What is the name of the police station in the long-running television series *The Bill*?
8 What nickname did the press give murderer Donald Nilsen, who carried out his crimes while wearing a black hood?
9 What nickname has been given to the coastal region of Spain where numerous criminals are said to live in comfortable exile?
10 Which garment commonly worn towards the end of the twentieth century became a symbol of street culture and criminal activity?

Half-time teaser
What is the record (in feet and inches) for the longest moustache ever grown?

Round 3: Art and Artists

1 Which artistic movement included among its founders Georges Braque and Pablo Picasso?
2 What nationality was Hieronymus Bosch?
3 Which Spanish artist is remembered for his melting clocks and long-legged elephants?
4 Antonio Canaletto is particularly associated with panoramic views of London and which other city?
5 Which artistic style of the 1920s and 1930s features geometrical shapes and zigzag forms?
6 Of which artistic movement were Edward Burne-Jones, John Everett Millais and William Holman Hunt leading members?
7 Of which monarch did Anthony van Dyck paint a celebrated portrait presenting three views of his subject's face?
8 Which British artist made an impact with such works as *The Hut* and *My Bed*?
9 On which Pacific island did Post-Impressionist Paul Gauguin paint many of his most famous works?
10 Where can you see Graham Sutherland's official portrait of Sir Winston Churchill?

Round 4: Pot Luck

1 Which country was awarded the George Cross for gallantry in 1942?
2 In bingo, which number is referred to as 'snake eyes'?
3 Which fictional character was born on St Valentine's Day, the daughter of Lord Henshingley Croft?
4 Who played the liberal Southern lawyer in the 1962 film *To Kill A Mockingbird*?
5 In which country was the Bofors anti-aircraft gun originally made?
6 Who won the 1997 Eurovision Song Contest with the song 'Love shine a light'?
7 Which planet in the solar system is the largest?
8 What was added to the Olympic swimming events in 1984?
9 Which is 'the windy city'? ✳
10 Which line on maps of the London Underground is coloured yellow?

Jackpot

Who became king of England in 1714?

✳ The nickname refers to the refreshing breezes that blow across the city, although there have also been suggestions that it referred originally to the habitual boasting of its inhabitants.

Quiz 32

Round 1: Pot Luck

1 According to the proverb, what is the greater part of valour?
2 Which English city had the Roman name Deva?
3 What sporting first did Susan Brown achieve in 1981?
4 Which kind of tea is flavoured with bergamot?
5 On the Olympic flag, what do the five rings represent?
6 Who were in 'bits and pieces' in 1964?
7 In rap slang, what is a 'homie'?
8 Which canal links the east and west coasts of Scotland via the Great Glen?
9 Who served as vice-president of the USA under Bill Clinton?
10 What ailments does London's Moorfields hospital specialise in?

Round 2: Great explorers

1 What was the legendary golden city sought by the conquistadors in South America?
2 Which city was Marco Polo from?
3 Which great English explorer was murdered in the Sandwich Islands?
4 Which Portuguese explorer gave the Pacific Ocean its name?
5 Which astronaut hit a golf ball on the moon?
6 Which European explorer discovered Jamaica?
7 Who led the first successful Antarctic expedition?
8 What were Scott of the Antarctic's first names?
9 What was the name of Christopher Columbus's flagship?
10 Which contemporary British explorer was considered as successor to Sean Connery in the role of James Bond?

Half-time teaser

'Buffalo Bill' Cody claimed the record for the number of bison killed in a single season – how many did he claim?

Round 3: 21st century Rock and Pop

1 Which pop star came to fame as frontman of the boy band 'N Sync?
2 Who was named Bestselling Female Vocalist of All Time at the 2000 World Music Awards, and then suffered a complete emotional and physical breakdown?
3 Which contemporary pop star has released the albums *Let Go*, *Under My Skin* and *The Best Damn Thing*?
4 Which pop star was born of Portuguese parentage in British Columbia, Canada in 1978?
5 Which member of the Clash died in 2002?
6 Which US pop star's career began with success in the 2002 television talent show *American Idol*?
7 Which single featuring a deranged amphibian topped the singles charts early in 2005?
8 What did the UK charts include from the start of 2007?
9 From which British city do the Kaiser Chiefs hail?
10 Whose album released in 2006 became the fastest-selling début album ever released in the UK?

Round 4: Pot Luck

1 Of which athletic event is the Fosbury flop a feature?
2 Where did the Flowerpot Men want to go in 1967?
3 Which amendment to the US constitution allows a defendant to withhold information that might damage their own case?
4 By what name is Allen Konigsberg better known?
5 Who was the creator of Jeremy Fisher?
6 Who observed that 'A week is a long time in politics'?
7 What did football goals lack before 1875?
8 Who starred opposite Trevor Howard in *Brief Encounter*?
9 Who wrote *Airport*, *Hotel* and *Wheels*?
10 What was the name of the world's first nuclear-powered submarine?

Jackpot

Alongside Lincoln, Kennedy and McKinley, who was the other US president to be assassinated?

✻ The explorer in question was rejected by Cubby Broccoli because his hands were too big and his face looked like that of a farmer.

Quiz 33

Round 1: Pot Luck

1 Who was the Iron Duke?
2 In which children's book were Homily, Pod and Arriety first introduced to readers?
3 Who played the US marshal facing a gang of outlaws in the classic 1952 western *High Noon*?
4 What is the capital of Somalia?
5 In what role did Ernest Hemingway participate in World War I?
6 In which year was Prince Edward born?
7 Which artist was accused in 1877 of 'flinging a pot of paint in the public's face'?
8 What was the name of the character played by Joan Collins in television's *Dynasty*?
9 Who rode a white swan in 1970?
10 Of which organisation is 'Think globally, act locally' the slogan?

Round 2: Around the World

1 What is the name of the hill outside Jerusalem at the foot of which the Garden of Gethsemane is situated?
2 Which African country is entirely surrounded by South Africa?
3 What is the name of the most famous bridge spanning the Grand Canal in Venice?
4 Which is the smallest independent state in the world?
5 Which city is sometimes called 'the city of dreaming spires'?
6 Where is the Copacabana beach?
7 Which of the following is not in Australia – Sydney, Brisbane or Wellington?
8 In which British town was the television sitcom *The Office* set?
9 In which Italian city is E. M. Forster's novel *A Room with a View* partly set?
10 In which country did the Contras and the Sandinistas compete for power in the 1980s?

Half-time teaser

According to a recent survey, how many times will the average American visit a McDonald's during their lifetime?

Round 3: Epitaphs

1 Whose gravestone bears the warning 'Good frend for Jesus sake forbeare, to dig the dust encloased heare! Blest be the man that spares thes stones, and curst be he that moves my bones!'?

2 Which poet's gravestone reads 'Here lies one whose name was writ in water'?

3 To which English king did an anonymous wit dedicate the epitaph 'Here lies our sovereign lord the king, whose word no man relied on, who never said a foolish thing, nor ever did a wise one'?

4 Who has the epitaph 'If you seek his monument, look around you'?

5 Whose gravestone bears an epitaph beginning 'Workers of all lands unite'?

6 Which US wit suggested for her own epitaph 'Excuse my dust'?

7 Whose epitaph was 'That's all, folks!'?

8 Which Irish poet wrote for himself the epitaph 'Cast a cold eye on life, on death, Horseman, pass by!'?

9 Which comedian suggested for his own epitaph 'I told you I was ill!'?

10 Whose gravestone bears the line 'Quoth the Raven, "Nevermore"'?

Round 4: Pot Luck

1 What is the name of the famous high-speed train that runs between Osaka and Tokyo in Japan?

2 By what title is Whistler's *Arrangement in Grey and Black* better known?

3 In which film are the two main characters called Charlie Allnutt and Rose Sayer?

4 By what name was US-born traitor William Joyce known for his broadcasts from Nazi Germany during World War II?

5 Who was arrested on suspicion of stealing a diamond and emerald bracelet during England's 1970 World Cup campaign?

6 What is a female deer known as?

7 What is the name of the pub in *Coronation Street*?

8 To whose skull does Hamlet deliver a famous speech?

9 Who won the 1998 Eurovision Song Contest for Israel?

10 By what name was escapologist Ehrich Weiss better known?

Jackpot

Which Spanish architect designed the Sagrada Familia cathedral in Barcelona, begun in the 1880s and still unfinished?

⋆ The US version of the programme relocated the action to Scranton, Pennsylvania, highlights of which include the Scranton Anthracite Museum.

Quiz 34

Round 1: Pot Luck

1 Which of the world's languages has the most speakers?
2 Which comet returns to earth every 75 years?
3 With which family of instruments would you associate James Blades and Evelyn Glennie?
4 Where is the Algarve?
5 From which Cole Porter show came such classic songs as 'I get a kick out of you' and 'You're the top'?
6 US presidential elections take place in November, but in which month does an incoming president take office?
7 Which Glenn Miller tune won the first gold disc?
8 What shape is something that is oviform?
9 In the Bible, who was David's father?
10 What was the BEF?

Round 2: Words from Abroad

1 Which French phrase is used by the English to describe a no-through road?
2 What Greek phrase refers in English to 'the common rabble'?
3 Which language contributed to English the words 'dinghy', 'juggernaut' and 'shampoo'?
4 What Latin phrase describes an illogical step in an argument?
5 Which language contributed to English the words 'commando' and 'trek'?
6 What Yiddish word means 'effrontery' or 'cheek'?
7 What French phrase is used in English to describe a social blunder?
8 What Swedish word describes an official who investigates a complaint against a local authority or other institution?
9 What German word refers to anything perceived to be pretentious or inferior or in bad taste?
10 Which French phrase describes clothes that are ready-to-wear?

Half-time teaser
How tall, in feet, is St Paul's Cathedral?

Round 3: Fictional Characters

1 In which novel is Frodo a central character?
2 Who marries Tess in Thomas Hardy's *Tess of the D'Urbervilles*?
3 Which book features a dog called Montmorency?
4 What was Winnie-the-Pooh's real name? ✳
5 In which Charles Dickens novel does Uriah Heep appear?
6 What is the name of Algernon's fictitious friend in *The Importance of Being Earnest*?
7 Where was Captain Hook educated?
8 In which adventure novel does Professor Challenger appear?
9 Which one of the Mr Men is a practical joker who lives in a teashop-shaped house and drives a shoe-shaped car?
10 Who played Horace Rumpole in the televised versions of the stories by John Mortimer?

Round 4: Pot Luck

1 What does the prefix trans- mean?
2 Which educational institution established in 1969 became known as 'the university of the air'?
3 In which sport was Wilf Mannion a well-known figure?
4 What name was subsequently given to the German counter-offensive in the Ardennes in late 1944?
5 What disappeared from the British coinage in 1960?
6 What is the mountain ash also known as?
7 What kind of plant is the source of vanilla?
8 Which British monarch was known as 'the Sailor King'?
9 Of which fellow-composer did Rossini remark that he 'has lovely moments but awful quarters of an hour'?
10 Which athlete won Olympic gold in the 800 metres and the 1500 metres in 2004?

Jackpot

If the nobility, the Church and the commons are the first three estates, what is the fourth estate?

✳ The original teddy bear that inspired the Winnie-the-Pooh stories can still be seen, in a New York library. In 1960, a Latin version of his adventures, *Winnie ille Pu*, became the first foreign-language book to appear in the *New York Times* Bestseller List.

Quiz 35

Round 1: Pot Luck

1 Of the Seven Wonders of the World, which are the only ones still standing?
2 What is the name of the RAF aerobatic display team?
3 What was the name of the shopping mall in Manchester destroyed by an IRA bomb in 1996?
4 For what television programme is 'Approaching menace' the theme tune?
5 Where was the classic 1960s television series *The Prisoner* filmed?
6 Tony Blair was not even born when Elizabeth II became queen – true or false?
7 Who shot Bobby Kennedy?
8 What was the occupation of John Tradescant?
9 Whose music is celebrated at the annual Aldeburgh Festival?
10 Who was the first non-royal personality to be depicted on a British postage stamp?

Round 2: The Body

1 What is the chief purpose of the eyebrow – to shield the eyes from bright light, to stop perspiration running into the eyes or to make the eyes more attractive?
2 How many ribs do humans have?
3 It takes more muscles to frown than it does to smile – true or false?
4 Which Australian supermodel is known as 'The Body'?
5 England's strategy in the 1932–33 Ashes tour of Australia led to a diplomatic row – what name did the tour acquire?
6 Which dance style of the 1980s was characterised by jerky, robotic movements?
7 What high street cosmetics chain was founded by Anita Roddick in 1976?
8 In which part of the body is the femoral artery?
9 There are 106 bones in the human body – true or false?
10 Who sought to protect Whitney Houston in the 1992 film *The Bodyguard*?

Half-time teaser

What is the record for the longest game of Monopoly ever played?

Round 3: Celebrities

1 On what 2004 reality television programme did Jordan and Peter André first form a relationship, eventually resulting in marriage?
2 In which country was the *Big Brother* celebrity show format originally devised?
3 On which Caribbean island did Princess Margaret have a holiday villa?
4 Who deserted his wife for Angelina Jolie in 2005?
5 Of which church is Tom Cruise a well-known member?
6 Who became Mrs Liam Gallagher in April 1997?
7 Which actress is film director Sam Mendes married to?
8 Who married Madonna in 1985?
9 Who became Mrs Michael Jackson in May 1994?
10 What surname do Brooklyn, Romeo and Cruz share?

Round 4: Pot Luck

1 Which artist born in Salford became famous for his 'matchstick' figures?
2 What style of music evolved in the 1960s from ska, calypso and rhythm and blues?
3 Which country lies to the immediate south of Egypt?
4 What is vodka made from?
5 Who does Babar the elephant marry in the children's books of Jean de Brunhoff?
6 In Australian slang, where do 'banana-benders' come from?
7 To which country does the island of Madeira belong?
8 What was the name given to the soft-soled suede shoes worn by Teddy boys in the 1950s?
9 Who, in 1972, promised to be your long-haired lover from Liverpool?
10 What was the name of the German shepherd dog that became a Hollywood star in the 1920s?

Jackpot

Which politician did Winston Churchill dismiss in 1931 as 'the boneless wonder'?

✷ The lead roles were originally intended for Diana Ross and Steve McQueen.

Quiz 36

Round 1: Pot Luck

1 In which city would you find the Palatine Hill?
2 In American football, what is the playing area called?
3 Who sang about a 'ballroom blitz' in 1973?
4 In George Orwell's *Animal Farm*, who is Napoleon, the leader of the pigs, thought to represent?
5 Which major sporting event takes place at the Roland Garros Stadium in Paris?
6 Which 1984 novel by Anita Brookner was set in a fashionable Swiss hotel?
7 Who was the first athlete to run 5,000 metres in under 13 minutes?
8 What did the Greek goddess Nike represent?
9 By what other name is the Spanish chestnut also known?
10 Of which radio programme is 'Barwick Green' the signature tune?

Round 2: Beginnings

1 Which novel begins 'It was the best of times, it was the worst of times'?
2 In which television western did Clint Eastwood begin his career?
3 Which bugle call is sounded at the beginning of the military day?
4 Which musical instruction means 'from the beginning'?
5 Which Shakespeare play begins 'If music be the food of love, play on'?
6 In skiing, which colour denotes a beginners' slope?
7 Who wanted to 'begin the beguine' in 1981?
8 What does the prefix 'tele-' mean?
9 British tanks are usually given names beginning with which capital letter?
10 Which children's classic begins 'Once there were four children whose names were Peter, Susan, Edmund and Lucy'?

Half-time teaser

How many legs does a woodlouse have?

Round 3: Rivers

1 In which river was Christ baptised?
2 Which river forms the border between Zambia and Zimbabwe?
3 Which celebrated fishing river flows from Basingstoke to Southampton Water?
4 On which river does New York City stand?
5 Which Russian composer attempted to drown himself in the River Neva as a result of his disastrous marriage?
6 Up which Chinese river did the Royal Navy frigate *Amethyst* find itself trapped in 1949?
7 Which major river has its source in the Black Forest?
8 On which river does Peterborough stand?
9 In which river did the Lorelei lure boatmen to their doom?
10 Which river forms the border between the USA and Mexico?

Round 4: Pot Luck

1 What name did Thomas Hardy give Dorchester in his novels?
2 Which sporting organisation is headed by Bernie Ecclestone?
3 What line on the hull of a ship indicates its maximum loading level?
4 What was Elvis Presley's middle name?
5 There are more calories in a glass of Coke than there are in a glass of lager – true or false?
6 Who wrote 'My guy'?
7 Which county cricket team plays at Trent Bridge?
8 Who released an album called *Hot Rats*? ✳
9 Which male tennis player was beaten by Billie Jean King in the famous 'Battle of the Sexes' match of 1973?
10 Who succeeded Harold Macmillan as prime minister?

Jackpot

Which British actor was the first to receive an Oscar?

✳ Other albums by the same artist included *Lumpy Gravy, Burnt Weeny Sandwich, Weasels Ripped My Flesh* and *Ship Arriving Too Late to Save a Drowning Witch.*

Quiz 37

Round 1: Pot Luck

1 What is the highest point in Africa?
2 What name did the press give to the female members of Tony Blair's first Cabinet when he took office in 1997?
3 Which one of the Spice Girls had hits with 'Feels so good', 'I want you back' and 'Tell me'?
4 By what name was Istanbul known outside Turkey until 1930?
5 Which yachting trophy was won every time it was competed for between 1851 and 1983 by the New York Yacht Club?
6 Who adopted 'Over the rainbow' as a signature tune?
7 There is a higher proportion of redheads in the Scottish Highlands than anywhere else – true or false?
8 Which poet wrote a celebrated poem inspired by the drowning of some nuns in a shipwreck?
9 What informal name is given to the red ensign flown by British merchant ships?
10 Who drew the illustrations for the first editions of A. A. Milne's *Winnie-the-Pooh*?

Round 2: The Wild West

1 Who directed the 1969 western *The Wild Bunch*?
2 Who were the original stars of the television western series *Alias Smith and Jones*?
3 Which Wild West outlaw was finally shot dead by Sheriff Pat Garrett?
4 Which pop group was named after a John Wayne western?
5 What single about a native American topped the charts in 1960?
6 Which native American tribe accepted Kevin Costner into its ranks in the 1990 film *Dances with Wolves*?
7 Which television western series had a theme tune based on Rossini's *William Tell* overture?
8 At which battle in South Dakota between the US army and the Sioux was Chief Sitting Bull killed?
9 In which television western series were Billy Blue, Buck and Manolito leading characters?
10 Who played the Waco Kid in the comedy western *Blazing Saddles*?

Half-time teaser

How many rooms are there in the White House?

Round 3: Newspapers and Magazines

1 Which newspaper boasted the slogan 'All human life is there'?
2 What 1956 society event inspired the headline 'Egghead weds hourglass'?
3 In which satirical magazine is Elizabeth II routinely referred to by the nickname Brenda? ✳
4 What first appeared in a British newspaper on 2 November 1924?
5 Which children's comic was home to Dennis the Menace and Lord Snooty?
6 In 2005 what society event inspired the *Bristol Evening Post* headline 'Tetbury man weds'?
7 In which newspaper was the Beachcomber column a regular feature for many years?
8 The 1982 *Sun* headline 'Gotcha!' greeted news of the sinking of which vessel?
9 In which children's comic was Desperate Dan a leading character?
10 Which rival publication sued *Hello!* magazine in 2003 for printing unauthorised pictures of the wedding of Michael Douglas and Catherine Zeta-Jones?

Round 4: Pot Luck

1 David Bowie was born on which other pop star's twelfth birthday?
2 In which novel does Captain Yossarian face a classic no-win situation?
3 What is the name of the Jedi knight who trains Luke Skywalker in the *Star Wars* films?
4 The Geoffrey Household thriller *Rogue Male* begins with a failed assassination attempt against which national leader?
5 Which city is capital of Australia?
6 Who was the first England football manager?
7 Who was the mother of actress Isabella Rossellini?
8 Which film was advertised with the slogan 'Be afraid. Be very afraid'?
9 Which is the most popular tourist attraction in London?
10 Which US general had the nickname 'Blood and Guts'?

Jackpot

What was the name of the censorship code applied to US movies from 1930?

✳ The same publication refers to the Prince of Wales as Brian, to Prince Philip as Keith, the late Princess Margaret as Yvonne and the late Princess Diana as Cheryl.

Quiz 38

Round 1: Pot Luck

1. Where is Henman Hill?
2. In cockney rhyming slang, what is an 'Auntie Ella'?
3. What is a mole's favourite food?
4. Which city is served by Charles de Gaulle airport?
5. Marlon Brando and George C. Scott both refused to accept what?
6. In which sport was Yogi Berra a well-known figure?
7. In which city might one see Leonardo da Vinci's *Last Supper*?
8. Of what band is Roy Wood frontman?
9. More tea is grown in China than in India – true or false?
10. Which organisation runs the Chelsea Flower Show?

Round 2: Flight

1. Who flew the Atlantic in *The Spirit of St Louis*?
2. Where in the UK would you find Benbecula airport?
3. What kind of animal is a flying fox?
4. Which country is home to Labrador Airways?
5. Who starred as US president James Marshall in the 1997 film *Airforce One*?
6. Of which US state is Concord the capital city?
7. In which county is the East Midlands airport?
8. What aeronautical first was achieved by Ellen Church in 1930?
9. Which US city is served by Logan International airport?
10. Which rank in the RAF is more senior – Squadron Leader or Flight Lieutenant?

Half-time teaser

How many lives were lost when the *Titanic* sank in 1912?

Round 3: Famous Addresses

1 Who lives at 11 Downing Street?
2 Besides Sherlock Holmes, which other notable fictional detective lived in Baker Street? ✴
3 In Monopoly, what kind of property is the Angel Islington?
4 Who works at Lambeth Palace?
5 Who lived at Mount Vernon?
6 What was the home of Arsenal football club from 1913 to 2006?
7 Which branch of the armed services trains its officers at Cranwell?
8 Which street in New York is home to the New York Stock Exchange?
9 Who was the first British monarch to live in Buckingham Palace?
10 Plaques of which colour are erected in London to identify the homes of famous people?

Round 4: Pot Luck

1 Which of the following is not one of the Seven Deadly Sins – pride, impatience or anger?
2 What name is given to outbursts of uncontrolled aggression among motorists?
3 Which US poet wrote *I Know Why the Caged Bird Sings*?
4 Of which city is Hollywood a suburb?
5 Which opera features a naval lieutenant called Pinkerton?
6 Andrew Fisher, Arthur Fadden and John Gorton have all served as prime minister of which Commonwealth country?
7 Who replaced Sir Edward Elgar on a £20 note in 2007?
8 Who composed the Eroica Symphony?
9 What does the Beaufort Scale measure?
10 In which sport are competitors vulnerable to 'the bonk'?

Jackpot

What disappeared from the British coinage in 1984?

✴ Sherlock Holmes lived at 221B Baker Street, ignoring the fact that in Conan Doyle's day the numbers only went as far as 100. Letters addressed to the detective are now delivered to the Sherlock Holmes Museum, at 239 Baker Street.

Quiz 39

Round 1: Pot Luck

1 By what nickname did Florence Nightingale become known?
2 What was the world's first cloned sheep called?
3 Who had a hit in 1970 with 'Gimme dat ding'?
4 Which Spanish football club won the European Championship every year from 1956 to 1960?
5 Who was shot by Kristen Shepard in 1980 in front of numerous witnesses?
6 Who starred in the 1975 film of Ken Kesey's *One Flew Over the Cuckoo's Nest*?
7 Which Regent Street store played a leading role in promoting the decorative style of art known as art nouveau in the early twentieth century?
8 The A3 connects which two cities?
9 What is the name of Prince Charles's home in Gloucestershire?
10 Who preceded Michael Howard as leader of the Conservative Party?

Round 2: Dogs

1 At which battle was Prince Rupert's dog Boy killed?
2 In which children's classic is the family pet dog called Nana?
3 What was the name of the pet dog that found the stolen World Cup trophy in 1966?
4 The adjective 'feisty' comes from the Old English for 'farting dog' – true or false?
5 Which cowboy film star took his nickname from that of his dog?
6 What is the most popular name for a dog in Britain?
7 How was life made easier for dog owners in 1984?
8 What is unusual about the basenji breed of dog?
9 Who was lead singer with the Bonzo Dog Doo-Dah Band?
10 What was the name of the dog that appeared in famous advertisements for His Master's Voice?

Half-time teaser

How many carats were there in the Cullinan diamond before it was cut up for use in the Crown Jewels?

Round 3: Murder Most Foul

1 Where was French Revolutionary leader Jean Paul Marat stabbed to death?
2 Which country has the highest murder rate in the world?
3 How did murderer John George Haigh dispose of the bodies of his victims?
4 Who plays Chief Inspector Tom Barnaby in television's *Midsomer Murders*?
5 James Hanratty was hanged in 1961 for a murder that took place in a lay-by on which main road between Luton and Bedford?
6 Who was the deranged murderer in Alfred Hitchcock's thriller *Psycho*?
7 Which murderer was arrested in 1910 after a telegraph message was sent to the ship on which he was attempting to flee Britain?
8 Notorious US murderer Charles Manson once auditioned for the Monkees – true or false?
9 On which moors did the Moors Murders take place?
10 At which infamous London address did John Christie murder at least eight women between 1943 and 1953? *

Round 4: Pot Luck

1 In American slang, what is a 'gumshoe'?
2 Who adopted 'Inka dinka doo' as a signature tune?
3 Who was the Jersey Lily?
4 The Hundred Years War actually lasted less than one hundred years – true or false?
5 What style of art and interior decoration involves the reduction of ideas to the barest essentials?
6 With which other pop star did Bob Geldof set up the Band Aid charity project of 1984?
7 What product is sold under the trade name Damart?
8 Who beat Scott to the South Pole?
9 Where is the University of Warwick located?
10 Which river flows through Shrewsbury and Gloucester?

Jackpot

Which style of art is characterised by figures with unnaturally elongated limbs and torsos?

* Such was the notoriety of this address that the street was later renamed Ruston Close before being demolished in the 1970s and rebuilt as Bartle Road: a garden now occupies the site of number 10.

Quiz 40

Round 1: Pot Luck

1 In which country is the battlefield of Waterloo located?
2 In horse racing, at what age does a colt become a stallion?
3 Which Shakespeare play has the subtitle *All Is True*?
4 What name was formerly given to the streets in London and New York where many music publishers had their headquarters?
5 Where did a peasant girl called Bernadette claim to have seen a vision of the Virgin Mary in 1858?
6 Which organisation looks after British lighthouses?
7 Which country has sovereignty over the Galapagos Islands?
8 Which is the most common blood group in Britain?
9 Which British monarch was advised by a group of ministers known as the Cabal?
10 Who, in 1988, famously instructed his audience to 'read my lips'?

Round 2: Biographies

1 Which English 'opium-eater' made a confession in 1821?
2 Who wrote an autobiography entitled *My Life and the Beautiful Game*?
3 Whose autobiography was entitled *My Struggle*?
4 Who wrote the autobiographical novel *Cider with Rosie*?
5 Which dancer called his autobiography *Precious Little Sleep*?
6 Who wrote a celebrated memoir about her rural childhood in the fictionalised Lark Rise?
7 Whose biography was called *Stand By Your Man*?
8 Who wrote autobiographical works entitled *Boy* and *Going Solo*?
9 Who wrote an autobiography about the two years, two months and two days he spent living on Walden Pond?
10 Who wrote *The Autobiography of Alice B. Toklas*?

Half-time teaser

How many chapters are there in the Bible?

Round 3: Fruit and Veg

1 If you were eating a Green William, what would you be consuming?
2 Which kind of fruit comes in Flower of Kent, Northern Spy and Rome Beauty varieties?
3 Which vegetable did George Bush senior admit to hating? ✳
4 Which fruit is a cross between an orange and a tangerine?
5 Mel Blanc, who provided the voice of Bugs Bunny, was allergic to carrots – true or false?
6 Which kind of vegetable is a Crimson Globe?
7 What kind of fruit do you get if you cross a raspberry with a blackberry?
8 What is quorn made of?
9 Potatoes are a plentiful source of which vitamin?
10 If you bit into an Elegant Lady, what would you be eating?

Round 4: Pot Luck

1 Which famous horse won the Derby by a record 10 lengths?
2 What is the largest ship in the modern Royal Navy?
3 Which football team is the subject of the central character's obsession in Nick Hornby's *Fever Pitch*?
4 Which children's classic begins with the line 'All children, except one, grow up'?
5 What is known as 'the kissing disease'?
6 Which European country was ruled by Joseph Bonaparte from 1808 to 1814?
7 Which song provided hits for Tears for Fears in 1982 and for Michael Andrews and Gary Jules in 2003?
8 The extinct thylacine of Australasia is better known by what other name?
9 In which event has the world record never been broken at the Olympic Games?
10 Who painted *The Laughing Cavalier*?

Jackpot

Which city was capital of the Confederacy during the US Civil War?

✳ Hardly had he done so than several tons of it were delivered to the White House by a body representing the growers.

Quiz 41

Round 1: Pot Luck
1 Who, in 1961, became the first man in space?
2 Who took a walk through the streets of London in 1974?
3 Which Hollywood actress collaborated with Robbie Williams on the chart-topping 2001 hit 'Somethin' stupid'?
4 Who was 'Big-Hearted Arthur'?
5 Which heart-throb of silent cinema first worked in Hollywood as a gardener and dancer?
6 Who, in 1668, became the first official Poet Laureate?
7 Which is the Hilary term at the universities of Dublin and Oxford?
8 What nationality was László Biró, the inventor of the Biro?
9 Who was the first footballer to receive a knighthood?
10 Which pop band borrowed its name from that of a South African football team?

Round 2: All at Sea
1 Which two seas are linked by the Suez Canal?
2 In Shakespeare's *Richard II*, what is described as a 'precious stone set in a silver sea'?
3 In 1995, Britons Jason Lewis and Steve Smith achieved the first crossing of the Atlantic in what kind of vessel?
4 Who starred in the 1953 film version of Nicholas Monsarrat's *The Cruel Sea*?
5 Which seabird inspired a 1968 number one hit by Fleetwood Mac?
6 Cleopatra's Needle on the Embankment in London is a copy made after the original was lost at sea – true or false?
7 At which battle did Nelson put his telescope to his blind eye and declare he could see no ships?
8 The prime minister of which country disappeared while swimming in the sea in 1967?
9 Which island country is located east of southern Africa?
10 Which British field marshal drowned in HMS *Hampshire* in 1915?

Half-time teaser
How far is it in miles from London, England to Sydney, Australia?

Round 3: Musicals

1 In *The Wizard of Oz*, what was the name of Dorothy's dog?
2 Who wrote the short stories about New York characters that provided the basis for the musical *Guys and Dolls*?
3 Which musical was loosely based upon the life of a real-life sharpshooting cowgirl?
4 What is the name of the nightclub singer who is the central character in *Cabaret*?
5 Which musical is based in an imaginary village in the Scottish highlands that comes to life for just one day every hundred years?
6 Which film musical set in the Black Hills of Dakota during the Gold Rush starred Doris Day?
7 Who is the main male character in the musical *Carousel*?
8 Which stage musical by Joan Littlewood featured songs from World War I?
9 Which film was the musical *High Society* based on?
10 From which musical comes the song 'My name is Tallulah'?

Round 4: Pot Luck

1 In which film did Marlon Brando play a Hell's Angel?
2 Which Arthur became a star of television's *Going for a Song*?
3 Which was the first country to grant women the vote?
4 What colour caps do members of the British military police wear?
5 Who, in 2004, denied the affair he had had with Petronella Wyatt?
6 Crockett and Tubbs were characters in which US television series?
7 Who chaired radio's *Any Questions?* programme from 1967 to 1984?
8 In which Shakespeare play does the phrase 'brave new world' appear?
9 Who were Larry Fine, Moe Howard, Jerry Howard and (later) Shemp Howard better known as?
10 Who became the first man to represent Great Britain in the Olympic ski jump event?

Jackpot

On which day of the week were both Abraham Lincoln and John F. Kennedy shot?

* His body has never been discovered, promoting rumours that he may have been kidnapped by a Russian or Chinese submarine or abducted by a UFO.

Quiz 42

Round 1: Pot Luck

1 Which is the Land of the Long White Cloud?
2 In which Disney cartoon film are Perdita and Pongo central characters?
3 What is a russophobic afraid of?
4 Which 2002 film concerned a Sikh teenager's dream of becoming a professional footballer?
5 Who was the first British monarch to fly in an aeroplane?
6 What is the name given to the play of light and dark in paintings?
7 Upon which Shakespeare play was the musical *Kiss Me Kate* based?
8 Who was the Flanders Mare?
9 Who preceded Rowan Williams as Archbishop of Canterbury?
10 Ralph Waldo Emerson, Rita Hayworth, Ronald Reagan and Charlton Heston have all been sufferers of which disease?

Round 2: Partners

1 Which musical pair parted after quarrelling over the choice of carpet for their theatre?
2 Charles Rolls and Henry Royce never met – true or false?
3 Which pair shared the 1993 Nobel Peace Prize?
4 Lucien B. Smith and Joseph Glidden introduced which obstacle to progress in the 1860s and 1870s?
5 Mervyn Bunter is manservant to which aristocratic British sleuth?
6 Under which US president did J. Danforth Quayle serve as vice-president?
7 Which cartoon character danced with Gene Kelly in the 1945 film *Anchors Aweigh*?
8 In which city did William Burke and William Hare provide the medical profession with fresh corpses?
9 Alongside Roy Jenkins, David Owen and Shirley Williams, who was the fourth member of the Gang of Four who founded the Social Democratic Party in 1981?
10 Were Alcock and Brown famous as men's outfitters, makers of sherbet fountains, or transatlantic aviators?

Half-time teaser

How many books are there in the Bible?

Round 3: Heavens Above

1 By what other name is the Pole Star known?
2 What may be classified as elliptical, irregular or spiral?
3 What was the name of the telescope put into orbit by the space shuttle *Discovery* in 1990?
4 Who, in 1979, provided hitchhikers with a guide to the galaxy?
5 What does an orrery show?
6 Which planet was discovered by Sir William Herschel in 1781?
7 In *Star Trek*, how long was the *Enterprise*'s original mission supposed to last?
8 What name is given to a cloud of gas and dust in space?
9 Which country achieved the first unmanned moon landing?
10 How old (to within two years) was John Glenn when, in 1998, he became the oldest man in space?

Round 4: Pot Luck

1 What, according to the proverb, is the thief of time?
2 Who is the assassin's target in the thriller *The Day of the Jackal*? ✳
3 Which jockey has won the most Classic races?
4 How many sides are there in a dodecagon?
5 Who was renowned as the Butcher of Broadway?
6 What is the name of the ritual dance performed by New Zealand's international rugby team before the start of play?
7 What did Oscar Wilde dismiss as 'the unspeakable in pursuit of the uneatable'?
8 Which dipsomaniac journalist is named in the title of a play by Keith Waterhouse?
9 Which supermarket chain was built on the slogan 'Pile it high, sell it cheap'?
10 Which is the most expensive property in Monopoly?

Jackpot

What is the secret language of beggars and tinkers called?

✳ The fictional assassin's methods, especially the technique by which he creates a false identity, have been copied by many later criminals. Yigal Amir, who assassinated Israeli premier Yitzhak Rabin in 1995, owned a Hebrew translation of the book.

Quiz 43

Round 1: Pot Luck

1 Who wrote the American Declaration of Independence?
2 In which Beatles film was the Blue Meanie a character?
3 Who was the author of the mammoth cycle of seven novels published in English as *Remembrance of Things Past*?
4 Which musical instrument did Django Reinhardt play?
5 Which country has the longest coastline?
6 In which film did Bette Davis deliver the line 'Fasten your seat belts, it's going to be a bumpy night'?
7 Which puppet character helped restore the fortunes of the commercial breakfast television company TV-am in the 1980s?
8 Which famous playwright wrote a 30-second play comprising a single breath and then a cry?
9 More people died in the Vietnam War than in World War I – true or false?
10 Which famous baseball player did film actress Marilyn Monroe marry?

Round 2: Motoring and Motorists

1 Who made the first petrol-fuelled car?
2 When Americans say 'hood', which part of a car are they referring to?
3 Which German-made car was originally intended as a car of the people during Hitler's Third Reich?
4 Which annual rally for veteran cars provided the backdrop for the 1953 film *Genevieve*?
5 Which singer was driving a fast car in 1988?
6 Where did an accident in 1969 cost the life of Mary Jo Kopechne in a car driven by Senator Edward Kennedy?
7 Whose hits included 'House of fun', 'It must be love' and 'Driving in my car'?
8 Which much-loved car was dubbed 'the plastic pig' when a new model was launched in 1989?
9 Who had their first hit in 1975 with a single about German motorways?
10 What aid to motorists made its first appearance in 1931?

Half-time teaser

How many men have landed on the Moon to date?

Round 3: Waging War

1 Who, on 28 June 1914, fired the 'shot that rang round the world'?
2 What public act of defiance on 16 December 1773 increased tension in the lead-up to the American War of Independence?
3 Who released an album called, simply, *War*?
4 What was the name given to the apparently divine warriors who were reported to have come to the aid of the Old Contemptibles when hard-pressed in August 1914?
5 During which war did soldiers first wear what became known as balaclavas?
6 What was the name of the herbicide dropped by US bombers to defoliate trees during the Vietnam War?
7 What was the nickname of the Seventh Armoured Division that fought in North Africa during World War II?
8 In 1991 which country was liberated in the course of Operation Desert Storm?
9 Which World War II operation had the code name Barbarossa?
10 Which war ended with the Treaty of Vereeniging?

Round 4: Pot Luck

1 On which Beatles album cover did Paul McCartney appear barefoot, leading to speculation that he had died?
2 In which horror film did Mia Farrow give birth to the Devil's child?
3 What was odd about the death of the Greek playwright Aeschylus?
4 What label was bestowed upon Oasis, Blur and other leading British rock and pop bands of the mid-1990s?
5 F. W. Woolworth opened his first store in Scotland – true or false?
6 With which city is the semi-legendary figure of Lady Godiva associated?
7 In which country will you find the largest pyramid in the world?
8 Who broadcast a series of 'Fireside Chats' in the early years of World War II?
9 Which major cultural institution opened in new premises in St Pancras, London in 1998?
10 What are studied in Rorschach tests in order to reveal the subject's underlying personality?

Jackpot

In which children's book is Anne Shirley the central character?

✳ More recently, a Beatles tribute band called the Blue Meanies has attracted a large following, despite the fact that they make no attempt to look like the Beatles and are all Mexican.

Quiz 44

Round 1: Pot Luck

1 In *1066 and All That*, who were described as 'right but repulsive'?
2 Who became famous with paintings of Flatford Mill and its surroundings?
3 In which opera are Jemmy Twitcher, Lucy Lockit and Polly Peachum characters?
4 Toronto is the capital of which Canadian province?
5 In which month is the first Beaujolais Nouveau delivered?
6 Vincenzo Perugia was imprisoned for one year, 15 days after stealing which work of art?
7 Who followed Jim Callaghan as prime minister?
8 In which television soap opera were Sinbad and Billy Corkhill characters?
9 What, in cricket, is the name given to a ball that is bowled along the ground towards the batsman?
10 Which country always leads the opening procession at the Olympic Games?

Round 2: Aliases

1 By what name is Frederick Austerlitz better known?
2 What was John Peel's real name?
3 By what name do pop fans know Gordon Sumner?
4 By what name was Captain Scarlet's deadly enemy Conrad Turner better known?
5 Joel Chandler Harris wrote celebrated animal stories under what pseudonym?
6 Which member of the Rolling Stones is really called William George Perks?
7 By what name was Anthony Dominic Benevetto better known?
8 What was Lonnie Donegan's real first name?
9 After which US film star did notorious British prison inmate Michael Gordon Peterson name himself?
10 Which international sportsman's real name is Edson Arantes do Nascimento?

Half-time teaser

The Trans-Siberian railway is the longest in the world – what is its length in miles?

Round 3: Presidents

1 Who was the first Roman Catholic president of the USA?
2 Who preceded Jacques Chirac as president of France?
3 Who was president of Egypt during the Suez Crisis of 1956?
4 Which president of the USA was the tallest?
5 Who was president of Germany from 1925 to 1934?
6 In which series did Martin Sheen play President Josiah Bartlet?
7 Which is the official residence of the president of France?
8 George Bush senior is older than Jimmy Carter – true or false?
9 Which march is traditionally played when the US president arrives at formal events?
10 On which mountain in the USA are carved the heads of four presidents?

Round 4: Pot Luck

1 Terpsichore was the Muse of what?
2 Which company made the Brownie box camera?
3 Who released an album called *The Song Remains the Same*?
4 Who became the first unseeded tennis player to win the men's singles title at Wimbledon?
5 Which footpath runs 105 miles from Beachy Head to Winchester?
6 Which day in the Church calendar marks the first day of Lent?
7 What does sago come from?
8 Which US state is known as the Heart of Dixie? ✳
9 Which London prison is the largest in Britain?
10 Who designed the lions in London's Trafalgar Square?

Jackpot

With what kind of weapon was Leon Trotsky murdered in exile in Mexico?

✳ The origins of the nickname Dixie for the southern USA are obscure. Some say it is a reference to the Mason–Dixon Line between north and south, others to the 10-dollar notes issued by the Louisiana banks (*dix* being ten in French) or else to a kindly slave-owner by the name of Dixy.

Quiz 45

Round 1: Pot Luck

1 For what discovery is Scottish scientist Sir Alexander Fleming remembered?
2 Who was the sworn enemy of Dan Dare in the 1950s comic *Eagle*?
3 What is the name of the vicious young gangster in the 1938 Graham Greene novel *Brighton Rock*?
4 Who wrote the play *Accidental Death of an Anarchist*?
5 What is a Snellen chart used for?
6 Which famous dish is comprised of raw steak?
7 Besides red and blue, which is the other colour of which all other colours are made?
8 Which restaurant chain was founded in South Wales in 1948 by the son of an Italian-born café owner?
9 Who wrote a trilogy of plays beginning with *Chicken Soup with Barley* in 1958?
10 Which Filipino leader was known for her large collection of shoes?

Round 2: Around Britain

1 Which English city had the Viking name Jorvik?
2 To which group of islands does Tresco belong?
3 What is the county town of Buckinghamshire?
4 Which is the most overweight city in the UK?
5 What is the main promenade at Blackpool known as?
6 What measure was introduced in London in 2003 to reduce the number of vehicles entering the city?
7 In which fictional south-east town was the comedy series *Dad's Army* set?
8 Of which city is Handsworth a district?
9 Where was Prince Charles invested as Prince of Wales?
10 Which fishing village near Penzance in Cornwall gave its name to a renowned group of British artists?

Half-time teaser

How many mountains are there over 8,000 metres?

Round 3: On the Stage

1 Which New York street is the centre of commercial theatre in the USA?
2 Which Samuel Beckett play features two tramps named Vladimir and Estragon?
3 Which major sporting event is staged annually at Sheffield's Crucible Theatre?
4 Which London theatre acquired its present name in 1833 when it was renamed in honour of a future monarch?
5 What name did playwright Terence Rattigan give to the typical conservative British theatregoer of the 1950s?
6 What was the name of the revolutionary new acting style developed by Konstantin Stanislavsky?
7 Which London-born comic actress enjoyed a successful stage partnership with Noël Coward in such plays as *Private Lives*?
8 What name was given to John Osborne and the other members of a new generation of young British playwrights who became famous in the late 1950s?
9 In which play do two kindly old ladies poison elderly guests in their home to relieve them of their loneliness, and then bury their bodies in the cellar?
10 Upon which Shakespeare play did Tom Stoppard base his own play *Rosencrantz and Guildenstern are Dead*?

Round 4: Pot Luck

1 How many countries does France share a border with?
2 Who formed the first commando forces?
3 How many stomachs does a cow have?
4 Which notable writer lived for many years in the village of Ayot St Lawrence in Hertfordshire?
5 Footballer Peter Bonetti and cricketer Phil Tufnell shared what nickname?
6 Under what name did George Michael and Andrew Ridgeley enjoy chart success?
7 In which county is Portland Bill?
8 What oath is traditionally sworn by newly qualified doctors?
9 What was the nickname of the place from which the first BBC programme was broadcast in 1926?
10 Which animal is mentioned more frequently than any other in the Bible?

Jackpot

What was the name of the former Italian prime minister kidnapped and murdered by the Red Brigades in 1978?

⁎ The person in question also owned works by Michelangelo, Canaletto and Botticelli, but decided against buying the Empire State Building because that would be 'too ostentatious'.

Quiz 46

Round 1: Pot Luck

1 By what other name do Americans refer to the 'Abominable Snowman' or 'Sasquatch'?
2 Which US president was nicknamed 'Old Hickory'?
3 What major change was introduced by the Church of England in 1994?
4 What was the name of the deranged castaway in Robert Louis Stevenson's *Treasure Island*?
5 Who composed the Trout Quintet?
6 Which part of the face is technically known as the columella?
7 Whose hits included 'My Ding-a-Ling' and 'No particular place to go'?
8 Which scientist observed, 'If I have seen further it is by standing on the shoulders of giants'?
9 A dotterel is a species of which bird?
10 Who became the first black footballer to captain England?

Round 2: Medical Matters

1 What is Joseph Lister remembered for?
2 Rickets is a condition caused by a lack of which vitamin?
3 What is myopia?
4 What is the medical name for German measles?
5 Which mobile medical innovation was introduced by Frenchman Jean Dominique Larrey in 1792?
6 What medical first did George Jorgensen endure in 1952?
7 What does the medical term hypertension refer to?
8 Which neurological disorder features a range of tics and compulsive swearing?
9 What is the medical term for phlegm?
10 What type of surgery does Papworth Hospital in Cambridgeshire specialise in?

Half-time teaser

How tall, in centimetres, is an Oscar statuette?

Round 3: The Boys in Blue

1 Which television policeman was reincarnated for a long television career after being killed in his only screen appearance?
2 Which well-known snooker player was a policeman before entering sport as a professional?
3 Which opera features an evil police chief called Scarpia?
4 What is the name of the headquarters of London's Metropolitan Police?
5 Who was the adventurer pursued by the police in John Buchan's thriller *The Thirty-Nine Steps*?
6 The Automobile Association was founded to warn drivers of police patrols – true or false?
7 What is the name of the chief of police in *The Simpsons*?
8 Which notorious villains were eventually brought to justice in 1969 by Detective Superintendent Leonard 'Nipper' Read?
9 Which of the following is not slang for a policeman – copper, rozzer or buzzer?
10 How did police panda cars get their name?

Round 4: Pot Luck

1 Who held Fay Wray in the palm of his hand? ✳
2 What is noise measured in?
3 The letter 'i' appears on which row of letters on a keyboard?
4 The Grand Slam in tennis includes the French, US Open, Wimbledon and which other championship?
5 Which biblical character changed his name from Saul?
6 What did the composers Beethoven, Fauré and Smetana have in common?
7 Which cricket team was the first to win both the County Championship and the Sunday League in the same season?
8 Which US city is home to the Tigers baseball team?
9 Who is golf's 'Great White Shark'?
10 Who drank a drink to Lily the Pink in 1968?

Jackpot

To which class of animals do skinks belong?

✳ When Fay Wray died in 2004, at the age of 96, the lights of the Empire State Building in New York were extinguished for 15 minutes in her honour.

Quiz 47

Round 1: Pot Luck
1 What is the capital of Libya?
2 There are more miles of canal in Birmingham than there are in Venice – true or false?
3 Whose hits included 'All I really want to do', 'If I could turn back time' and 'Love can build a bridge'?
4 Which lake does the Ugandan capital Kampala overlook?
5 Who wrote *The Caretaker*?
6 Which drug prescribed to pregnant women in the early 1960s caused serious deformities in newborn children?
7 Which country was the first to have a female prime minister?
8 What is the name of the monstrous soldiers created by Sauron in J. R. R. Tolkien's *The Lord of the Rings*?
9 What was Che Guevara's profession before he became a political figurehead?
10 Which king of Babylon was warned of his own death by the writing on the wall?

Round 2: The USA
1 Which US city is known as 'the Big Apple'?
2 Which US state has as its motto 'Eureka'?
3 Which opera singer was fined in 1906 for pinching a woman's bottom in the monkey house of New York's Central Park Zoo?
4 When the Noddy books of Enid Blyton were published in the USA, which character was renamed Whitebeard to avoid causing offence?
5 Which is bigger – the US state of Georgia or the republic of Georgia?
6 Which US state has just one syllable in its name?
7 Where is the bulk of the USA's gold reserve kept?
8 There are more vehicles than drivers in the USA – true or false?
9 Which fictional character fell asleep as a subject of George III and awoke 20 years later to find himself a free American citizen?
10 In the UK Remembrance Day falls on 11 November, but what is the same date known as in the USA?

Half-time teaser
Which name appears more than any other in the Bible?

Round 3: Rascals, Rogues and Villains

1 How did Tom Keating and Hans van Meegeren become notorious?
2 In 1997, Marcus Harvey caused a stir with his portrait of which infamous murderer?
3 According to the popular rhyme, how many whacks did Lizzie Borden give her father in 1892? ✳
4 Who was the last person to be hanged under British law on a charge of treason?
5 Which fictional murderer disposed of his victims by using them as ingredients in meat pies?
6 Which anti-Western Islamic terrorist network was founded in the early 1990s by Osama Bin Laden?
7 Which classic romantic adventure story describes how Exmoor was terrorised by a family of outlaws in the late eighteenth century?
8 What was the nickname of gangster Al Capone?
9 Who starred as television's rascally master sergeant Ernest G. Bilko?
10 By what name was the Nazi officer Klaus Barbie known?

Round 4: Pot Luck

1 What do you get if you mix grated coconut with sugar syrup?
2 Los Del Rio had just one major chart hit, in 1996 – what was it called?
3 Which is 'the sweet you can eat between meals'?
4 In *The African Queen*, what was 'The African Queen'?
5 In 1994 which famous sporting event came to the UK for the first time?
6 What is measured by the Mohs scale?
7 For whom was Buckingham Palace originally built?
8 Where is Sir Arthur Conan Doyle's *The Hound of the Baskervilles* chiefly set?
9 What is the name given to an additional storey inserted between two other floors?
10 Who played television's Buffy the Vampire Slayer?

Jackpot

Which is the largest art gallery in the world?

✳ The rhyme is not a very accurate version of the real events: in fact, Lizzie Borden's stepmother (not her real mother) received 18 blows, while her father received just one – and it may not have been Lizzie at all (she was acquitted and died in 1927).

Quiz 48

Round 1: Pot Luck

1 Which company are jewellers to the Crown?
2 Under what name did Luke and Matt Goss enjoy chart success?
3 The Blackwall, Rotherhithe and Dartford are all examples of what?
4 In which Arthur Miller play is Willy Loman a central character?
5 Which British film star died when his plane was shot down in 1943? ✻
6 On which river does Washington DC stand?
7 Which US president had the motto 'The buck stops here'?
8 Who was 'the Galloping Gourmet'?
9 How many magpies for a wedding?
10 Which was the only part of the mythological hero Achilles that was
   vulnerable?

Round 2: Rail Travel

1 Which British city is served by Spa railway station?
2 Which British railway station has the most platforms?
3 Which high street chain opened its first store in Euston railway station?
4 Which company operates the US rail system?
5 Which character from Tolstoy kills herself by throwing herself under a train?
6 The world's first underground railway opened in which year – 1843, 1863 or
   1883?
7 Who was the driver of the ill-fated Cannonball Express?
8 Which is the largest railway station in the world?
9 In which city is Connolly railway station?
10 In *Ivor the Engine*, what powered Ivor's engine?

Half-time teaser

How many metres are there in a nautical mile?

Round 3: Sport and Leisure

1 Which country has ice hockey as its national sport?
2 Alongside the British Open, US Open and US Masters, which other tournament makes up golf's Grand Slam?
3 How heavy does a professional heavyweight boxer have to be – 86 kilograms, 96 kilograms or 106 kilograms?
4 In Monopoly, what colour is the Strand?
5 Which two sporting pursuits does the biathlon combine?
6 Which construction toy was invented by Frank Hornby in 1900?
7 How many penalty points does a show jumper get if he or she falls off the horse?
8 Who lost to Virginia Wade in the 1977 women's singles final?
9 In which sport are a foil and an épée used?
10 By what royal nickname was German footballer Franz Beckenbauer known?

Round 4: Pot Luck

1 Which of the following is not the title of a royal duke – Cornwall, Gloucester, Wales or York?
2 Who was Hercule Poirot's assistant?
3 The *Mabinogion* is a sacred Indian text – true or false?
4 Which notable figure did Winston Churchill describe as 'Indomitable in retreat; invincible in advance, insufferable in victory'?
5 Alongside Martin Van Buren, who was the other bald US president?
6 What did both Lambert Simnel and Perkin Warbeck make claims to?
7 What is the modern name of Van Diemen's Land?
8 Of which country is the menorah a symbol?
9 What were the Amati family famous for making?
10 Which ingredient distinguishes a Pontefract cake from other cakes?

Jackpot

What is the source of agar agar?

⋆ Suggestions that the star in question died because the Germans thought Winston Churchill was on his plane have since been discounted. It appears that the Germans knew perfectly who was on board and targeted him for his outspoken support for the Allied cause.

Quiz 49

Round 1: Pot Luck

1 The 14 most venomous snakes in the world live in which continent?
2 What does 'asbo' stand for?
3 Who issued an invitation to 'come on over to my place' in 1965 and again in 1972?
4 By what name did Mary Mallon become notorious in New York early in the twentieth century?
5 Which heavily pregnant actress received an Oscar for *Chicago*?
6 Which Belgian cyclist was known as 'the Cannibal' because he 'ate up' his opponents?
7 What is the capital of Jordan?
8 What invention of Percy Shaw in 1934 greatly improved road safety?
9 Cardington in Bedfordshire is associated with what type of transport?
10 Which famous English prophetess lived in a cave at Knaresborough in North Yorkshire?

Round 2: Clothing

1 Which item of clothing was famously likened to a barbed-wire fence, because 'it protects the property without obstructing the view'?
2 Where was denim first made?
3 Who, in the late 1970s, teamed up with Malcolm McLaren to sell punk fashion clothing from a boutique called Sex in London's King's Road?
4 What did the press call the trade dispute that broke out in 2005 over imports of cheap Chinese clothing?
5 Where do Panama hats come from?
6 What item of clothing do Australians call 'budgie-smugglers'?
7 What colour berets do peacekeeping soldiers with the United Nations wear?
8 Who had 'baggy trousers' in 1980?
9 What name was given to the ankle-length socks worn by American teenage girls in the immediate postwar period?
10 Who released an album called *New Boots and Panties!*?

Half-time Teaser

How many monarchs occupied the English throne between the Battle of Hastings in 1066 and the execution of Charles I in 1649?

Round 3: Leaders

1 Who led his followers on a Long March in 1934?
2 Which French military commander was known as 'the bravest of the brave'?
3 Who was the leader of the Gunpowder Plot of 1605?
4 Which British monarch was the last to lead his troops into battle?
5 Who was the last Liberal Party leader?
6 What is the adult leader of a pack of Cub Scouts called?
7 Who was the leader of the National Union of Mineworkers in the 1983 Miners' Strike?
8 Who led the March on Rome in 1922?
9 Who was the leader of the Mongols who established a huge empire in the early thirteenth century?
10 Who, until he hanged himself in 1999, was the leader of the Monster Raving Loony Party?

Round 4: Pot Luck

1 How many legs do adult insects have?
2 Who publicly declared in 1916 that 'History is bunk'? ✳
3 Which British sitcom of the early 1990s was set in a leisure centre?
4 Which English queen was sometimes referred to mockingly as Mrs Brown?
5 Who wrote the novel *Wilt*?
6 The Sahara desert is getting smaller each year – true or false?
7 What is the name of the river over which Julius Caesar led his troops in 49 BC, in defiance of Roman law?
8 What is the seventeenth letter of the alphabet?
9 Who caused a scandal by turning up at a fancy-dress party in a Nazi uniform?
10 In which 1956 film did Virginia McKenna seek to protect a group of children from invading Japanese forces?

Jackpot

In what field are chevron, bend, fess and saltire technical terms?

✳ Other notable sayings by the same person included 'If you think you can, you can. And if you think you can't, you're right.'

Quiz 50

Round 1: Pot Luck

1 What name is given to a Scout rally?
2 Which pope was the first to visit Britain?
3 In speedway, how many times do riders go round the track in a single race?
4 How were Charles II and James II related?
5 Of which Canadian province is Halifax the capital?
6 If something is vulpine, which animal does it resemble?
7 What is the highest point of a triangle called?
8 How many shots does each player take in succession in curling?
9 From which legendary founder of Rome did Julius Caesar claim to be descended?
10 By what name was Soeur Sourire better known?

Round 2: Cities of the World

1 Which is the Eternal City?
2 In which US city is the television comedy *Frasier* set? ✶
3 By what name is the city of Byzantium known today?
4 Casablanca is a city in Algeria – true or false?
5 Which city grew from the pioneer settlement of Botany Bay?
6 In which Italian city would you find the Bridge of Sighs?
7 Which city is known as 'the Athens of the North'?
8 Which US city is served by Dulles International airport?
9 In which northern English city was the 1997 film *The Full Monty* set?
10 Alongside London, Liverpool and Newcastle, which other British city is served by an underground railway system?

Half-time teaser
What is the world record for the longest kiss?

Round 3: The World of Work

1 What does a milliner make or sell?
2 In *Dad's Army*, what was Corporal Jones's job in civilian life?
3 With which job is the disease pneumoconiosis particularly associated?
4 Which US president worked as a male model earlier in his career?
5 In days gone by, what did a wainwright make?
6 In *A Midsummer Night's Dream*, what is the profession of Nick Bottom?
7 Which Hollywood star worked as a lumberjack before entering the film business?
8 Bill Giles, John Ketley and Ian McCaskill are all employed as what?
9 Which policeman swapped his old job for that of a figure skater?
10 What role in a film crew is performed by the best boy?

Round 4: Pot Luck

1 Which US artist is better known for his invention of the electric telegraph?
2 What name is given to a potential building site that has been built on before?
3 What does copra come from?
4 Who named his first child Zowie?
5 Which two cities are connected by the M1?
6 Which disease is known as the Royal Disease?
7 Who had a number one hit in the UK in 1995 with 'Some might say'?
8 Who wrote *The Bonfire of the Vanities*?
9 William Fox Talbot is remembered as a pioneer in which field?
10 Which ancient Chinese dynasty held power from AD 1368 to 1644?

Jackpot

In which sport might a player 'dig' to defend against a 'spike'?

✳ In reality, only one episode of the series was filmed in the city in which it was supposedly set: the rest were filmed in and around the Paramount Studios in Los Angeles.

Quiz 51

Round 1: Pot Luck

1 Which is the world's smallest continent?
2 Which can survive longer without water – a camel or a rat?
3 By what name was Thailand known until 1939?
4 Who was the lead singer with the Pretenders?
5 Who played the emperor Claudius in the 1976 television adaptation of *I, Claudius* by Robert Graves?
6 Which Viking leader settled Greenland in the tenth century?
7 Which animal has a bill like a duck, a tail like a beaver and lays eggs?
8 In what year was the Apollo programme to land a man on the Moon announced?
9 What is 'triskadekaphobia' the fear of?
10 From which Mediterranean island did the emperor Napoleon escape in 1815?

Round 2: Famous Firsts

1 Who was the first person to swim the English Channel?
2 Which national team won the first World Cup competition in 1930?
3 'Dimwit', 'twit', 'wally' and 'wimp' were all first recorded as insults in which decade of the twentieth century?
4 Who was the first scientist to split the atom?
5 Which was the first of the comic operas of Gilbert and Sullivan?
6 What was the first full-length animated film made by Walt Disney?
7 What was first introduced to Britain by Sir Walter Raleigh on 27 July 1586?
8 What was British architect 'Capability' Brown's real first name?
9 Who became the first English bride of an heir to the British throne since 1659?
10 What means of escape did bank robbers in Paris use for the first time on 27 October 1901?

Half-time teaser

By the time of what would have been his seventieth birthday in 2005, Elvis Presley had reached number one in the UK charts more times than any other artist – how many chart-toppers had he had?

Round 3: Shopping

1 What shopping innovation was introduced in an Oklahoma supermarket in June 1937?
2 What brand is advertised with the slogan 'Bread wi' nowt taken out'?
3 What does the English word 'gift' mean in German?
4 Complete the slogan: 'Melts in your mouth . . .'
5 Which magazine is sold in shopping streets 'to help the homeless help themselves'?
6 What innovation terrified shoppers when introduced for the first time at Harrods in Knightsbridge?
7 What was the name of the department store in the television sitcom *Are You Being Served?*
8 Under what name did Chris Lowe and Neil Tennant have a series of chart hits?
9 Which London department store adopted the slogan 'The customer is always right'?
10 What was the name of Arkwright's shop assistant in the sitcom *Open All Hours?*

Round 4: Pot Luck

1 Of which country was Constantine II the last king?
2 What kind of music did Scott Joplin play?
3 In which Beijing square were hundreds of students massacred by Chinese troops in June 1989?
4 Who, in his 1991 song 'Stay away', sang 'I'd rather be dead than cool'?
5 Which poet wrote the poem 'Not waving but drowning'?
6 Which of the world's lakes has the largest surface area?
7 What is the common name for the medical condition *tinea pedis*?
8 Which British city was heavily bombed on 14 November 1940 in Operation Moonlight?
9 By what name are members of the Society of Friends better known?
10 In which sport is the Walker Cup contested?

Jackpot

Who succeeded Nelson Mandela as president of South Africa in 1999?

* It is also one of the few venomous mammals, with a spine on its foot capable of causing severe pain in humans.

Quiz 52

Round 1: Pot Luck

1 By what name is 14 July known in France?
2 Which car manufacturer makes the Brava, Ducato and Tipo?
3 Who is the central character in James Joyce's *Ulysses*?
4 To which post was Joseph Ratzinger elected in 2005?
5 What was the *Spruce Goose*?
6 Which contemporary political leader is a descendant of William IV and a fifth cousin twice removed of Elizabeth II?
7 What name is given to people (usually civilians) kept near a potential target to deter attack?
8 By what name is Aden now known?
9 In British place names, what does 'scar' mean?
10 Which one of rugby's Six Nations has never won a Home Nations, Five Nations or Six Nations championship?

Round 2: Kings and Queens

1 In which country did Elizabeth II receive the news that she was queen?
2 Who was the last of the reigning Stuart kings and queens of Britain?
3 Of which country did Albert II become king in 1993?
4 Who was the first Danish king of England?
5 Humbert II was the last king of which European country?
6 How many prime ministers, up to and including Tony Blair, have there been during the reign of Elizabeth II?
7 Which European country has been ruled by queens called Christina and Ulrika?
8 In which English city is King John buried?
9 Who was 'the King of Swing'?
10 Which mythological king suffered the misfortune of seeing everything he touched turned to gold?

Half-time teaser

In 2001 the diameter of a tennis ball was increased to how many millimetres?

Round 3: Music

1 Who is the odd one out musically – Geraint Evans, Enrico Caruso or Mario Lanza?
2 Who wrote 'Alexander's Ragtime Band'?
3 With which band was Jim Morrison lead singer? *
4 Who suggested 'bending it' in 1966?
5 From which show does the song 'Climb every mountain' come?
6 Westlife's first seven releases all reached number one – true or false?
7 In which film did Cliff Richard sing 'Bachelor boy'?
8 According to the song, why should one thank heaven for little girls?
9 Which Indian instrument was made popular in the West by Ravi Shankar?
10 Which work by Tchaikovsky incorporates 'La Marseillaise'?

Round 4: Pot Luck

1 Which European explorer discovered Hawaii?
2 In which sport is the Waterloo Cup contested?
3 Which island group includes Praslin, Silhouette and Bird islands?
4 Where would you find crenels and merlons?
5 Which of the following is the odd one out – hara-kiri, sushi or sashimi?
6 Where is the University of Hertfordshire based?
7 Who was the first actor to be knighted – David Garrick, Edmund Kean or Henry Irving?
8 Which English county has the motto 'Much in little'?
9 In World War II, what did the Germans call their defences on the Channel coast?
10 What are Boodle's, Groucho's and Pratt's?

Jackpot

What does the American word 'scuttlebutt' refer to?

* The causes of Morrison's death in Paris at the age of 27 have never been properly explained. There has been much speculation that he is still alive, living in India, Africa or South America, above a supermarket in New Jersey or as a cowboy in Oregon.

Quiz 53

Round 1: Pot Luck
1 What is the last letter of the ancient Greek alphabet?
2 In CD-ROM, what does ROM stand for?
3 What is the popular name for the Indian film industry?
4 At which Scottish school were Princes Charles, Andrew and Edward educated?
5 Where did the record-breaking Brinks-Mat robbery of 1983 take place?
6 What was a 'boneshaker'?
7 Of what country is Biafra a part?
8 Who directed James Stewart in the classic 1946 film *It's a Wonderful Life*?
9 Who formed the French National Party in 1972?
10 Which member of the Rolling Stones died in 1969?

Round 2: The 1960s
1 Who was the third member of the 1969 Apollo moon landing mission, alongside Neil Armstrong and Buzz Aldrin?
2 What, since 1967, has been sold under the slogan 'Because I'm worth it'?
3 Which US artist and film-maker in 1968 was shot and wounded by an actress who had appeared in one of his films?
4 In 1967, which British football club became the first to win the European Championship?
5 Which popular television sitcom of the late 1960s starred Derek Nimmo as an accident-prone clergyman?
6 With which political figure did the phrase 'the wind of change' become associated?
7 In which television series of the 1960s was Cathy Gale a character?
8 Which 1968 Beatles song was originally given the title 'I'm backing Britain'?
9 Where did an anti-Castro invasion end in fiasco on 17 April 1961?
10 Who, in 1963, proclaimed to a large German audience 'I am a doughnut'?

Half-time teaser
According to the 2001 census, what percentage of homes in the UK are one-person households?

Round 3: Colours

1 Who had a 'blue period' from 1901 to 1904?
2 Copper nitrate is blue, but what colour is copper chloride?
3 Who sang about a lady in red in 1986?
4 What colour did the Rolling Stones suggest it should be painted in 1966?
5 Who shot to stardom in the 1930 film *Blue Angel*?
6 Which real-life hero played a young Union soldier in the American Civil War in the 1951 film *The Red Badge of Courage*?
7 Into which large green creature does Dr David Banner transform when angered?
8 What colour cards are used for history questions in the board game Trivial Pursuit?
9 At which school was the fictional Tom Brown educated in the novel *Tom Brown's Schooldays*?
10 What colour is absinthe?

Round 4: Pot Luck

1 What do the initials ACAS stand for?
2 A television drama series about the police is sometimes known as a police periodical, a police procedural or a police epidural?
3 Who had a number one hit in the UK in 1982 with 'Save your love'?
4 Who created the Edinburgh policeman Inspector Rebus?
5 Which organisation is based at Langley, Virginia?
6 For which team did Eric Cantona play immediately before joining Manchester United?
7 What are Boy Scouts between the ages of six and eight called?
8 In which country are more people beheaded than in any other?
9 What did the neo-Impressionists call their technique of using small dots of pure colour to form a picture?
10 In the music-hall song, where did Burlington Bertie come from?

Jackpot
Which team did Roy of the Rovers play for?

✳ The woman, a feminist called Valerie Solanas, was apparently annoyed with her victim because he had lost a film script she had lent him.

Quiz 54

Round 1: Pot Luck
1 In which sport is the Super Bowl played?
2 What is the UAE?
3 What element gives Mars its red colour?
4 In which language was the New Testament originally written?
5 Which charitable organisation was founded in Oxford in 1942?
6 In which country might you find the John Paul II airport?
7 Jimmu, Hanzel and Konin were early rulers of which empire?
8 Which boxer became a champion at five different weights?
9 From which show does the song 'Bewitched, bothered and bewildered' come?
10 In which country did the Velvet Revolution of 1989 take place?

Round 2: Classic British Television
1 Who was the so-called 'Father of Television'?
2 What was Patrick McGoohan's number in *The Prisoner*?
3 How much did a UK television licence cost when introduced in 1946?
4 Which medieval hero was played on television in the 1950s by Conrad Phillips?
5 Valerie Singleton co-presented the first edition of *Blue Peter* – true or false?
6 Which radio and television series was set in Tannochbrae?
7 What was the name of the prison in the comedy series *Porridge*?
8 Which disease afflicted the central character in Dennis Potter's *The Singing Detective*?
9 Which quiz programme has been hosted by Bamber Gascoigne and Jeremy Paxman?
10 What was the name of the horse in *Steptoe and Son*?

Half-time teaser
In 2007 Steve Milton of Oregon established a new world record for a ball made solely of rubber bands – how many rubber bands did he use?

Round 3: Sea Life

1 Bladderwrack is a form of what?
2 A killer whale is a member of the dolphin family – true or false?
3 Which sea creature changes its sex annually?
4 To which species of fish does the central character in the 2003 film *Finding Nemo* belong?
5 What is the name of the seaside resort plagued by a great white shark in *Jaws*?
6 What is a young whale called?
7 What kind of seabird comes in Arctic, common, little and Sandwich varieties?
8 The 1997 movie *Fierce Creatures* was the unsuccessful follow-up to which earlier film?
9 To which family of fishes does the anchovy belong?
10 Which bird is sometimes referred to as a sea parrot?

Round 4: Pot Luck

1 Tarquinius Superbus was the last king of where?
2 On which date is Burns Night celebrated in Scotland?
3 From whose reign does Jacobean architecture date?
4 Which county cricket team has the nickname Gladiators?
5 What is the name of the emperor of Japan whose reign began in 1989?
6 Who adopted 'Thanks for the memory' as a signature tune?
7 Where is the US Open tennis tournament held?
8 Who solved the challenge of the Gordian Knot, said to be so intricate that no man could unravel it?
9 Is Kerry Blue a type of cheese, a breed of dog or a shade of light blue?
10 In cockney rhyming slang, what are you if you are 'elephant's trunk'?

Jackpot

What did the ancient Greeks call a pillar built in the shape of a woman?

⋆ The name Super Bowl was never intended to be a permanent name for the event but just to be used as a stopgap while something better was thought of. It was coined in the 1970s through reference to the Rose Bowl game contested by US colleges and the bouncy Super Ball toys then very popular with children.

Quiz 55

Round 1: Pot Luck

1 Great Britain comprises how many countries?
2 Who wrote 'Summertime'?
3 From which film comes the line 'I'll have what she's having'?
4 Who was captain of the England rugby union team from 1988 to 1996?
5 In astronomy, what are classed as spiral, elliptical or irregular?
6 Who topped the charts with 'I'd like to teach the world to sing'?
7 What is the name of the stretch of water that divides Alaska from Russia?
8 Which famous designer worked on the costumes for the film *My Fair Lady*?
9 Who wrote *The Call of the Wild*?
10 What is sake brewed from?

Round 2: Children

1 What, according to a recent survey, is the most popular sandwich filling among British schoolchildren?
2 Which English king sired the most illegitimate children?
3 Which popular long-running BBC radio programme included among its presenters Uncle Mac?
4 Which pop group comprising Beyoncé Knowles, Kelly Rowland and Michelle Williams broke up in 2005?
5 Which trilogy of novels follows the adventures of a young girl called Lyra?
6 Which member of the Monkees was a former child star whose credits included *Coronation Street* and the stage musical *Oliver!*?
7 The child depicted in the famous painting *Bubbles* by John Everett Millais was the artist's son – true or false?
8 Which popular children's television series of the 1970s was set in a Victorian magic shop?
9 What kind of animal formed the subject matter of Damien Hirst's *Mother and Child Divided*?
10 Who appeared both as one of the children and, in the remake, as the mother in film versions of E. Nesbit's *The Railway Children*?

Half-time teaser
How tall (in feet) is the Canary Wharf Tower?

Round 3: Trains

1 Who took the midnight train to Georgia in 1973?
2 Who was the chairman of the British Railways Board who carried out closures of less well-used lines in the early 1960s?
3 In which real-life railway station was much of the classic 1945 movie *Brief Encounter* filmed?
4 Which first in railway history did William Huskisson MP achieve in 1825?
5 Who lived at 23 Railway Cuttings, East Cheam?
6 What was the name of the big express train in the *Thomas the Tank Engine* stories of the Reverend W. Awdry?
7 By what name did the rail service between King's Cross, London and Edinburgh become known?
8 Who embarked on a love train in 1971?
9 In 1988 French politicians demanded the renaming of which London railway station?
10 Which Scottish rail disaster was commemorated in verse by William McGonagall?

Round 4: Pot Luck

1 Who sang about Lucy in the sky with diamonds in 1974?
2 Which comedy show, cancelled in 1989, always closed with a chase sequence involving scantily clad women?
3 Who created the air ace Biggles?
4 On which continent would you find the country of Suriname?
5 At which theme park can be found the Nemesis and Oblivion rides?
6 Which country came under the dictatorial control of Papa Doc and Baby Doc Duvalier?
7 Which swimmer dominated the Olympic swimming events in 1972?
8 Who played television's Doctor Kildare in the 1960s?
9 Who released the album *Obscured by Clouds* in 1972?
10 Which year did Elizabeth II call her 'annus horribilis'?

Jackpot

Of which town in California did Clint Eastwood become mayor in 1986?

⁎The part of the lady who delivers the line was actually played by director Rob Reiner's mother.

Quiz 56

Round 1: Pot Luck

1 Which three colours appear on the Italian flag?
2 What does a fletcher make?
3 Who is the creator of Tracy Beaker?
4 Stanley Rous was known as 'the Father of English – ' what?
5 By what other name is the peewit or green plover known?
6 Which part of the body is vulnerable to alopecia?
7 Over which empire did Xerxes and Darius reign?
8 Who wrote the play *What the Butler Saw*?
9 Under what name did Annie Lennox and Dave Stewart have a series of chart hits?
10 Which territory in north-west India is disputed between India and Pakistan?

Round 2: Lifestyles

1 Who observed that life is too short to stuff a mushroom?
2 Which instrument did Sherlock Holmes play in his spare time?
3 Instant coffee was introduced by Nestlé in which year – 1917, 1927 or 1937?
4 How did Mrs W. A. Cockran ease the lot of housewives in 1889?
5 In which city did Beau Nash become a celebrated social figure and fashion icon?
6 When was the first microwave oven made – 1945, 1955 or 1965?
7 Which company introduced the first waterproof watch in 1927?
8 Who was the founder of Habitat?
9 The world first suntan cream was developed in which year – 1926, 1936 or 1946?
10 How did Steve Wozniack and Steve Jobs change the modern way of life in 1977?

Half-time teaser

How many episodes were made of the *Dad's Army* comedy series?

Round 3: Books

1 Which book of the Bible describes the flight of the Israelites from Egypt?
2 How old was Adrian Mole when he wrote the first volume of his secret diary?
3 Whose books include *When the Wind Blows* and *Fungus the Bogeyman*?
4 What was voted Book of the Century in a 1997 survey held by Waterstone's and Channel Four?
5 Who wrote books with the titles *Gentlemen Marry Brunettes* and *Gentlemen Prefer Blondes*?
6 In which book was Dolores Haze the object of an older man's obsession?
7 Whose books have included *Down Among the Women* and *The Life and Loves of a She-Devil*?
8 Which is the only Charles Dickens book that has a female narrator?
9 In which book does a ship called the *Pequod* feature prominently?
10 What was the title of the first of the Harry Potter books?

Round 4: Pot Luck

1 In which London building would you find Poets' Corner? ✻
2 What is the heaviest weight division in wrestling, for men over 100 kilograms, called?
3 Which chemical element has the symbol K?
4 What type of animal are loons and potoos?
5 Which British MP was killed by an IRA bomb in the House of Commons car park?
6 What is the name of the marbles that Greece would like back from the British Museum?
7 Of which Australian state is Melbourne the capital?
8 Who was prime minister of Russia until swept away in the Bolshevik Revolution of October 1917?
9 In which Shakespeare play are Malcolm, Hecate and Fleance characters?
10 Who is Richard Penniman better known as?

Jackpot

Of which country was Queen Liliuokalani the last monarch?

✻ Not everyone buried in Poets' Corner was a poet. Also buried there is Thomas Parr, who achieved fame through his great age. Having married for the second time at the age of 122, he finally died in 1635 reputedly aged 152.

Quiz 57

Round 1: Pot Luck

1 Who performed 12 mythological labours?
2 Which singer was nicknamed 'the Queen of Soul'?
3 To whom did Don McLean dedicate his classic hit single 'American Pie'?
4 Which British film company specialising in horror was founded in 1947?
5 Where was chocolate first made?
6 What was the tune blasted out by US helicopters going into the attack in the 1979 film *Apocalypse Now*?
7 Whose long-jump world record established in 1968 remained unbroken until 1991?
8 Who played opposite Clint Eastwood in the 1995 film *The Bridges of Madison County*?
9 Who adopted 'Bring me sunshine' as a signature tune?
10 What is an LED?

Round 2: Smells and Bells

1 Which institution is sometimes referred to by the nickname 'smells and bells'?
2 What nationality was Pope Adrian IV?
3 What name was given to the split that occurred in the Roman Catholic Church in 1378, leading to the establishment of rival popes?
4 Which to date has proved the most popular name among popes?
5 Which 1959 film was the first film ever to be blessed by the Pope?
6 Who played Pope Julius II in the 1965 film *The Agony and the Ecstasy*?
7 Which pope of the twentieth century reigned for just 33 days?
8 Which Roman Catholic organisation was founded in 1928 to promote Christian principles throughout the world?
9 Which city in Northern Ireland has a Catholic district called Bogside?
10 Where was the Vatican banker Roberto Calvi found hanging in 1982?

Half-time teaser

How many countries (by the end of 2005) had abolished the death penalty for all offences?

Round 3: Birds

1 Which popular television sitcom starred Pauline Quirke and Linda Robson as two Essex girls?

2 In golf, what is the name given to a hole that a player completes in three strokes less than par?

3 On which day are birds traditionally believed to choose their mates?

4 Which infectious disease is caused by the H5N1 virus?

5 Who had everyone dancing to the 'Birdie Song' in 1981?

6 By what name did imprisoned US murderer Robert Stroud become better known?

7 Which pop group had hits with cover versions of Bob Dylan's 'Mr Tambourine Man' and 'Turn, turn, turn'?

8 Barnacle geese were formerly eaten by Catholics during Lent because it was thought that they hatched from barnacles and could thus be classed as fish – true or false?

9 By what bird-related nickname are the football clubs Newcastle United and Notts County known?

10 Which French singer was known as 'the little Sparrow'?

Round 4: Pot Luck

1 Who killed Shakespeare's Macbeth?

2 Who led a mutiny against Captain Bligh on the *Bounty* in 1787?

3 Which boy band were at number one in the UK charts on 1 January 2000 with the double-A side 'I have a dream/Seasons in the sun'?

4 Who founded Amstrad in 1968?

5 Charles Dickens was an enthusiastic player of croquet – true or false?

6 Who wrote the lyrics for Elton John's single 'Candle in the wind'? ✳

7 Only women take part in Olympic synchronised swimming competitions – true or false?

8 Which character in Greek tragedy unknowingly killed his father and married his mother?

9 Which organisation sells artificial poppies to mark Remembrance Day?

10 Which one of King Arthur's knights found the Holy Grail?

Jackpot

Which is the highest mountain in Europe?

✳ Although initially addressed to Marilyn Monroe, and later rewritten in memory of Diana, Princess of Wales, it was originally inspired by a tribute to the singer Janis Joplin.

Quiz 58

....

Round 1: Pot Luck

1 What do the initials GPS stand for?
2 How many sides are there in a heptagon?
3 What relation is film director Francis Ford Coppola to actor Nicolas Cage?
4 Who were urging on Eileen in 1982?
5 Is a ship's mizzenmast at the front or rear of the vessel?
6 Where is the English Derby horse race held?
7 Who wrote music criticism under the pseudonym Corno di Bassetto?
8 By what alternative name is the eggplant also known?
9 What was the name of Britain's first commercial jet airliner?
10 Which footballer became, in 1979, the subject of the first one-million-pound transfer?

Round 2: Traitors

1 How many pieces of silver did Judas get for betraying Christ?
2 What was the name of the rock from which traitors were thrown in ancient Rome?
3 Against which monarch was the Rye House Plot aimed?
4 Under what name did Margaretha Geertruida Zelle become notorious?
5 Which English monarch did Edward Oxford, John William Bean, John Francis, William Hamilton, Robert Pate, Arthur O'Connor and Roderick Maclean all try to murder?
6 Which American general was branded a traitor after changing sides during the American War of Independence?
7 In which war was the term 'fifth column' first used?
8 Where in London would you find Traitor's Gate?
9 Against whom was the Babington Plot organised?
10 Who was imprisoned as a traitor after World War II as head of the Vichy regime in France?

Half-time teaser

How long, in metres, is the world's longest bicycle?

Round 3: The 1980s
1 Which newspaper was founded by Eddie Shah in 1986?
2 Who won the Booker Prize for Fiction in 1980 with *Rites of Passage*?
3 What royal title was bestowed upon Princess Anne in 1987?
4 What first did Kevin Moran of Manchester United achieve during an FA Cup final in 1985?
5 Which jockey's struggle against cancer and subsequent Grand National triumph inspired a 1983 film starring John Hurt?
6 What finally disappeared from the British coinage in 1980?
7 What event provoked a boycott of the 1980 Moscow Olympics?
8 Who was dancing on the ceiling in 1986?
9 Who left the European Economic Community in 1985?
10 Who succeeded Ron Greenwood as England football manager in 1982?

Round 4: Pot Luck
1 Who wrote the plays *Volpone* and *Bartholomew Fair*?
2 Which is darker in colour – fino or amontillado sherry?
3 By what English name is the Ursa Major constellation also known?
4 The Romans used concrete in their buildings – true or false?
5 What shape is a lateen sail?
6 To which post were John Flamsteed, Sir Martin Ryle and Sir Martin Rees all appointed?
7 Of which organisation was John Reith the first director-general?
8 On 4 February 1504 James IV of Scotland took part in the first officially documented match in which sport?
9 What nationality is pop musician Manfred Mann?
10 Which television soap opera included among its cast dogs called Willy and Wellard?

Jackpot
Of whom did Buster Keaton say 'Chaplin wasn't the funniest, I wasn't the funniest, this man was the funniest'?

✳ It may help to know that the actor's real name is Nicholas Kim Coppola. He changed his name to avoid accusations of favouritism, borrowing his new one from Luke Cage, a superhero in Marvel Comics.

Quiz 59

Round 1: Pot Luck
1 In which street did the Great Fire of London break out in 1666?
2 What nationality was artist René Magritte?
3 Who wrote the novels *Silas Marner*, *Romola* and *Middlemarch*?
4 Who, in 1986, was 'addicted to love'?
5 Who founded the cult of scientology?
6 Which country took offence when lampooned by comedian Sacha Baron Cohen in a film released in 2006?
7 Which major art prize was won by Gilbert and George in 1986 and by Damien Hirst in 1995?
8 In which film does a troubled former marine called Travis Bickle befriend a young girl called Iris?
9 With which pop group was Errol Brown lead singer?
10 On what fictional island do the *Thomas the Tank Engine* stories of the Reverend W. Awdry take place?

Round 2: Gold
1 What is the chemical symbol for gold?
2 Which brand of cigarettes was sold under the slogan 'pure gold'?
3 Which singer had the nickname 'the Golden Foghorn'?
4 Which comedy team of the 1930s and 1940s included the duos Flanagan and Allen, Nervo and Knox, and Naughton and Gold?
5 What was the name of the political party founded by Sir James Goldsmith in 1994?
6 Upon which popular US television show did comedienne Goldie Hawn get her big break?
7 In which John Huston film do three gold miners fall out in their search for a lost gold mine in central Mexico?
8 At which film festival is the Golden Bear awarded?
9 What is the popular gold-related name for iron pyrite?
10 Who sang the theme song for the James Bond film *Goldeneye*?

Half-time teaser
In his memoirs, how many women does the legendary womaniser Casanova admit to having seduced?

Round 3: Funny Folk

1 Which comedian was known as 'the Cheeky Chappie'?
2 Which British comedians assumed the roles of Jeeves and Wooster in 1990?
3 Which film by the Monty Python team created a furore in religious circles on its release in 1979?
4 Who wrote an autobiography entitled *Don't Laugh at Me*?
5 To which *Carry On* star was John Le Mesurier married?
6 From which Spanish city did the waiter played by Andrew Sachs come in the hit sitcom *Fawlty Towers*?
7 Which of the Marx Brothers pretended he was mute? ✳
8 Where was the comedy series *Father Ted* set?
9 What was the name of the informal lunch club at a hotel in New York that was regularly attended by Dorothy Parker, George S. Kaufman and other legendary wits of the 1920s and 1930s?
10 Who is the Big Yin?

Round 4: Pot Luck

1 Who lived at Hill Top in the Lake District?
2 Which US rock group includes bassist Gene Simmons?
3 On whose life was the film biography *Shadowlands* based?
4 By what Arthurian name was John F. Kennedy's administration popularly known?
5 German V-1 flying bombs were variously known as 'buzz bombs' or by what other nickname?
6 What is the name given to the grassland that covers 40 per cent of Africa?
7 How many individuals were there in the Osmonds pop group?
8 What was the name of the fictional holiday camp in the sitcom *Hi-de-Hi!*?
9 In which African country is the native currency the birr?
10 What was the sequel to the Clint Eastwood film *Every Which Way But Loose*?

Jackpot

Which country has a national flag that is not rectangular in shape?

✳ He performed solely in mime after an early reviewer praised his physical comedy but disliked his voice. Later in life, though, he became a popular after-dinner speaker.

Quiz 60

....

Round 1: Pot Luck

1 What is the maximum number of points that a player can score with three darts?
2 What is the symbol of the Republican Party in the USA?
3 With which racing team did Jim Clark spend his entire Formula One career?
4 In which opera does the ill-fated central character invite a statue to dinner?
5 What colour is celandine?
6 Which English football league club was the first to install artificial turf?
7 Which thriller by Erskine Childers concerned German preparations to invade Britain before World War I?
8 Hypnos was the Greek god of what?
9 What is Crichton's job in J. M. Barrie's play *The Admirable Crichton*?
10 The Perseids, the Leonids and the Geminids are all what?

....

Round 2: Celebrities

1 Which two Hollywood stars made their last appearances in the 1961 film *The Misfits*?
2 What is Ozzy Osbourne's first name?
3 Which pop star in 2007 notoriously cut off her own hair after the staff at a hair salon refused to do so?
4 In 1994 Michael Jackson became the son-in-law of which deceased pop star?
5 US singer Tommy Lee was married to which US film and television actress?
6 Who is godfather to, among others, Sean Lennon, Liz Hurley's son Damian and Brooklyn Beckham?
7 Who caused a stir in 2006 by adopting David Banda?
8 Which contemporary pop star has the married name Shelly Kearns?
9 Who was the victim of allegedly racist comments made by Jade Goody in *Celebrity Big Brother* in 2007?
10 What were the Tamworth Two?

....

Half-time teaser

Jackie Bibby and Rosie Reynolds-McCasland share the record for sitting in a bath with rattlesnakes – how many snakes did each share their bath with?

....

Round 3: Nicknames

1 What nickname did singer Vera Lynn acquire during World War II?✳
2 Which disc jockey had the nickname 'Fluff'?
3 Who is golf's 'Golden Bear'?
4 Who was the so-called 'Madame Sin' who offered intimate encounters in exchange for luncheon vouchers?
5 Which pop musician had the nickname 'Killer'?
6 By what nickname was singer Jenny Lind widely known?
7 Which public figure became known in the press as 'Lord Porn'?
8 Who, in track athletics, became known as 'the Ebony Antelope'?
9 Which member of the royal family was dubbed 'Princess Pushy'?
10 Who was 'America's Sweetheart'?

Round 4: Pot Luck

1 Which London building is famous for its Whispering Gallery?
2 What is the name of the fictional town in which *Coronation Street* is set?
3 What do the initials AONB stand for?
4 In tennis, who was the 'Bouncing Basque'?
5 Which great work of English literature includes 'The Knight's Tale'?
6 In Judaism, which festival commemorates the flight of the Israelites from Egypt?
7 Which US president first announced the development of the space shuttle?
8 On which lake did Donald Campbell die?
9 In which Thomas Hardy novel does Bathsheba Everdene marry Sergeant Troy?
10 If a Cornishman offered you some yarg, what would you be eating?

Jackpot

In which sport are 'kip' and 'Arab spring' technical terms?

✳In modern cockney rhyming slang, 'Vera Lynn' variously stands for 'skin' and thus 'cigarette paper' or, more ominously, 'heroin'.

Quiz 61

....

Round 1: Pot Luck

1 What was the name of the grumpy central character in television's *One Foot in the Grave*?

2 In which English county is the city of Carlisle?

3 Who was known as the Nine Days' Queen?

4 Who released an album called *The Great Rock 'N' Roll Swindle*?

5 Which prison is guarded by the ghostly Dementors in the Harry Potter books of J. K. Rowling?

6 What notable date in history was recorded in the diary of George III with the words 'Nothing of importance happened today'?

7 All polar bears are left-handed – true or false?

8 Of which artistic movement was Roy Lichtenstein a leading member?

9 What was the name of the Mexican leader who captured the Alamo in 1836?

10 Who explained his defeat in a 1923 world heavyweight boxing match with the words 'I forgot to duck'?

....

Round 2: The 1990s

1 Which 1990s television series followed the escapades of a group of young lawyers?

2 What landmark figure did the world's population pass around 6.33 pm on Monday 9 August 1999?

3 Who played the female lead opposite Hugh Grant in the 1995 film of Jane Austen's *Sense and Sensibility*?

4 For which film did Steven Spielberg win his first Oscar in 1993?

5 Who won the World Rally Championship every year from 1996 to 1999?

6 Which Italian fashion-wear company caused a stir in the 1990s with a series of advertisements featuring an inmate on death row and other controversial images?

7 Whose government, in 1993, urged everyone to get 'back to basics'?

8 Which Malibu-based television series prominently featuring red bikinis was first broadcast in 1990?

9 What nickname did the press bestow upon the works of young British artists such as Damien Hurst and Tracey Emin in the 1990s?

10 Who disrupted proceedings at the 1996 Brit Awards ceremony by invading the stage in protest at a performance by US pop star Michael Jackson?

....

Half-time teaser

How large, in square miles, is the principality of Wales?

....

Round 3: Toys and Games

1 After whom was the teddy bear named?
2 By what name was 'bingo' known before it acquired its modern (US) name in the 1960s?
3 The toy balloon was invented in 1824 by scientist Michael Faraday – true or false?
4 Who won the 1967 Eurovision Song Contest with the song 'Puppet on a string'?
5 Under what name were Action Man toy figures sold in the USA?
6 What children's toy began life as a throwing weapon used by hunters in the Philippines?
7 Which brand of children's soft toys, featuring such characters as Quackers the Duck and Waddle the Penguin, was launched in 1994 and sparked an enduring collecting craze?
8 To what game does the Acol bidding system apply?
9 Which company makes the Playstation?
10 Which singer played 'Games without frontiers' in 1980?

Round 4: Pot Luck

1 Who starred in *Gladiator*?
2 Two great footballers, Eusebio and Pelé, shared the same nickname – what was it?
3 Who had hits with 'Lady Eleanor' and 'Meet me on the corner'?
4 Who observed that hell is other people?
5 Which stretch of water lies between Cumbria in England and Dumfries and Galloway in Scotland?
6 What is Batman's real name?
7 Which notorious head of the Teamsters Union in the USA disappeared in 1975 and is generally thought to have been murdered?
8 How many fences are there in the Grand National course?
9 Who released an album called *Pet Sounds*?
10 Which biblical character was said to have lived to the age of 969?

Jackpot

What is the name given in Norse mythology to the battle in which the world will end?

* Many years later the same words were famously repeated by US President Ronald Reagan after he was wounded in an assassination attempt.

Quiz 62

Round 1: Pot Luck

1 What is a young deer called?
2 What ailment is sometimes referred to by the French terms 'petit mal' or 'grand mal'?
3 For which children's cartoon series did the Goodies provide the voices?
4 Where does the falabella breed of horses originally come from?
5 What hours does the middle watch at sea cover?
6 What is the administrative centre of Wiltshire?
7 In which sport do teams compete for the Swaythling Cup?
8 With which band was Rick Wakeman the keyboard player?
9 Which award did poet Benjamin Zephaniah turn down in 2003 because of its imperialistic connections?
10 Which crop is damaged by the boll weevil?

Round 2: Travel

1 What was the name of the yacht in which Sir Francis Chichester sailed single-handed round the world in 1966 and 1967?
2 What name do Muslims give to the pilgrimage the faithful are expected to make to Mecca at least once in their lives?
3 In which ship did Britain's first West Indian immigrants arrive in 1948?
4 Which two Italian cities are linked by the Appian Way?
5 It is further by road from Glasgow to Exeter than it is from Southampton to Stranraer – true or false?
6 Who, in 1991, became the first Briton in space?
7 What make of car proved capable of time travel in the *Back to the Future* films?
8 What is unusual about the journey taken by the cast in the 1966 film *Fantastic Voyage*?
9 In which popular musical do the performers move about on roller skates?
10 Who is the patron saint of travellers?

Half-time teaser

Retired ratcatcher Ken Edwards holds the record for the number of cockroaches eaten in one minute – how many did he eat?

Round 3: Cinema

1 To which actress did Humphrey Bogart deliver the line 'Here's looking at you, kid' in *Casablanca*? ✳

2 Which was the first of the long-running *Carry On* film series?

3 Who played Beatrix Potter in the 2006 film *Miss Potter*?

4 Who directed the films *Barry Lyndon* (1975) and *Full Metal Jacket* (1987)?

5 In which 1978 film did Gregory Peck play the notorious Josef Mengele?

6 Who directed the 1959 comedy *Some Like It Hot*?

7 Which 1979 war film was inspired in part by Joseph Conrad's 'Heart of Darkness'?

8 What was the name of the character played by Michael Caine in *The Ipcress File*?

9 In which film did David Essex play a fairground worker who escapes this life to become a pop star?

10 In which 1956 film did Charlton Heston play Moses?

Round 4: Pot Luck

1 Shortage of which vitamin leads to the condition of scurvy?

2 On which Greek island did King Minos keep the Minotaur?

3 Which US president issued Fourteen Points?

4 Which classic musical was based on Shakespeare's *Romeo and Juliet*?

5 Who was music's Man in Black?

6 Which cricket competition was renamed the Twenty20 Cup in 2003?

7 Which radio play begins 'To begin at the beginning, it is spring, moonless night in the small town, starless and bible-black'?

8 Which of the following monarchs is not buried in Westminster Abbey – Elizabeth I, Charles II or Queen Victoria.

9 What is the sternum more commonly known as?

10 Which is the largest city in California?

Jackpot

Members of which Scottish football club are nicknamed the Jam Tarts?

✳ In 2005 this was voted the fifth most memorable line in film history in an American Film Institute survey. Most memorable of all was 'Frankly, my dear, I don't give a damn' from *Gone With the Wind*.

Quiz 63

Round 1: Pot Luck

1 What do Australians refer to as a 'dunny'?
2 Who, in 1997, became the youngest golfer to win the US Masters?
3 In which children's programme was the Soup Dragon a character?
4 In text messaging, what do the initials FWIW stand for?
5 Who wrote the Whitney Houston hit 'I will always love you'?
6 What was the name of the oil tanker that hit a reef in Prince William Sound in 1988, causing a damaging oil spill?
7 What was the name of the site in north-western Guyana where 913 members of the People's Cult died in 1978?
8 Oxygen is the largest constituent of the air we breathe – true or false?
9 By what name is the USA's B-52 bomber also known?
10 Who was the Brown Bomber?

Round 2: Gods and Goddesses

1 Who, in Greek mythology, was the king of the gods?
2 By what name did the Greeks know the Roman god Mercury?
3 After whom was Thursday named?
4 Which royal figure is considered a god by Rastafarians?
5 Who was the England goalkeeper beaten by Diego Maradona's 'hand of God' goal in the World Cup in 1986?
6 Who is the Hindu goddess of death?
7 What was the name the Romans gave to the Greek goddess Aphrodite?
8 Which David Bowie song contains the line 'It's a god-awful small affair, to the girl with the mousy hair'?
9 Who directed the *Godfather* films?
10 In which kind of building is the uppermost level popularly referred to as 'the gods'?

Half-time teaser

To the nearest thousand, how many species are there of butterflies and moths?

Round 3: The Weather

1 On whose head did raindrops keep falling in 1970?
2 What name is given to the mental stress suffered by people forced by the weather or other factors to remain indoors for a long period?
3 Who was the presenter of BBC television's *That Was the Week That Was*?
4 By what name is 15 July known in reference to the legend that the weather on that date will remain unchanged for the next 40 days?
5 Which communications satellite launched by the USA in 1962 became the subject of a hit single by the Tornados?
6 Which blockbuster novel published in 1936 was nearly given the alternative title *Tomorrow is Another Day*?
7 What was the name of the hurricane that devastated New Orleans in 2005?
8 Who, in 1962, observed that 'it might as well rain until September'?
9 Who had his one and only chart success with the single 'Seasons in the sun' in 1974?
10 Who, in 1999, wanted to know why it always rained on them?

Round 4: Pot Luck

1 Which tune provided both Judy Collins and the Royal Scots Dragoon Guards with a hit?
2 In which novel does Nick Carraway play the role of narrator?
3 A giraffe cannot cough – true or false?
4 What is the collective noun for a group of porpoises?
5 What was Elvis Presley's first UK number one hit single?
6 Which racehorse won the Grand National in 1977?
7 Who joined Luciano Pavarotti and Placido Domingo to make up the Three Tenors?
8 Who succeeded Sir Thomas Fairfax as head of the New Model Army in 1650?
9 What is graphology the study of?
10 What name is given to a piece of chicken cooked with a filling of garlic butter?

Jackpot

In which country did the Orange Revolution of 2004 take place?

✴After England beat Argentina in the 2002 World Cup, some fans celebrated by wearing T-shirts bearing the legend 'Look, no hands!'

Quiz 64

....

Round 1: Pot Luck

1 What is the capital of Cuba?
2 Which motor-racing circuit near Weybridge in Surrey hosted top race events before World War II?
3 What is the Scottish equivalent of a judge?
4 Which car manufacturer makes the Boxster and the Carrera?
5 Who directed the *Death Wish* films starring Charles Bronson?
6 Which modern delicacy made its first appearance in a chip shop in Stonehaven, western Scotland in the mid-1990s?
7 Which 2000 film told the story of a working-class lad's ambition to become a ballet dancer?
8 How many farthings were there in a shilling?
9 In which sport is the Britannia Shield a leading competition?
10 What sport do the Barmy Army follow?

....

Round 2: Africa

1 Cape Town is overlooked by which mountain?
2 Which East African country was once known as Abyssinia?
3 By what nickname is South Africa's rugby union team known?
4 The 1990 film *White Hunter, Black Heart* was based on the filming of which earlier movie?
5 Which African ruler included among his titles 'Lord of All the Beasts of the Earth and Fishes of the Sea, and Conqueror of the British Empire in Africa'?
6 What name did Southern Rhodesia take when it won independence from Britain in 1980?
7 Which animal is responsible for the most human deaths on the African continent?
8 If a South African offered you biltong would you drink it, eat it or put it in your wallet?
9 In which modern country might you find the ruins of ancient Carthage?
10 Algeria lies to the west of Libya – true or false?

....

Half-time teaser

Ashrita Furman holds the record for walking continuously with a milk bottle balanced on top of the head – how many miles did he manage?

....

Round 3: Booze

1 What is perry made from?
2 In which country is ouzo a national drink?
3 What is mixed with vodka and cola to make a Black Russian?
4 Which Mexican liqueur is made from the juice of the agave plant?
5 What is the dominant flavour of curaçao?
6 Which liqueur of French origin was allegedly introduced to Scotland by Bonnie Prince Charlie?✳
7 Which fruit is used to make kirsch?
8 How many bottles are there in a methuselah?
9 If a wine is described as tough, what is wrong with it?
10 Which cocktail consists of one part vodka, two parts orange juice and two teaspoons of Galliano?

Round 4: Pot Luck

1 Who is remembered as the inventor of the pneumatic tyre?
2 In 1960s television, where did the *Seaview* sail to under Admiral Nelson?
3 Who adopted 'I got rhythm' as a signature tune?
4 Which strait links the Aegean Sea with the Sea of Marmara?
5 Pearl is a derivative form of which first name?
6 How many innings are there in a game of baseball?
7 Who, in the role of *Little Britain*'s Emily Howard, repeatedly and unconvincingly protests 'I'm a laydee'?
8 Who came first – Julius Caesar, Nero or Caligula?
9 In which century did the population of the world pass one billion?
10 What was the original title of the television soap opera *Emmerdale*?

Jackpot

In 2002, when the British public were invited to choose a wildflower to represent their county, which flower was selected more often than any other?

✳ Legend has it that the Bonnie Prince handed over the recipe to the Mackinnon family of Skye in gratitude for their hospitality after his defeat against the English in 1746. The drink in question has only been produced commercially since 1912.

Quiz 65

Round 1: Pot Luck
1 What is the name of the fantasy land where Peter Pan lives?
2 Which fictional character was inspired by the real-life Alice Liddell?
3 Who had a 'beautiful day' in 2000?
4 Who was King Lear's other daughter, beside Goneril and Cordelia?
5 What is the anthem of the European Union?
6 What nationality are the pop group Rush?
7 Which aristocratic family have their ancestral seat at Althorp in Northamptonshire?
8 What is a ziggurat?
9 Which sport was rocked by the Black Sox scandal in 1919?
10 Who crowned Napoleon Bonaparte as emperor in 1804?

Round 2: La Belle France
1 Which French town remained in English hands from 1347 to 1558?
2 Which quay, located on the left bank of the Seine in Paris, is often taken to represent the French government as a whole?
3 Who played the title role in the hit 2001 film *Amélie*?
4 Which French artist, influenced by Degas, is celebrated for his paintings of performers at the Moulin Rouge in Paris?
5 Who played Monsieur Hulot in a series of celebrated French film comedies that began in 1953?
6 What was the name of the French commander who died fighting General Wolfe at Quebec?
7 Who provided the heavy breathing on French singer Serge Gainsbourg's 1967 hit 'Je t'aime . . . moi non plus'?
8 What did the French call the massive gun with which the Germans shelled Paris in 1918?
9 Which famous French Impressionist had a son who in his turn became a celebrated film director?
10 Who wrote *The French Lieutenant's Woman*?

Half-time teaser
How many symphonies did Wolfgang Amadeus Mozart write?

Round 3: Family Matters

1 Apart from being husband and wife, how are Prince Philip and Elizabeth II related?
2 Who wrote *My Family and Other Animals?*
3 To which family of insects do glow-worms belong?
4 Which member of the Russian royal family did Mrs Anna Anderson claim to be?
5 Who played numerous members of the D'Ascoigne family in the Ealing comedy *Kind Hearts and Coronets?*
6 What was the name of the family cook in *Upstairs Downstairs?*
7 In which J. B. Priestley play does a mysterious policeman interrogate each member of the Birling family about the suicide of a young woman?
8 The king of which country was machine-gunned with most of his family by his own son in 2001?
9 Who played James Bond's ill-fated wife in the film *On Her Majesty's Secret Service?*
10 Were the Walker Brothers, whose hits included 'No regrets', actually brothers?

Round 4: Pot Luck

1 How many squares does a chessboard have?
2 Who painted *Girl with a Pearl Earring?*
3 Who was 'blinded by the light' in 1976?
4 Jayne Torvill was born a year before Chistopher Dean – true or false?
5 What nationality were the parents of Mother Teresa?
6 In which television series is Nora Batty a character?
7 If a person is described in the press as 'tired as emotional' what are they likely to be really?
8 What battle took place on Senlac Hill?
9 Whose best friends include Bill Badger, Algy Pug, Edward Trunk and Bingo the Brainy Pup?
10 In which war did the Battle of the Clouds take place?

Jackpot

Who created the Daleks for television's *Doctor Who?*

⁎ It was named after the great-granddaughter of the founder of the German Krupp company that originally made the gun.

Quiz 66

Round 1: Pot Luck
1 By what other name is the buddleia commonly known?
2 From which show does the song 'Ding dong the witch is dead' come?
3 Which theatre on London's South Bank was rebuilt largely through the efforts of Sam Wanamaker?
4 How many sides are there in a trapezium?
5 What is William Harvey remembered for discovering?
6 Who said, when entering US Customs, 'I have nothing to declare but my genius'?
7 Which Basque and Spanish ball game is usually identified as the fastest ball sport besides golf?
8 Who sang about Enola Gay in 1980?
9 Who wrote the novel *High Fidelity* about a struggling record shop owner?
10 Where in the UK is New Street station?

Round 2: Tourist Destinations
1 Where might you view the Horseshoe Falls and the Rainbow Falls?
2 What material was used to construct the Statue of Liberty?
3 In which country was the first Disneyland resort in Asia opened?
4 Where would you be if you visited 'the Athens of Ireland'?
5 Which lies further north – Majorca, Ibiza or Madeira?
6 Where might tourists view the Venus de Milo?
7 Where did tourists flock in 1851 to see the Great Exhibition?
8 Where can tourists see the Crown Jewels?
9 Which spectacular waterfalls are situated on the border between Zambia and Zimbabwe?
10 Where might the local population call a tourist a 'grockle'?

Half-time teaser
Kharagpur in West Bengal boasts the longest railway platform in the world – how long is it in metres?

Round 3: Handbags and Glad Rags

1 What name is given to the protective leather trousers worn by cowboys in the American West?
2 What kind of garment is a glengarry?
3 What was the name given to the sleeveless tops fashionable in the early 1970s?
4 Where would a man wear dundrearies?✶
5 By what name is the Scottish filibeg better known?
6 What kind of garment is a mantilla?
7 What colour cap do goalkeepers in water polo wear?
8 In greyhound racing, what colour is worn by the dog in trap two?
9 What is a wide-awake?
10 Which language gave us the word 'anorak'?

Round 4: Pot Luck

1 If something is simian, what animal does it resemble?
2 Alongside the juniper and the Scots pine, which is Britain's other native conifer?
3 Which singer began his career backed by the Jordanaires?
4 What is measured in pascals?
5 What was tennis player Evonne Goolagong's married name?
6 Who, in 2006, ended his career holding the record for goals scored in the Premiership?
7 Anton Edelman, Jean-Christophe Novelli and Robert Carrier are all what?
8 Who plays Harry Potter in the films of the adventure stories by J. K. Rowling?
9 What nationality is the central character in *Schindler's List*?
10 What colour is heliotrope?

Jackpot

Where would you find a tittle?

✶ The word itself comes from the name of Lord Dundreary, a vacuous aristocrat in the 1858 play *Our American Cousin* by Tom Taylor. He was particularly relished by audiences for his nonsensical sayings, such as 'Birds of a feather gather no moss'. It was while watching this play that Abraham Lincoln was assassinated.

Quiz 67

Round 1: Pot Luck

1 Which Great Dane kept company with Fred, Velma, Shaggy and Daphne?
2 Who got to number two in the UK charts with 'I did what I did for Maria'?
3 In which children's novel is a rabbit called Hazel a central character?
4 Which is the most common day of the week for heart attacks?
5 Which Beatles track is said to have inspired Charles Manson to go on a murder spree in 1969?
6 In which English county is the city of Exeter?
7 Why did the conviction of a 54-year-old Norwegian for drunken driving make headlines around the world in 1995?
8 Which is the biggest country in Africa?
9 In *Peter Pan*, what did J. M. Barrie call 'an awfully big adventure'?
10 Where did Napoleon die in 1821?

Round 2: Food and Drink

1 What two words were combined to form the word 'brunch'?
2 When is simnel cake eaten?
3 Which cut of beef was supposedly knighted by an English king?
4 What is tofu made from?
5 What allegedly causes Chinese Restaurant Syndrome?
6 What is rum made from?
7 With how many fish did Jesus feed the five thousand?
8 A Bakewell tart is made with jam, sugar, eggs, butter and what other essential ingredient?
9 Which English king died of 'a surfeit of lampreys'?
10 How many pints are there in a flagon?

Half-time teaser

How many emperors of Japan were there before Emperor Akihito succeeded to the throne in 1989?

Round 3: School

1 Who are the gang of riotous schoolchildren whose escapades have long been a star feature of the *Beano* comic?
2 What is the name of the government body set up in 1992 to inspect schools?
3 Who is the best friend of the schoolboy Jennings in the novels of Anthony Buckeridge?
4 Which fictional schoolboy was created by Frank Richards?
5 Which sensational 1954 novel presented a shockingly realistic picture of life in an American urban high school?
6 Which 1961 novel by Muriel Spark described the efforts of a Scottish schoolmistress to inspire her gifted pupils?
7 What is the name of the school in the Charles Dickens novel *Nicholas Nickleby*?
8 Which actor put together a school rock band in the 2003 film *School of Rock*?
9 Who wrote *The School for Scandal*?
10 In which Charlotte Brontë novel is the 10-year-old central character sent to the inhuman Lowood school?

Round 4: Pot Luck

1 From which sport comes the phrase 'ballpark figure', meaning 'an approximate figure'?
2 What is the central wedge-shaped stone in an arch called?
3 Who sang lead vocals with the Pogues until replaced by Joe Strummer?
4 Which classical instrument does Woody Allen play in his spare time?
5 Who wrote 'Nothing compares 2 U'?
6 Only three films have ever won 11 Academy Awards – *Ben-Hur*, *The Lord of the Rings: Return of the King* and which other?
7 Who was taller – Lewis Carroll or J. M. Barrie?
8 Who introduced the concept of 'Big Brother'?
9 Who did the Baha Men let out in 2000?
10 Which historical figure is supposed to have provided the inspiration for Bram Stoker's Dracula?

Jackpot

In which range of hills would you find Hedgehope Hill, Windy Gyle, Cushat Law and Bloodybush Edge?

⁎ According to Manson himself, he was one of five angels who would eventually rule the world. The other four angels were the Beatles.

Quiz 68

Round 1: Pot Luck

1 What is the leading female singer in an opera called?
2 What was the Pink Panther in the first film of that name?
3 What was the only thing left in Pandora's box after she opened it?
4 Whom did film actress Janet Leigh marry in 1951?
5 Which country administers the Azores island group?
6 Paul Weller achieved fame as lead man with which new wave rock band?
7 Which national football team was the first to win two successive World Cup titles?
8 To Americans, are 'pot holders' china ornaments, oven gloves or bras?
9 Hawthorn and may are the same plant – true or false?
10 Who was the first of the Roman emperors?

Round 2: Sport and Leisure

1 In which sport might you use a niblick?
2 Who enjoyed Olympic success on Goodwill?
3 Which England cricketer and Arsenal footballer appeared in advertisements for Brylcreem?
4 Who, in 1955, scored the first official maximum break in snooker?
5 Which Olympic gymnast recorded a perfect score in 1976?
6 In which year was there no winner of the Grand National?
7 How many Formula One world championships did Stirling Moss win?
8 In which century was the jigsaw puzzle invented – the seventeenth century, the eighteenth century or the nineteenth century?
9 What is the maximum score in a tenpin bowling game?
10 How long does an American football match last?

Half-time teaser

In 2004, a new world record was set by an individual playing the drums non-stop – how long did he manage to keep going?

Round 3: Animals

1 What is a boomslang?
2 Which animal, closely related to the llama, is famous for its luxurious wool?
3 What was the dog in Enid Blyton's *Famous Five* books called?
4 What kind of creature is an alewife?
5 What do silkworms feed on?
6 How many humps does a Bactrian camel have?
7 A dugong is a bird with a large curved bill – true or false?
8 What kind of animal comes in eared, elephant and grey varieties?
9 Which animals leave droppings called spraints?
10 At what age under British law does it become legal for a person to buy a pet?

Round 4: Pot Luck

1 What does a cartographer do?
2 In which sport might a competitor execute an Eskimo roll?
3 Which car company was founded by Colin Chapman?
4 In which film does one character tell another 'We're going to need a bigger boat?'
5 In which European city was the 1959 film *La Dolce Vita* set?
6 The Battle of Borodino was fought in which war?
7 Which British prime minister attended the Treaty of Versailles in 1918?
8 What was Buddy Holly's first name? ✳
9 What was the name given to the revived Band Aid project staged in July 2005 to draw attention to Third World poverty?
10 What was the name of David Cassidy's character in television's *Partridge Family*?

Jackpot

Which poetic surname goes with Ezra and Loomis?

✳ Items connected with Buddy Holly continued to be found at the scene of his fatal air crash in 1959 for some years. His famous black-rimmed glasses were located in a local sheriff's office in 1980 and were returned to his family. They were sold in 1998 for $80,000, making them the world's most expensive pair of glasses.

Quiz 69

Round 1: Pot Luck

1 Which Greek scientist is famous for shouting 'Eureka!'?
2 Who designed the Albert Memorial?
3 In 1992 the reputation of Galileo was restored when the Vatican made what concession?
4 Whose best-known paintings included one entitled *Whaam!*?
5 Who wrote the children's story *The Old Man of Lochnagar*?
6 Which former transatlantic liner is now moored at Long Beach, California?
7 Apart from Brazil, which is the only country to have won two successive World Cup football titles?
8 Hendrick Avercamp, Vanessa Bell and Sidney Nolan were all famous as what?
9 Who was the senior British church representative who was kidnapped by Muslim extremists in Beirut in 1984?
10 Who died trying to break a water speed record on Lake Windermere in 1930?

Round 2: Big Business

1 What term describes a level beyond which an employee is unlikely to be promoted?
2 In business jargon, what do the initials PDQ stand for?
3 'Taking care of business' was the motto of which internationally famous pop star?
4 What is the name given to the process of buying up a company and then selling off anything of value?
5 Which company was bought by Victor Kiam because he liked its products so much?
6 In business jargon, what does the acronym 'yuppie' stand for?
7 What name was given to the often unscrupulous traders who descended upon the southern states at the end of the US Civil War in search of easy profits?
8 In what play does a dimwitted apprentice called Willie Mossop rise to riches as a shoe salesman?
9 Which successful diet expert suffered a loss of credibility when he died overweight of a heart attack in 2003?
10 What name was given to the modernisation of the London Stock Exchange, which came into effect on 27 October 1986?

Half-time teaser

What is the metric equivalent, in square metres, of 300 square feet?

Round 3: Love and Marriage

1 With whom does Quasimodo fall in love in Victor Hugo's *The Hunchback of Notre Dame*?
2 Who wrote the play *When We Are Married*?
3 Who had just one big chart hit with 'Lovin' you' before her untimely death in 1979?
4 In England in 1576, how old did a person have to be before they could marry?
5 Which of the following does not make an appearance in the classic Beatles song 'All you need is love' – 'La Marseillaise', 'Greensleeves', 'God save the queen', 'In the mood'?
6 What happened when Napoleon tried to kiss his wife Josephine after their wedding?
7 Which year witnessed the so-called 'Summer of love'?
8 Which sculptor's most famous work shows two people kissing?
9 Who embarked on a 'caravan of love' in 1986?
10 What substance when drunk in tea or coffee is supposed to reduce sexual desire?

Round 4: Pot Luck

1 At which battle was General Custer killed?
2 Which fictional character was inspired by the adventures of Alexander Selkirk?
3 Who had hits with 'If I were a carpenter', 'Reach out I'll be there' and 'Walk away Renée'?
4 Who was 'the Milk Snatcher'?
5 Who provided the voice of Shrek?
6 Wild Bill Hickock, Al Jolson and Buster Keaton all died while engaged in what activity?
7 Ben Travers was the author of a series of highly successful West End comedies – by what name did they become known?
8 What nationality was Henry Stanley, the man who found the explorer David Livingstone in deepest Africa in 1870?
9 Who released an album called *Goat's Head Soup*?
10 By what name is the Mafia also known in the USA?

Jackpot

Who died in the same plane crash as Richie Valens and Buddy Holly?

⁂ The vessel is well known for its many ghosts. Particularly notorious is the first-class swimming pool, which is supposedly haunted by several female ghosts in 1930s swimming costumes.

Quiz 70

Round 1: Pot Luck

1 In which city did Roger Bannister break the four-minute mile?
2 Which US state is bordered by Arizona, Nevada and Oregon?
3 Which car manufacturer makes the Perdana, the Persona and the Satria?
4 How many people are there in an American football team?
5 Which US showman claimed 'There's a sucker born every minute'?
6 How were Elizabeth I and Mary, Queen of Scots related?
7 Which sport was formerly called battledore?
8 The composer J. S. Bach had how many children – 10, 15 or 20?
9 Who was the first black English football international?
10 Which international women's organisation is traditionally associated with 'jam and Jerusalem'?

Round 2: Science and Technology

1 Which chemical element has the symbol Fe?
2 In British electric plugs, what is the brown wire?
3 In food science, what do the initials GM stand for?
4 How many square centimetres are there in one square metre?
5 How many sides does a trapezium have?
6 What is the weight of a litre of water?
7 How should 0.07 be expressed in fractions?
8 How many degrees are there in a semicircle?
9 What unit is used to measure force?
10 How many noughts are there in a million when written as numerals?

Half-time teaser

John Cassidy holds the record for balloon sculptures modelled in one hour – how many did he manage?

Round 3: Young and Old

1 What is a young kangaroo called?
2 Which British order of chivalry is the oldest?
3 Who was the 'Grand Old Man' or 'GOM' of British politics?
4 Is the Old Man of Hoy a type of tobacco, a novel by Walter Scott or a rock stack in Orkney?
5 Only three players have won the PFA Young Player of the Year two years running – Ryan Giggs, Robbie Fowler and who else?
6 Which US president was the youngest to achieve office?
7 Which is the oldest royal residence still in regular use?
8 Who became the youngest world heavyweight champion?
9 Which controversial US general observed 'Old soldiers never die, they simply fade away'?
10 By what name is the 'Stars and Stripes' also known?

Round 4: Pot Luck

1 Which lady famously declared that she was not for turning?
2 What colour is *Wisden Cricketers' Almanac*? ✳
3 From which show does the song 'Hopelessly devoted to you' come?
4 In which part of the British Commonwealth was Edward VIII Governor after his abdication?
5 Which sign of the zodiac covers a person born on 28 October?
6 If something is cooked at Gas Mark 6, what temperature is it cooked at?
7 Which sailing ship was painted by Turner on its way to be broken up?
8 In which Italian city does most of the 1969 film *The Italian Job* take place?
9 What was the preferred mode of transport among mods in the 1960s?
10 In which fictional country was Anthony Hope's *The Prisoner of Zenda* (1894) set?

Jackpot

What was special about the construction of HMS *Wilton*, commissioned into the Royal Navy in 1972?

✳ John Wisden himself was considered the best all-rounder in English cricket in the middle of the nineteenth century. In 1850 he clean-bowled all ten wickets in an innings at Lord's, a feat that remains unmatched in first-class cricket to this day.

Quiz 71

Round 1: Pot Luck

1 In which James Bond adventure is Oddjob an evil henchman?
2 Which poet wrote 'The Pied Piper of Hamelin'?
3 What has been 'good to the last drop' since 1907?
4 Which supergroup of the 1960s consisted of drummer Ginger Baker, bassist Jack Bruce and guitarist Eric Clapton?
5 What was the name of the umpire who became involved in an acrimonious ball-tampering row involving the Pakistan national team in 2006?
6 Who took over from Terry Wogan as host of the television game show *Blankety-Blank*?
7 From which fruit is calvados made?
8 Who adopted 'Sally' as a signature tune?
9 By what name is the country of Zaire now known?
10 What chivalric rank does a person with KT after their name hold?

Round 2: China

1 By what name did the political reorganisation of Chinese society on Maoist principles in the 1960s become known?
2 Which desert extends over a large area of northern China and south-eastern Mongolia?
3 Where do Chinese gooseberries come from?
4 What was the name given to the notional political barrier that grew up between communist China and the non-communist world in the late 1940s?
5 Which Chinese dish has a name that means 'fried flour'?
6 What was the name of the violent uprising directed against foreigners that erupted in China in 1900?
7 Who had china in their hand in 1987?
8 What name has been given to the rows of lifesize model soldiers found in the tomb of the early Chinese emperor Shi Huangdi?
9 The date of the Chinese New Year is judged by the solar calendar – true or false?
10 What is the second longest river in China, after the Yangtze?

Half-time teaser

How many verses are there in the Bible?

Round 3: Flight

1 What is the name given to the official aircraft assigned to the president of the USA?

2 What was the name of the aircraft from which an atomic bomb was dropped on Hiroshima in 1945?✳

3 By what name is the Boeing 747 better known?

4 In RAF bombers of World War II, what name was given to a rear gunner in the tail of an aircraft?

5 Which flammable gas was used to fill the R101 airship, ultimately with disastrous results?

6 In RAF slang what height did an 'angel' (as in 'angels one five') represent?

7 After what is the Chinook helicopter named?

8 Who was manager of Manchester United at the time of the Munich air crash of February 1958?

9 What is the aerial sport played by two teams of seven players in the Harry Potter novels of J. K. Rowling?

10 By what name was air ace Manfred von Richthofen better known?

Round 4: Pot Luck

1 Where is the home of the Northern Ireland Assembly?

2 Who released an album called *Don't Shoot Me, I'm Only the Piano Player*?

3 Which of the 'Carry On' films was set against the background of the Indian Mutiny?

4 What was the name of Bertie Wooster's most formidable aunt?

5 What do the initials VSOP stand for?

6 How many syllables are there in a Japanese haiku?

7 Which member of parliament earned the nickname 'the Beast of Bolsover'?

8 Which annual US sporting event attracts more spectators than any other?

9 Who were Clotho, Atropos and Lachesis?

10 Where in New Mexico was a UFO rumoured to have crashed in 1947?

Jackpot

Which founder-member of Pink Floyd died in 2006?

✳ It was named after the pilot's mother, who in turn had been named after the heroine in a novel.

Quiz 72

Round 1: Pot Luck

1 For what is designer Alec Issigonis usually remembered?
2 Who was 'the Teflon President'?
3 From whom did the USA buy Louisiana in 1803?
4 Where is the Royal Navy's Officer Training School?
5 In which sport does the playing area include a 'popping crease'?
6 What is the process by which water is absorbed by plants?
7 In which film did Ryan O'Neal and his daughter Tatum star as a father and daughter?
8 Which football team plays at the Stadium of Light in Lisbon?
9 Which novel begins with the line 'Last night I dreamt I went to Manderley again'?
10 Of which newspaper was William Rees-Mogg editor until 1981?

Round 2: Children's Television

1 Who was the first actor to play Doctor Who on television?
2 Which classic series featured the World Aquanaut Security Patrol?
3 Whose best friends were Zaza and Mrs Kiki?
4 Which song was Huckleberry Hound constantly singing?
5 Which programme included the characters Colonel Steve Zodiac and Robert the Robot?
6 Who were Fleegle, Bingo, Drooper and Snorky?
7 In television's *Thunderbirds*, by what name was Hiram Hackenbacker better known?
8 What was the name of the first *Blue Peter* guide dog, introduced to the show in 1964?
9 What did the acronym *TISWAS* stand for?
10 In which city is the television series *Byker Grove* set?

Half-time teaser

The world's tallest sandcastle was constructed in Falmouth, Maine in 2003 – how tall was it, in metres?

Round 3: First and Last

1 In which city was the world's first skyscraper built?
2 Which US state would come last in an alphabetical list?
3 What Michael made the first album to be released on the Virgin record label?
4 What type of paint was first marketed by Reeves Ltd in 1964?
5 Whose last words were 'Yet it still moves'?
6 At which battle did the British army stage its last full-scale cavalry charge?
7 Who became the first female Speaker of the House of Commons?
8 The pencil made its first appearance in which year – 1695, 1795 or 1895?
9 Of which country was Zog I the last king?
10 Which was the first sound film?

Round 4: Pot Luck

1 Which character in television's *Star Trek* had green blood (T positive)?
2 Which Christian feast is celebrated on 28 December? *
3 Why was it impossible to put the ball in the back of the net before 1890?
4 Which part of the eye gives it its colour?
5 Which group of writers and artists included the Woolfs, the Bells and Lytton Strachey?
6 What name refers to the practice of making uninvited telephone calls to potential customers in order to sell them something?
7 Whose hits have included 'Breathless', 'Runaway' and 'What can I do'?
8 In which year was the Irish Free State founded – 1916, 1919 or 1949?
9 For what television programme was 'That's living alright' the theme tune?
10 Which football team did television's Alf Garnett support?

Jackpot

Who was Nazi Germany's foreign minister?

* This day is traditionally considered the unluckiest day of the year and a very bad time to take risks or start new projects. The superstitious are also recommended to avoid washing themselves or trimming their fingernails on this date.

Quiz 73

Round 1: Pot Luck

1 Which country lies to the west of Argentina?
2 By what name is the Leonardo da Vinci painting *La Gioconda* also known?
3 Who succeeded Oliver Cromwell as head of England, Scotland and Ireland?
4 What do the initials T. S. stand for in poet T. S. Eliot's name?
5 Which sportsman was variously known as the Brockton Bomber, the Blockbuster or the Rock from Brockton?
6 What is the main ingredient of a Molotov cocktail?
7 Who had a number one hit in the UK in 1974 with 'The streak'?
8 What was the code name of the beach in Normandy entrusted to Canadian invasion forces on D-Day 1944?
9 The Egyptians were plagued by locusts, flies – and which other insects?
10 Which country has a plain green flag?

Round 2: Ships

1 Who sailed the seas in the *Calypso*?
2 In which ship did the Pilgrim Fathers sail to the New World?
3 Nelson's flagship *Victory* is now preserved in dry dock in which port – Southampton, Portsmouth or Falmouth?
4 Which Royal Navy battlecruiser was sunk by the German battleship *Bismarck* on 24 May 1941, with the loss of all but three hands?
5 On sailing ships of the Royal Navy, what was the name given to the upper deck to which only officers had free access?
6 What was the name of the ship upon which Charles Darwin voyaged to the Pacific?
7 Which Greek shipping magnate abandoned his long-term mistress Maria Callas to marry Jackie Kennedy in 1968?
8 What was the name of the Greenpeace vessel sunk by French secret agents in 1985?
9 Who commanded the British fleet at the Battle of Jutland in 1916?
10 What was the name of the oil tanker that sank off Cornwall in 1967, spilling oil on Cornish beaches?

Half-time teaser

How old, in years and days, was Aaron Lennon when, in 2003, he became the youngest player ever to appear in a Premier League match?

Round 3: High Society

1 In which month does Elizabeth II celebrate her official birthday?
2 In *Brideshead Revisited*, what was the name of Sebastian Flyte's teddy bear?
3 Which classic 1941 film starring Orson Welles was based on the life of William Randolph Hearst?
4 Which well-known London night-club was dedicated to socialite Lady Annabel Vane-Tempest-Stewart in 1963?
5 What was the title that Anthony Wedgwood Benn gave up in 1963 in order to continue as a member of parliament?
6 What was the name of the self-proclaimed holy man who exercised great influence over the Russian royal family before the Russian Revolution of 1917?
7 What royal title was bestowed upon Camilla Parker Bowles on her marriage to Prince Charles?
8 Which 1975 album by Queen included the track 'Bohemian rhapsody'?
9 What was the real name of Oscar Wilde's lover Bosie?
10 How many of Henry VIII's wives were beheaded? ✶

Round 4: Pot Luck

1 In which novel is Alan Breck a fugitive from the English?
2 Which is the only country in Africa that is split into two time zones?
3 Which sport did Mark Twain famously dismiss as 'a good walk spoiled'?
4 What nationality are the pop group the Stereophonics?
5 Who became president of Ireland in 1997?
6 Who wrote the *Enigma Variations*?
7 Who played the lead role opposite Leslie Caron in *An American in Paris*?
8 What innovation was introduced to scoring in tennis in 1970?
9 What was the name of the nuclear plant that exploded in April 1986, releasing large amounts of radioactive material?
10 Singer Barry Alan Pincus is better known by what name?

Jackpot

What was introduced to British football on 2 October 1976?

✶ As four of Henry's marriages were annulled, meaning they never took place legitimately, technically he had only two wives.

Quiz 74

Round 1: Pot Luck

1 Whereabouts in France is the Hall of Mirrors?
2 How long does it take the Earth to go round the Sun?
3 Which post has been occupied by Cosmo Gordon Lang, Geoffrey Fisher and Arthur Ramsey?
4 Of which sport is a 'garryowen' a feature?
5 With which single did the Rolling Stones first get to number one?
6 What was the name of the horse that collapsed under Dick Francis in the Grand National?
7 William Wordsworth was one of several prominent poets to refuse the post of Poet Laureate – true or false?
8 Which mythological beast had a lion's body and an eagle's head and wings?
9 Which two US states share no borders with other US states?
10 If something is described as annular, what shape is it?

Round 2: The 1970s

1 Which boys were back in town in 1976?
2 Which new county was formed in 1974 from parts of Somerset and Gloucestershire?
3 Who did Muhammad Ali fight in the famous 'Rumble in the Jungle' bout staged in Zaire in 1974?
4 Which composer's music provided the soundtrack for the 1971 film *Death in Venice*?
5 Who was football's Supersub in the 1970s?
6 What controversial innovation was introduced in the British press in 1970?
7 Which country, in 1976, became the only one to fail to win a gold medal while hosting an Olympic Games?
8 Which country was until 1979 ruled from the so-called Peacock Throne?
9 How were refugees from Vietnam in the 1970s referred to in the press?
10 The coastline of which country was damaged in 1978 by oil from the *Amoco Cadiz*?

Half-time teaser

Emilio Florin of Uruguay has the world's largest collection of key rings, all different – how many does he own?

Round 3: The British Isles

1 Sark is part of which island group?
2 Which island is home to Grimsetter airport?
3 On which island did King John agree the Magna Carta?
4 Which footballer helped Lindisfarne out with 'Fog on the Tyne' in 1990?
5 Which island is governed by the Tynwald?
6 In which islands is 10 January set aside as Maggie Thatcher Day?
7 On which island would you find Fingal's Cave?
8 From which island did Hereward the Wake lead a rebellion against William the Conqueror?
9 On which island is the town of St Helier?
10 Of which island is Portree the largest town?

Round 4: Pot Luck

1 How many red ballons did Nena see go by in 1984?
2 In motor-racing, what does a yellow flag mean?
3 Whose nicknames have included 'The Sultan of Spin' and 'Mandy'?
4 What part of Europe did the Romans know as Lusitania?
5 Who designed the *Great Western*, the *Great Britain* and the *Great Eastern*?
6 What is the name of ITV's teletext system?
7 What nationality is pop singer Enya?
8 Which German commander suffered a reversal in fortunes at El Alamein in 1942?
9 The Skagerrak lies between which two countries?
10 What emergency procedure involves a sufferer being firmly gripped from behind around the ribcage and jerked?

Jackpot

What was the name of the Christian Democrat leader of West Germany for 14 years from 1949?

✳ The throne itself was stolen from the Red Fort at Delhi in a raid of 1793.

Quiz 75

Round 1: Pot Luck

1 What began on 18 June 1940?
2 Who was Europe's first woman prime minister?
3 What starts at Cheriton?
4 Who provided the singing voice of Audrey Hepburn in the film *My Fair Lady*?
5 Which mountain, crowned by an ancient monastery, was the scene of fierce fighting 80 miles south of Rome in February 1944?
6 Queen Victoria's reign was the longest reign in history – true or false?
7 In cricket, what is a 'baggy green'?
8 What physical disability did poets Homer and John Milton have in common?
9 What was the name of Phileas Fogg's manservant in the Jules Verne novel *Around the World in Eighty Days*?
10 Who had a number one hit in the UK in 1999 with 'Millennium prayer'?

Round 2: The Scots

1 Who was the Scottish hero played by Mel Gibson in *Braveheart*?
2 Soldiers of which Scottish clan carried out the massacre at Glencoe in 1691?
3 Who, in Scottish football, was the Big Man?
4 In which film did Edward Woodward come to a fiery end on a Scottish island?
5 What was the name of the leading Nazi who flew to Scotland in 1941 in an attempt to negotiate peace between Britain and Germany?
6 In which pop group have Angus Young, Malcolm Young, Cliff Williams, Bon Scott and Brian Johnson been leading figures over the years?
7 Who wrote the novel *Tender is the Night*?
8 Which dictator included among his titles 'Big Daddy' and 'King of Scotland'?
9 What is Mons Meg – a Scottish bread roll, a large fifteenth-century cannon at Edinburgh Castle or a Scottish folk dance?
10 The last time a bagpiper accompanied Scottish troops into battle was in 1945 – true or false?

Half-time teaser
How many ships of the line took part in the Battle of Trafalgar?

Round 3: Wonderful Words

1 What two words were combined to form the word 'motel'?
2 In the phonetic NATO alphabet beginning Alpha, Bravo, Charlie, which word represents the letter Y?
3 What is the only word in English that begins and ends with the letters 'und'?
4 What is the correct spelling of the word ecstasy?
5 What does the dialect word 'mouldiwarp' refer to – an old cow, a mole or a grassy field?
6 The hypothetical particle called the quark takes its name from which work of literature?
7 In the limericks of Edward Lear, what is a 'runcible'?
8 A 'clowder' is the collective name for a group of what kind of animals?
9 An ancient Greek word meaning 'kingfisher' now means in English 'peaceful' or 'calm' – what is it?✳
10 Which foreign language contributed to English the words 'howitzer', 'pistol' and 'robot'?

Round 4: Pot Luck

1 What colour is the Central Line on maps of the London Underground?
2 A tiger has striped skin – true or false?
3 Which male striptease group was originally founded in Los Angeles in the 1970s?
4 Which is 'the Lone Star State'?
5 Which US rock musician is known as 'the Boss'?
6 Who drew on her own experience of mental breakdown in the 1963 novel *The Bell Jar*?
7 Who had a number one hit in the UK in 1991 with 'Bring your daughter to the slaughter'?
8 Which of the following was not an Anglo-Saxon kingdom – Wessex, Mercia or Anglesey?
9 Which Anthony Burgess novel became a notorious film directed by Stanley Kubrick?
10 Who was known as 'the Welsh Wizard'?

Jackpot

What colour jersey is worn by the winner of the Mountain Stage of the Tour de France?

✳ The ancient Greeks identified the kingfisher with a mythical bird that could supposedly calm the waves by magic during the winter solstice in order to nest at sea, hence the modern meaning of the word in question.

Quiz 76

Round 1: Pot Luck

1 Which war provided the setting for the television series *M.A.S.H.*?
2 In which month is the US Masters golf competition always held?
3 What should you do with bombazine – eat it, wear it or take out the pin and throw it?
4 Upon which Shakespeare play was the 1966 film *Chimes at Midnight* based?
5 Who is Warren Beatty's actress sister?
6 Who wrote *The Unbearable Lightness of Being*?
7 Which martial art has a name that translates as 'way of the empty hand'?
8 Only males can suffer from haemophilia – true or false?
9 Cumbria is the most northerly county in England – true or false?
10 What is unusual about fossils of the dinosaur known as archaeopteryx?

Round 2: Scandals

1 What was exposed by Bernstein and Woodward?
2 Which top jockey was sentenced to three years in prison in 1987?
3 Which scandal was relived in the 1989 film *Scandal*?
4 Which well-known figure was lost overboard from the *Lady Ghislaine* in 1991?
5 Which Nobel Prize-winning German novelist caused a stir in 2006 when he revealed he had been in the Waffen SS?
6 How did Tommie Smith and John Carlos cause a scandal at the 1968 Mexico Olympics?
7 Which European football club was stripped of the 1993 European Champion Clubs' Cup title because of a bribery scandal?
8 Who called the Lonrho Affair the 'unacceptable face of capitalism'?
9 Who was the ghillie with whom Queen Victoria was scandalously linked?
10 Who, when threatened with exposure in the press, thundered 'Publish and be damned!'

Half-time teaser

Lauren and David Blair, who married in 1984, hold the world record for the number of times they have renewed their vows – how many times have they done so?

Round 3: The Weather

1 Who was the Norse god of thunder?
2 Which chilly wind blows off the Alps into southern France and northern Italy for as many as 100 days a year?
3 On the Beaufort scale, which number denotes a whole gale?
4 For whom does Hayley Mills mistake a fugitive on the family farm in the 1961 film *Whistle Down the Wind*?
5 Which weather-related band has released such albums as *Songs for Polar Bears*, *Final Straw* and *Eyes Open*?
6 What is a wind-operated harp called?
7 Which 1969 film featured the song 'Raindrops keep falling on my head'?
8 Which clouds occur higher in the atmosphere – cirrus or cumulus?
9 Which British politician owned a yacht called *Morning Cloud*?
10 What is the literal meaning of the Japanese word 'kamikaze'?

Round 4: Pot Luck

1 Which country is governed by the Knesset?
2 Who composed the opera *Tosca*?
3 Michael and Vincent Hickey, James Robinson and Patrick Molloy were known as what?
4 Deep Purple started life as the New Yardbirds – true or false?
5 Who was the first Briton to win the Formula One World Championship?
6 At which ground does Warwickshire county cricket team play?
7 Alongside Will Smith, who was the other Man in Black?
8 What medical term describes the feigning of symptoms to gain admission to hospital?
9 Against which similar vessel did the ironclad *Virginia* fight an epic battle in 1862?
10 What was the name of the brutal political movement led by Pol Pot?

Jackpot

During which month does the action of Shakespeare's *Romeo and Juliet* take place?

✳ Among other services, the queen's ghillie devised for the monarch a cocktail of claret wine and Scotch whisky, which became her favourite drink. In the 1980s, Queen Elizabeth the Queen Mother is said to have admitted finding documents suggesting the pair actually married – and to have burned them.

Quiz 77

Round 1: Pot Luck

1 What is the name of the prime minister's official country residence?
2 What was the nickname of General Erwin Rommel?
3 Which song on the *Abbey Road* album by the Beatles was sung by Ringo Starr?
4 What phobia does a person suffer from if he or she is afraid of spiders?
5 Alongside Leinster, Munster and Ulster, which is the fourth province of Ireland?
6 Simon and Garfunkel were originally called Tom and Jerry – true or false?
7 In which country was the famed library of Alexandria?
8 What did the actor whose real name was River Bottom change it to?
9 A kangaroo cannot walk backwards – true or false?
10 Which product 'does exactly what it says on the tin'?

Round 2: US Presidents

1 Which scandal resulted in the resignation of US president Richard Nixon?
2 What is the name of the rural retreat used by US presidents?
3 What is the only surname that has been shared by a president of the USA and a prime minister of Britain?
4 The Bushes were the first father and son to serve as US president – true or false?
5 Who played the US president in the 1996 Tim Burton film *Mars Attacks*?
6 Which US president acquired the nickname 'the Great Communicator'?
7 Which US president was elected to office four times?
8 In which speech did US president Abraham Lincoln speak of 'government of the people, by the people, for the people'?
9 Who, despite winning more votes overall, was narrowly beaten by George W. Bush in the US presidential election of 2000?
10 What did the S in Harry S. Truman stand for?

Half-time teaser

How far is it in miles from Moscow to Beijing?

Round 3: Pop Groups

1 Of which band were Rick Parfitt and Francis Rossi founding members?
2 Which band was led by Kurt Cobain until 1994?
3 What was the name of the skiffle group led by John Lennon that in due course became the Beatles?
4 Which pop group had a line-up comprising Benny Anderwear, Agnetha Falstart, Frida Longstokin and Bjorn Volvo-us?
5 Who sang lead vocals with Roxy Music?
6 Under what name did Bob Dylan, George Harrison, Jeff Lynne, Roy Orbison and Tom Petty form their own supergroup in 1988?
7 Who was manager of the Sex Pistols?
8 In which city was Black Sabbath lead singer Ozzy Osbourne born?
9 With which 1970s pop group did Dave Hill play lead guitar?
10 Who was lead singer with the Smiths?

Round 4: Pot Luck

1 Who was Ol' Blue Eyes?
2 What do the initials RADA stand for?
3 Which West Indian batsman was sometimes called 'the black Bradman'?
4 Which US television series featured investigators Mulder and Scully?
5 What did the Jacksons blame it on in 1978?
6 In 1938 fishermen netted a fish that had supposedly been extinct for 70 million years – what was it called?
7 Which drug is sometimes referred to as 'brown sugar'?
8 Which film actress was nicknamed the Iceberg?
9 Who directed *Pulp Fiction*?
10 What was the name of the character played by George Cole in the television series *Minder*?

Jackpot

In 1975, following the unification of Vietnam, what new name was given to the city of Saigon?

✳ All three of the other Beatles are recorded as having described Ringo as the best rock 'n' roll drummer in the world. On one occasion, however, when asked whether Ringo was the best drummer in the world, Lennon joked 'He's not even the best drummer in the Beatles!'

Quiz 78

....

Round 1: Pot Luck

1 Who was 'the Godfather of Soul'?
2 Which dark-leaved evergreen tree is often planted in churchyards?
3 Which English cathedral has a Bell Harry Tower?
4 To whom did Theodore Roosevelt lose the 1912 US presidential election?
5 What is the home ground of Rangers football club?
6 In which sport do teams contest the Vince Lombardi trophy?
7 Which Oscar-winning film director made his début as an actor in the 1942 film *In Which We Serve*?
8 In which opera does Figaro pursue Rosina?
9 Which kingdom was reigned over by Queen Wilhelmina?
10 What was the cargo of the *Bounty* when mutiny broke out in 1789?

....

Round 2: Birds

1 What is an eagle's nest called?
2 The hummingbird is the only bird that can fly backwards – true or false?
3 What kind of bird is a hobby?
4 Which kind of bird comes in emperor, fairy and Galapagos species?
5 Which British bird can run the fastest?
6 Only female ducks quack – true or false?
7 What name is given to manure made from bird or bat droppings?
8 Which is Britain's smallest bird?
9 In which part of their stomach do birds grind their food?
10 By what other name are Mother Carey's chickens known?

....

Half-time teaser

In 2005, a record number of people dressed up as gorillas in London to raise money for the Dian Fossey Gorilla Fund – how many attended?

....

Round 3: Castles and Cathedrals
1 Windsor is the largest castle in England – true or false?
2 Which cathedral houses the largest bell in the UK?
3 In which notorious castle near Leipzig were Allied prisoners of war kept during World War II to prevent them making further escape attempts?
4 In which British city is there a Roman Catholic cathedral nicknamed 'Paddy's Wigwam'?
5 Salisbury cathedral is the oldest in Britain – true or false?
6 Which stately home became Brideshead in the 1981 television production of Evelyn Waugh's *Brideshead Revisited*?
7 In which British city is there a cathedral dedicated to St Mungo?
8 Which English cathedral has the tallest spire? ✶
9 In which county is the prehistoric earthwork known as Maiden Castle?
10 What name was given to the central structure in a medieval castle?

Round 4: Pot Luck
1 At whose trial did journalist Martin Bashir give evidence in 2005?
2 In 1962 the Metropole in Brighton became Britain's first licensed what?
3 What did the Shadows call themselves until they realised there was already a US band of the same name?
4 Which country cricket team plays at Old Trafford?
5 The Kiel Canal links Kiel with which sea?
6 Which 10-year-old actress in 1974 became the youngest ever to win an Oscar?
7 Which English football league club originally played as Thames Ironworks FC?
8 What do golfers call a free shot awarded after a poor shot?
9 Who had hits with 'Army of me' and 'It's oh so quiet'?
10 Which extreme sport originated as a rite of passage for young men on the South Pacific island of Pentecost?

Jackpot
In the phrase 'mind your ps and qs', what are the 'ps and qs'?

✶ Lincoln cathedral had the highest spire (at 524 feet) until it was blown down in 1584.

Quiz 79

Round 1: Pot Luck
1 Who, in 1971, sang about 'the fastest milkman in the west'?
2 Which street in New Orleans is traditionally identified as the birthplace of jazz music?
3 In which country was Osama Bin Laden born?
4 Who won the 1970 Eurovision Song Contest with the song 'All kinds of everything'?
5 To what was Ian Botham referring when he issued the challenge 'Bet you can't eat three!'?
6 Who, according to Winston Churchill, was 'the bullfrog of the Pontine marshes'?
7 Which US theatrical awards were named after US actress and manager Antoinette Perry?
8 Who released an album with the title *Are You Experienced*?
9 In which country did Austrian psychoanalyst Sigmund Freud die?
10 Which film director has won more Oscars than any other?

Round 2: Ireland and the Irish
1 By what name did Irishman Fingal O'Flahertie Wills become better known?
2 In which county would you find the Giant's Causeway?
3 What is the real name of U2's singer Bono?
4 Ireland has won the Eurovision Song Contest more times than any other country – true or false?
5 Which Irish nationalist leader was assassinated on 22 August 1922, plunging Ireland into mourning?
6 Which is the longest river in Ireland?
7 What was the informal name of the military police force that ruthlessly suppressed Irish Republicans in the early 1920s?
8 Which horse won both the Derby and the Irish Derby in 1981?
9 Where in County Mayo did the Virgin Mary allegedly make an appearance in 1879?
10 Who, in 1995, became the fourth Irishman to win the Nobel Prize for Literature?

Half-time teaser
The first heart transplant patient survived for 18 days after the operation – how long did the second patient survive?

Round 3: Sport and Leisure

1 In football, who holds the record for the most England caps?
2 Who directed the film *Chariots of Fire*?
3 Which British golfer was the first to win the US Masters?
4 Who captained the England cricket team when it suffered a five-nil whitewash against Australia in 2006, its worst defeat in the Ashes since 1921?
5 In 1983, which Second Division football team decided to sell all its players?
6 Which World Heavyweight boxing champion is believed to have died from a heroin overdose in 1970?
7 Which country has hosted the modern Summer Olympics the most times?
8 In which athletic event does Ashia Hansen specialise?
9 Which batsman retired with a record test average of 99.4 runs?
10 Which motor-racing circuit has been home to the British Formula One Grand Prix since 1987?

Round 4: Pot Luck

1 Where was the German fleet scuttled in 1919?
2 What was the name of the manager of the Beatles who died in 1967?
3 What is the Latin name for the Northern Lights?
4 What is the capital city of Nepal?
5 By what name was the tomato known when first introduced to Europe? ✳
6 Which is the hottest planet in the solar system?
7 Archie Bunker was the US equivalent of which British television character?
8 Who wrote the novel *Of Mice and Men*?
9 Which prominent US politician is known by such nicknames as 'Hilla the Hun' and 'Wicked Witch of the West Wing'?
10 Who got to number one in 1975 with 'Tears on my pillow'?

Jackpot

In which country were the Tonton Macoutes a feared private militia?

✳ No one was quite sure what to make of the tomato when it was first introduced. Many people avoided eating them, suspicious of their alleged aphrodisiac properties.

Quiz 80

Round 1: Pot Luck

1 Which Shakespeare play begins 'When shall we three meet again?'
2 Which sport involves making parachute jumps from high buildings or clifftops?
3 With which band did Jools Holland first enjoy success, playing keyboards?
4 Which team won the first Premier League football championship in 1993?
5 What is the Agatha Award presented for?
6 What name is given to a piano that has had the felt removed from its hammers, resulting in a more percussive, tinny sound?
7 Which member of Hollywood's Rat Pack claimed 'You're not drunk if you can lie on the floor without holding on'?
8 In which opera does a gypsy girl fall in love with a toreador?
9 In which city is the Paragon railway station?
10 Which well-known cricket ground is situated in St John's Wood, London?

Round 2: Body Matters

1 Which is the largest internal organ in the human body?
2 What is the clavicle better known as?
3 In Greek mythology, which beast had a woman's head and a lion's body?
4 Which English queen said 'I know I have the body of a weak and feeble woman, but I have the heart and stomach of a King'?
5 Which part of the body is technically called the hallux?
6 What is the light-sensitive part of the eye called?
7 Which gland produces insulin within the body?
8 What are a person's eye teeth otherwise known as?
9 How much skin does an average male adult human have – 10 square feet, 20 square feet or 30 square feet?
10 How many pairs of chromosomes are there in a human cell?

Half-time teaser

In 2005, a 115-year-old pair of jeans was sold for what record sum?

Round 3: War and Peace

1 Which army rank is the most senior – Captain, Lieutenant or Major?
2 In which war was the Battle of Marston Moor fought?
3 Which naval weapon was invented by Robert Whitehead in 1866?
4 Which organisation publishes the *War Cry*?
5 Who replaced Sir John French as commander of the British Expeditionary Force in 1914?
6 In which war did Leo Tolstoy fight?
7 William Shakespeare's play *Troilus and Cressida* is set against the background of which war?
8 With which country did the UK fight the Cod War in the 1960s?
9 How did Gavrilo Princip, the man who assassinated Franz Ferdinand and triggered World War I, die – by hanging, cyanide or tuberculosis?
10 Which king hid in an oak tree after the Battle of Worcester? ✳

Round 4: Pot Luck

1 Who succeeded Richard Nixon as US president?
2 Who released the album *Talking with the Taxman about Poetry*?
3 What term refers to the illicit practice of attempting to recruit a professional football player without the permission of his current club?
4 Which animal has a name that means 'earth pig'?
5 The formidable Margaret Dumont made appearances in the films of which comedy team?
6 Tennis-player Fred Perry was also a noted player of which other sport?
7 Whose music is closely associated with the annual Bayreuth Festival?
8 Which sport was invented in Canada by native Americans some time before the seventeenth century?
9 Buster Bloodvessel was lead singer with which pop group?
10 In which sport might a participant perform a veronica?

Jackpot

Who was the last British monarch to die in battle?

✳The original oak, at Boscobel House, died after tourists removed many of its branches as souvenirs. Its replacement was badly damaged by a storm in 2000, so a new sapling, grown from an acorn from the old tree, was planted by Prince Charles in 2001.

Quiz 81

Round 1: Pot Luck
1 By what name did Lesley Hornby become better known?
2 Who painted *The Monarch of the Glen*?
3 Which well-known television quiz show presenter who died in 2007 was born in Iceland?
4 Which US film actress of the 1920s became known as the 'It Girl'?
5 By which of the following names did the common British soldier become known around the end of the nineteenth century – Billy Smith, Tommy Atkins or Johnny Jones?
6 Whose hits included 'Charmless man', 'Parklife' and 'Country house'?
7 Which was the last battle to be fought on British soil?
8 What is the currency of Tunisia?
9 Which role did Anne Bancroft play in the 1967 film *The Graduate*?
10 By what name did Shirley Crabtree become famous?

Round 2: Sudden Deaths
1 Name the only British prime minister to be assassinated.
2 How did Brutus, assassin of Julius Caesar, die?
3 Which television drama series began as a quest to discover who murdered Laura Palmer?
4 What was the name given to the murder of some 50,000 French Protestants on 24 August 1572?
5 The Roman emperors Tiberius and Claudius, Tsar Alexander I of Russia, Pope Clement II and Charles V of France all died the same way – how?
6 Where did gunman Michael Ryan shoot 28 people on 20 August 1987?
7 Which soul singer was shot dead by his own father?
8 Whose assassination by Czech resistance fighters in 1942 provoked the murder of hundreds of ordinary Czechs in retaliation?
9 By what means was Bulgarian writer Georgi Markov assassinated in London in 1978?
10 Russian dissident Alexander Litvinenko was poisoned by which radioactive element?

Half-time teaser
Mars has the shortest year of any planet in the solar system – how many days does it have?

Round 3: Cartoons

1 What was Mickey Mouse's original name?
2 Which Disney cartoon character provided a nickname for prime minister Tony Blair?
3 Who provided the voice of Bugs Bunny?
4 Which was the first cartoon character to attract the attention of the censors?
5 In which Hanna-Barbera cartoon did Officer Charlie Dibble appear?
6 Which actor provided the voice for Shere Khan in the Disney version of *The Jungle Book*?
7 Who created the cartoon character Charlie Brown?
8 With which cartoon character is the catchphrase 'Yabba-dabba-doo!' associated?
9 Who created Tom and Jerry?
10 What was the name of the cavemen-racers in *Wacky Races*? ✳

Round 4: Pot Luck

1 Checkpoint Charlie was a crossing point in which notorious barrier?
2 Which US highway connects Chicago with Los Angeles?
3 In which country are the Tamil Tigers a powerful rebel force?
4 Who, in 1986, pointed out that 'anyone can fall in love'?
5 What invention of Sir John Harington's in 1589 proved a great convenience?
6 Who wrote the opera *Peter Grimes*?
7 Who lost the Battle of the Spurs?
8 What was the name of the vacuum cleaner in *The Teletubbies*?
9 Who played Michael Corleone in *The Godfather*?
10 Which US federal prison situated on a rocky island in San Francisco Bay housed Al Capone among other dangerous criminals?

Jackpot

The alphabet of the Rotokas language, spoken in Papua New Guinea, is the smallest in the world – how many letters does it have?

✳ Formula One ace Michael Schumacher was nicknamed Dick Dastardly after the character in *Wacky Races* on account of both his prominent chin and his employment of ruthless tactics on the track against other drivers.

Quiz 82

....

Round 1: Pot Luck

1 Who had a hit with 'Stairway to heaven' in 1993?
2 Which Roman emperor competed in the Olympic Games?
3 Which World War II cruiser is moored today at Symon's Wharf in London?
4 In golf, which club was formerly known as a 'mashie'?
5 Which is the only country that is ahead of the USA in World's Strongest Man competitions?
6 Which artist's masterpieces include *La Primavera* and *The Birth of Venus*?
7 What does Zorro mean in Spanish?
8 What is the maximum number of rounds possible in a boxing match?
9 What food was offered to trade unionists attending talks at 10 Downing Street to avert strike action in the 1960s and 1970s?
10 What name is given by cricketers to an over in which no runs are scored?

....

Round 2: Foreign Parts

1 What, in a German town, is the Rathaus?
2 Motorists in Thailand drive on the left – true or false?
3 Of which country is Tallinn the capital?
4 To which country does Easter Island belong?
5 On what island was Freddie Mercury born?
6 What is the capital of Uruguay?
7 Which city is serviced by the John O'Hare airport?
8 Who wanted to know the way to San José in 1968?
9 In which continent do the Berbers live?
10 In which country may be found the stone-cut city of Petra?

....

Half-time teaser

What is the world record in hours and minutes for standing continuously on one foot?

....

Round 3: Disasters

1 Which US volcano erupted in 1980 after lying dormant since 1857?
2 Supporters of which two football clubs were involved in the Heysel Stadium disaster of 1985?
3 Which Russian town was evacuated in 1986 as the result of a man-made disaster?
4 In which country did the R101 airship crash?
5 Which film and television superhero role is said to be jinxed because of the disasters connected with it?
6 Whose missed penalty sent England out of the 1996 European Championships?
7 In 1966 the US air force dropped four hydrogen bombs on southern Spain – true or false?
8 What disastrous fate befell Peter Rabbit's father?
9 By what make of missile were the *Coventry* and the *Sheffield* sunk during the Falklands War?
10 What German word refers to the taking of pleasure in the misfortunes of others?

Round 4: Pot Luck

1 Which famous cricketer first completed the double of 1,000 runs and 100 wickets in a season?
2 Which US political party is often referred to as 'the Grand Old Party'?
3 In which county is the RAF base Biggin Hill?
4 Which author invented the name Wendy? *
5 Which two races constitute racing's 'spring double'?
6 What name is given to a flat-bottomed Chinese sailing vessel?
7 Which American became the first non-European to win the Tour de France?
8 What is 'Magic' Johnson's real first name?
9 In the Royal Navy, which rank is senior – Captain or Commodore?
10 In which part of a castle would you find an oubliette?

Jackpot

Which German city is known as 'the Florence of the Elbe'?

* The name apparently came about through a young girl calling the author her 'fwendy-wendy'.

Quiz 83

Round 1: Pot Luck

1 What was the name of the Underworld in Norse mythology?
2 Which prime minister was known as 'Sunny Jim'?
3 In which sphere was Binkie Beaumont a prominent figure – aircraft manufacture, ice-skating or the theatre?
4 The elephant is the only animal with four knees – true or false?
5 Who, in the eighteenth century, made a series of famous paintings entitled *The Rake's Progress*?
6 Who sang about 'another suitcase in another hall' in 1997?
7 What treasure does Harrison Ford seek in the first of the *Indiana Jones* films?
8 Which politician was once described by Labour MP Michael Foot as 'a semi-trained polecat'?
9 A nautical mile is shorter than a terrestrial mile – true or false?
10 How many hoops do you need to play a game of croquet?

Round 2: Kings and Queens

1 Which English king was shot by an arrow while hunting in the New Forest?
2 Who played the king in Alexander Korda's 1933 film *The Private Life of Henry VIII*?
3 Which monarch has been played by Flora Robson, Glenda Jackson, Miranda Richardson and Cate Blanchett?
4 Who was the father of George V?
5 What kind of sporting accident is popularly supposed to have led to the death of Frederick Louis, eldest son of George II, in 1751?
6 Which English queen was born with six fingers on one hand?
7 Which English king as an adult was just four feet nine inches (1.4 metres) tall?
8 Which English king died after being shot by an arrow while besieging a castle in France?
9 Which King had a dream in 1963?
10 Which group had a hit with 'Kings of the wild frontier'?

Half-time teaser

A Fender-Stratocaster guitar signed by Paul McCartney, Brian May, Eric Clapton, Jimmy Page, Keith Richards and others and sold for charity in 2005 became the most expensive guitar ever bought – how much did it go for?

Round 3: Hollywood Hunks

1 Which Hollywood star was nicknamed 'the Hunk'?
2 By what name did Hollywood actor Bernard Schwartz become famous?
3 Which European actor earned the nickname 'the Austrian Oak' for his wooden acting performances?
4 Which James Bond actor worked as a milkman and coffin polisher before finding work as an actor?
5 Which Hollywood hunk had a renowned cabaret singer for an aunt?
6 Which Hollywood leading man had a chart hit in 1987 with 'Respect yourself'?
7 Who was offered shelter by an Avon lady in *Edward Scissorhands*?
8 Which Hollywood hunk made his last major appearance in *Field of Dreams* in 1989?
9 Which Hollywood hunk once admitted that he developed his distinctive vocal delivery from study of the breathy whispering of Marilyn Monroe?
10 Which Hollywood hunk has also spent time as frontman with the rock bands 30 Odd Foot of Grunts and The Ordinary Fear of God?

Round 4: Pot Luck

1 Which product is 'soft, strong and very long'?
2 In 1986, what was replaced by a red rose as the symbol of the Labour Party?
3 Which 1960s pop group was led by the Davies brothers?
4 In World War II, what was the LRDG?
5 Which outlaw has been played in the cinema by Mick Jagger and Heath Ledger?
6 In business jargon, what does the acronym 'glam' stand for?
7 Where would you find a jib?
8 To what rank did Adolf Hitler rise in World War I?
9 The name of the man with the longest beard in the heavily bearded US band ZZ Top is Frank Beard – true or false?
10 Who plays Hagrid in the Harry Potter films?

Jackpot

Who founded the celebrated Ballets Russes in 1909?

⁎ In fact, the legend is probably an invention. Though passionately fond of the sport in question, the person in question actually died from an abscess in the lung.

Quiz 84

Round 1: Pot Luck

1 On which river does Liverpool stand?
2 At which bar does Homer Simpson drink?
3 A porpoise is larger than a dolphin – true or false?
4 Oxides of which two chemicals create acid rain?
5 Which part of London was terrorised by Jack the Ripper in 1888?
6 What is a coney?
7 Who was the first athlete to hold the Olympic, World and Commonwealth titles and the world record simultaneously?
8 Who had a UK number one in 1999 with 'When you say nothing at all'?
9 What began at Fort Sumter in 1861?
10 What name was given to football's League Cup when it was sponsored for the first time in 1982?

Round 2: The 1950s

1 Who seized power in Cuba on 1 January 1959?
2 What was Genevieve in the 1953 film of the same name?
3 Who was the woman whose refusal to give up her seat led to the Montgomery Bus Boycott of 1955?
4 Which magazine was founded by Hugh Hefner in 1953?
5 In which country were the Mau-Mau active in the 1950s?
6 What name came to be applied to the youth of 1950s America, as described in the books of Jack Kerouac, Allen Ginsberg and William Burroughs?
7 Who scored an FA Cup hat trick during the so-called 'Matthews Final' of 1953?
8 How did controversial US artist Jackson Pollock die in 1956?
9 Which working-class cartoon character, never without his cap, made his first appearance in the *Daily Mirror* in 1957?
10 Who wrote a song about blue suede shoes in 1956?

Half-time teaser

When the Marcos regime was overthrown in 1986, how many handbags belonging to Imelda Marcos were discovered?

Round 3: Before They Were Famous

1 By what name did Farrokh Bulsara become well known?
2 Which English football league club originally played as Small Heath Alliance?
3 Which political leader did his war service on PT 109?
4 Which member of the Rolling Stones was born William Perks?
5 Which famous French artist worked as a labourer on the Panama Canal?
6 Which US president was famously born in a log cabin?
7 Which English novelist worked as a child in a boot-blacking factory?
8 Which Lancashire-born comedian served as Charlie Chaplin's understudy as a young man?
9 The Spitfire fighter plane might have been called the Shrew – true or false?
10 Who predicted that in the future everyone would be famous for 15 minutes?

Round 4: Pot Luck

1 What is the main constituent of glass?
2 Which arts festival was founded in August 1947 by Rudolf Bing?
3 In which sport was Roger Clark a leading figure in the 1960s and 1970s?
4 Timothy McVeigh was executed for which terrorist outrage?
5 What is Margaret Thatcher's middle name?
6 Which letter is positioned between F and H on a computer keyboard?
7 When was chewing-gum first patented – 1869, 1899 or 1919? ✳
8 Which English city was originally known as Sarum?
9 What does the musical direction 'tacet' mean?
10 At which racing circuit is the Italian Grand Prix held?

Jackpot

Which novel begins with the words 'It was a bright cold day in April, and the clocks were striking thirteen'?

✳ People chewed gum long before this, as far back as the ancient Greeks. According to scientists, people who chew gum while performing memory tests (such as quizzes) score significantly higher than those who do not.

Quiz 85

Round 1: Pot Luck

1 Who was 'Tricky Dicky'?
2 What is depicted in a calvary?
3 Which former captain of England ended his playing career with Newcastle United in 2006?
4 Who wrote the classic ghost story 'The Signal-Man'?
5 Which British conductor was known as 'Old Timber'?
6 What is the name of the valley that runs from Mozambique through East Africa and as far north as Syria?
7 Which specialist unit commanded by Major General Orde Wingate operated behind enemy lines in Burma during World War II?
8 Whose number one hits included 'Kon-Tiki', 'Please don't tease' and 'Travellin' light'?
9 What new name was given to Idlewild airport in New York in 1963?
10 In which US state is Boston?

Round 2: Spies

1 Which US intelligence organisation was set up in 1947?
2 In the films based on the novels by Ian Fleming, by what initial is the officer who provides James Bond with his lethal gadgets known?
3 Which English architect, builder of Blenheim Palace, was once imprisoned in the Bastille as a spy?
4 Which radio series of the 1940s featured such characters as Mrs Mopp, Funf the spy, and Claude and Cecil?
5 What was the code name of George Smiley's adversary in the John Le Carré spy thriller *Tinker, Tailor, Soldier, Spy*?
6 Which Soviet double agent fled to the USSR after escaping from Wormwood Scrubs prison in London in 1966?
7 What was the name of the art expert who in 1979 was publicly unveiled as the fourth man in the Cambridge Spy Ring alongside Philby, Burgess and Maclean?
8 Francis Walsingham acted as spymaster for which English monarch?
9 Who succeeded Roger Moore as James Bond in 1987?
10 What is the name of the boy spy created by Anthony Horowitz?

Half-time teaser

How far is it in miles from Penzance to Dover?

Round 3: Wildlife

1 What kind of crab shelters in the discarded shells of other animals?
2 Pregnant women attract double the number of mosquitoes that other women do – true or false?
3 What was the name of the horse ridden by Roy Rogers?
4 Who wrote the poems on which Andrew Lloyd Webber's musical *Cats* was based?
5 Of which plant did singer Gracie Fields claim to have the world's largest example?
6 Penguins fall over backwards when looking upwards at an aeroplane flying overhead – true or false?
7 Against whom was the so-called Cat and Mouse Act of 1913 aimed?
8 Who sang vocals with the Animals?
9 Which biblical character was swallowed by a whale?
10 Who released an album called *Journey through the Secret Life of Plants*?

Round 4: Pot Luck

1 Is an ankle-biter a small dog, a young child or a kind of bicycle?
2 Who provided the narrator's voice in the comedy series *Little Britain*?
3 Who briefly succeeded Richard Whiteley as presenter of television's *Countdown* programme?
4 What was the name of the central character in the 1971 film *First Blood*?
5 Who wrote the *Gormenghast* trilogy?
6 Who sang 'Moon river' in *Breakfast at Tiffany*'s?
7 Which river flows through the Grand Canyon?
8 Which African country was named after a profitable export?
9 What was the name of the US Defense Secretary who resigned his post in 2006 in the wake of criticism of US policy in Iraq?
10 Against which German city was the first RAF 'thousand-bomber raid' directed?

Jackpot

In which British city was the first Odeon cinema opened in 1930?

✳ In millions of years' time this valley is expected to expand until it divides the continent of Africa into two.

Quiz 86

Round 1: Pot Luck

1 What is the colour of the gemstone known as jet?
2 Who is television's 'domestic goddess'?
3 Which country is home to Aeroflot?
4 Which Gilbert and Sullivan operetta takes place in the Tower of London?
5 Which character was introduced in Nintendo's Donkey Kong game?
6 Why did Frank Sinatra junior hit the headlines in 1963?
7 Who was football's 'Galloping Major'?
8 How many hours are there in a week?
9 Which celebrity died at the hands of Kenneth Halliwell?
10 What name is given to an otters' den?

Round 2: Countries of the World

1 Which country is nearest to the North Pole?
2 Which country has the largest Roman Catholic population?
3 The 2003 mountaineering drama *Touching the Void* was set in which country?
4 In which country is the Ataturk Dam?
5 Of which Commonwealth country did William Lyon Mackenzie King serve three terms as prime minister?
6 Which country is serviced by Qantas Airlines?
7 Of which country is Manama the capital?
8 Which country has taken part in every Olympic Games, both summer and winter?
9 Which country was split in 1945 along the so-called Thirty-Eighth Parallel?
10 In which country are the most alcoholic spirits drunk?

Half-time teaser

The Life and Times of Joseph Stalin, in seven acts, holds the record for the longest opera of all time – how long does it take to perform?

Round 3: Television

1 What innovation was introduced to television in 1967?
2 Where was television's *Bergerac* set?
3 Which cult series included among the cast the 'Cigarette-Smoking Man'?
4 What was the name of the neurotic lawyer played on television by Calista Flockhart?
5 Which popular television programme has included among its hosts Angela Rippon, Hugh Scully and Michael Aspel?
6 On which programme did Nick Bateman attract the headlines in 2000?
7 At what number do the Kumars live?
8 Where is *Last of the Summer Wine* filmed?
9 Who were television's original badly behaved men?
10 Len Goodman, Arlene Phillips, Bruno Tonioli and Craig Revel Horwood are the panel in which television talent show?

Round 4: Pot Luck

1 What do chandlers make?
2 Is a peruke a hat, a cigar or a wig?
3 What does the mathematical symbol comprising a triangle of three dots mean?
4 Which road connects Oxford Circus with Piccadilly Circus?
5 In the James Bond stories, what is the first name of the villain Goldfinger? ✳
6 The vernal equinox marks the end of which season?
7 In which country did balti cooking evolve?
8 What was the name of Harare until 1982?
9 What is the equivalent of a try or goal in American football?
10 How many stars are there on the flag of New Zealand?

Jackpot

For which novel did Roddy Doyle win the Booker Prize for Fiction in 1993?

✳ Ian Fleming borrowed the name Goldfinger from a neighbour, the architect Erno Goldfinger, who went straight to his lawyers, forcing Fleming to make an out-of-court settlement. In the novel, the lovely Jill dies after being painted in gold, apparently from 'clogged pores'. Having clogged pores, however, would not have killed her.

Quiz 87

....

Round 1: Pot Luck

1 What is sometimes called 'the Conservative Party at prayer'?
2 What was the name of Radio Four before 1967?
3 Who became the first man to win five successive Wimbledon Men's Singles titles?
4 In which Scottish city are the football clubs Heart of Midlothian and Hibernian based?
5 Which battle began on 1 July 1916?
6 Who starred in the films *The Sound of Music*, *Waterloo* and *The Royal Hunt of the Sun*?
7 From which Broadway show comes the song 'Bewitched'?
8 Is a quango a large flightless bird, an administrative organisation or a fizzy orange drink?
9 What was the name of the theme tune of David Lean's 1965 film *Doctor Zhivago*?
10 How many locks are there on the Suez Canal?

....

Round 2: Ancient History

1 Which British archaeologist located the tomb of Tutankhamun?
2 In which county is Stonehenge?
3 What were the scroll-shaped tablets called in which the names of ancient Egyptian pharaohs were inscribed?
4 Who was the first Christian emperor of Rome?
5 Which style of classical column was decorated with carvings representing acanthus leaves?
6 What is the English name for the Roman town of Camulodunum?
7 Which Mediterranean island was the scene of a volcanic explosion that destroyed the Minoan civilisation around 1450 BC?
8 Who set sail in the *Argo*?
9 What was the name of the race of giants that Zeus defeated in order to rule on Olympus?
10 According to the Old Testament, how did the priests of Joshua destroy the walls of Jericho?

....

Half-time teaser

The world's largest sandwich was made at Wild Woody's Chill and Grill in Roseville, Michigan in 2005 – what did it weigh in kilograms?

....

Round 3: Top of the Pops

1 Who had a number one hit in the UK in 1961 with 'Runaway'?
2 What was the title of the chart-topping single released by the England World Cup squad in 1970?
3 Who won the 1988 Eurovision Song Contest for Switzerland?
4 Who had a number one hit in the UK in 1975 with 'If'?
5 Who, in 1979, got to number one because they didn't like Mondays?
6 Which opera singer reached number two in the UK charts in 1992 with 'Nessun dorma'?
7 Who had number one hits with 'I'll stand by you' and 'Sound of the underground'?
8 Which Spice Girl topped the charts with 'Bag it up', 'Lift me up' and 'Mi chico Latino'?
9 Whose number one hits included 'Babe', 'Everything changes' and 'Pray'?
10 Who topped the UK charts with 'Unchained melody' and 'The man from Laramie'?

Round 4: Pot Luck

1 What is Ceylon's modern name?
2 In the nursery rhyme, who marched his men to the top of the hill? ✳
3 In which year was the Berlin Wall constructed?
4 Who created the naval hero Horatio Hornblower?
5 In which novel by Virginia Woolf does the central character change sex at the age of 30?
6 Which is 'the city that never sleeps'?
7 Which, according to T. S. Eliot in *The Waste Land*, is 'the cruellest month'?
8 In the 1945 film *Brief Encounter*, which stage and film actor makes the railway announcements?
9 What is the documented history of a work of art known as?
10 Who, in 1975, had a funky moped?

Jackpot

Who played Watson to Basil Rathbone's Sherlock Holmes in a series of films made in the 1930s and 1940s?

✳ The rhyme is thought to refer to a brief invasion of the Netherlands staged by British forces in 1793. The hill in the rhyme is probably that on which the town of Cassel stands in the middle of the otherwise flat Flanders countryside.

Quiz 88

Round 1: Pot Luck

1 Who wrote *Water Music* for George I?
2 Where does rioja come from?
3 Which country lies between Niger and Sudan?
4 Who owns a celebrated fish restaurant in Padstow, Cornwall?
5 What was the name of Elvis Presley's house?
6 Who created the detective Jack Frost?
7 Whereabouts in the UK is Osborne House?
8 Which acid gives a nettle its sting?
9 Which road in 2003 became Britain's first toll-paying motorway?
10 What fail-safe mechanism prevents a locomotive crashing if something happens to the driver?

Round 2: Husbands and Wives

1 What was the name of William Shakespeare's wife?
2 Who married Sophie Helen Rhys-Jones in 1999?
3 Who, according to Jewish folklore, was Adam's first wife?
4 To whom has Princess Anne been married since 1992?
5 Which US state was named in honour of Charles II's wife Henrietta Maria?
6 What was the name of Mikhail Gorbachev's wife?
7 To whom was film actress Anne Bancroft married until her death in 2005?
8 Which former child star married Joan Collins in 1963?
9 To whom did Beatle Paul McCartney become engaged in 1967?
10 In which Thomas Hardy novel does Michael Henchard sell his wife and daughter for five guineas?

Half-time teaser

The record for the number of instances of swearing in an animated film is held by the 1999 film *South Park: Bigger, Longer and Uncut* – how many were there?

Round 3: Current Affairs

1 Which constituency does Tony Blair represent as an MP?
2 After the 2005 general election which well-known figure had the biggest majority?
3 Which British political party has its headquarters in Victoria Street, London?
4 Who served as the first leader of the Scottish parliament?
5 Which system of nuclear weaponry replaced Polaris in the UK in the 1990s?
6 Which protest organisation has as its symbol a circle containing an inverted V bisected by a vertical line?
7 Which British chancellor pulled Britain out of the Exchange Rate Mechanism in 1992?
8 Which state is the first to produce a result in US presidential primary elections?
9 How old must a US president be?
10 Who, in 2000, became the second president of the Russian Federation?

Round 4: Pot Luck

1 What colour are the flowers of St John's Wort?
2 What is a smolt?
3 Which US city was named after a British prime minister?
4 How many bottles of wine are there in a case?
5 Where were General Custer and his command wiped out in 1876?
6 What nationality was the composer Sibelius?
7 Which is the largest state of the USA?
8 Who did Muhammad Ali beat to win his third world title?
9 For which team did both Nigel Mansell and Damon Hill win the Formula One World Championship?
10 In which war did W. H. Auden serve as a stretcher-bearer?

Jackpot

Who shot Martin Luther King?

* Elvis evidently loved his home. It was reported that he would spend many hours in his bedroom gazing at screens linked to the various CCTV cameras positioned around the building.

Quiz 89

Round 1: Pot Luck

1 Who had a sword called Excalibur?
2 Which British politician became known as 'the Quiet Man'?
3 Who were the first European winners of football's World Cup?
4 Napoleon's favourite horse was named after which of his great victories?
5 Which state most recently became part of the USA?
6 What is a campanile?
7 What awards are presented annually for outstanding contributions to British film and television in imitation of Oscars in the USA?
8 Where would you find a glass pyramid designed by the architect Ieoh Meng Pei?
9 Which British footballer was the first to earn £100 a week?
10 Which part was played by Tyne Daly in the US television series *Cagney and Lacey*?

Round 2: Fabulous Firsts

1 Which was the first single to sell a million copies?
2 The first recorded use of the word 'baseball' is in Jane Austen's *Northanger Abbey* – true or false?
3 What kind of international competition was first held in Folkestone in August 1908?
4 Which sport was the first to have an official world championship (first held in 1873)?
5 Which football club won the first FA Cup competition following World War II?
6 Who promised to build 'a country fit for heroes' at the end of World War I?
7 In which year did Rowntree's Fruit Gums first go on sale – 1893, 1903 or 1913?
8 On 11 June 1953, which famous cricketer became the first professional player to captain England?
9 How did the Countess Constance Markievicz make political history in 1918?
10 Which author is usually identified as the first to use a typewriter?

Half-time teaser

Dutchman Niek Vermeulen holds the record for the world's largest collection of airline sick bags – how many does he have?

Round 3: Numbers

1 No number between one and 99 contains the letter A – true or false?
2 Which number in the National Lottery is chosen less often than any other?
3 In George Orwell's novel *Nineteen Eighty-Four*, what is the name of the room in which people are tortured by their greatest fear? ✳
4 In Roman numerals, which number is represented by the letter M?
5 How many Horsemen of the Apocalypse are there?
6 In *The Hitchhiker's Guide to the Galaxy*, what is the answer to the question 'what is the meaning of life, the universe and everything?'
7 What was US murderer John Dillinger known as?
8 By what number do members of the Royal Navy refer to their working dress?
9 What number refers to an ice-cream with a chocolate flake stuck in it?
10 According to the Bible, what is the Number of the Beast?

Round 4: Pot Luck

1 Which Charles Dickens character is always expecting something to turn up?
2 For what television programme was 'This wheel's on fire' the theme tune?
3 What style of jazz erupted in New York after World War II in the hands of such exponents as Charlie Parker, Dizzie Gillespie and Miles Davis?
4 Which is 'probably the best lager in the world'?
5 What are the Port of Liverpool Building, the Royal Liver Exchange Building and the Cunard Building in Liverpool collectively known as?
6 Which treaty formally ended World War I?
7 Which war did Muhammad Ali refuse to fight in?
8 According to a recent survey, what is the average Briton's favourite smell?
9 Which prime minister was accused of ignoring reality in the *Sun* headline 'Crisis? What crisis?'?
10 Which is the longest single-span suspension bridge in the world?

Jackpot

Which location in Essex became notorious in the 1930s as 'the most haunted place in Britain'?

✳ The story goes that the number was the same as that of the room at Broadcasting House in which Orwell had to endure many boring meetings when working for the BBC.

Quiz 90

Round 1: Pot Luck

1 Which is the only country that occupies an entire continent?
2 What is a hydrophobic afraid of?
3 Which major US sporting event has been held every January since 1967?
4 Who led the anti-communist witch-hunts of the 1950s in the USA?
5 What stage name did pianist Wladziu Valentino adopt?
6 What is a buttress – a folding chair, a supporting structure in buildings or a tight-fitting dress?
7 What gender are worker ants?
8 Which queen ruled first – Elizabeth I or Mary I?
9 In which country did violence erupt between Tutsis and Hutus in 1994?
10 How does an operetta differ from an opera?

Round 2: Names

1 Sean is an Irish equivalent of which first name?
2 In British place names, what does 'Chipping' mean?
3 By what name are the ports of Dover, Hastings, Hythe, Romney and Sandwich collectively known?
4 Which English city had the Roman name Aquae Sulis?
5 What, according to a survey of 2005, overtook the Red Lion as the most common pub name in Britain?
6 What was the name of the film company co-founded by George Harrison?
7 What colour name did Harvey Keitel have in the 1991 film *Reservoir Dogs*?
8 What is the first name of footballer Nobby Stiles?
9 By what name is Kampuchea now known?
10 In the Jeeves and Wooster stories of P. G. Wodehouse, what is Jeeves's first name?

Half-time teaser

Tomas Lundman holds the record for heading a football continuously without dropping it – how long did he manage to keep going?

Round 3: Entertainment

1 What was Mickey Mouse's dog called?
2 Whose hits included 'Endless love' and 'Touch me in the morning'?
3 Which Hollywood hunk was the first man to appear on the cover of *Vogue*?
4 Which popular novel includes among its main characters the sisters Amy, Beth, Jo and Meg?
5 From which play comes the line 'Brazil, where the nuts come from'?
6 In which country was US songwriter Irving Berlin born?
7 Which of Gilbert and Sullivan wrote the music?
8 Alongside the Lyttelton and the Cottesloe, what is the Royal National Theatre's third stage? *
9 Which role was played in the cinema by Michael Caine in 1966, by Alan Price in 1975 and by Jude Law in 2004?
10 From which musical does 'You'll never walk alone' come?

Round 4: Pot Luck

1 Lack of which hormone causes diabetes?
2 How did the Getty family make their fortune?
3 Which 14-year-old famously got himself into trouble for ordering a cherry brandy?
4 Which language is spoken most widely in Chile?
5 What does the Great Barrier Reef consist of?
6 Who was the first Frenchman to win the Formula One championship?
7 What is measured with a theodolite?
8 By what other name are althaea plants popularly known?
9 To what did the Test and County Cricket Board (TCCB) change its name in 1996?
10 In which sport might you 'catch a crab'?

Jackpot

In the 2002 BBC poll of the Greatest Britons of all time, Winston Churchill came top – who came second?

* The modernistic style of the theatre was praised by Sir John Betjeman and others, but incurred the disapproval of Prince Charles, who called it 'a clever way of building a nuclear power station in the middle of London without anyone objecting'.

Quiz 91

Round 1: Pot Luck
1 What is the name of the lion in the Narnia books of C. S. Lewis?
2 In which long-running series are David, Ruth and Eddie central characters?
3 Who won three consecutive Wimbledon men's singles titles in the years 1934 to 1936?
4 What was the name of the pop group of which Boy George was frontman?
5 In which film did Katy Johnson play a little old lady who unwittingly plays host to a desperate gang of robbers led by Alec Guinness?
6 Which Iraqi city stands on the Shatt al-Arab waterway?
7 What is the name of Postman Pat's cat?
8 Which international pressure group has as its symbol a candle wrapped in barbed wire?
9 In what manner was the English Channel swum for the first time in 1962?
10 What is the name of the Gaulish Druid in the adventures of Asterix?

Round 2: Modern Art
1 What purpose did the building in which the Tate Modern art gallery is housed originally serve?
2 What is the name of the giant Antony Gormley statue in Gateshead?
3 What is the name given to a work of art in which the picture is built up wholly or partly using pieces of paper, cloth or other material stuck to a canvas or other backing?
4 Which artist painted the double portrait *Mr and Mrs Clark and Percy*?
5 Which famous art collector lost much of his collection in a disastrous fire in May 2004?
6 Which British artist provided a coloured pattern to be used as a test card for cameras on board the space probe *Beagle 2* in 2003?
7 Who included among his masterpieces the 1944 painting *Three Studies for Figures at the Base of a Crucifixion*?
8 Which sculptor provided a statue of St Michael to be mounted on the new Coventry Cathedral in 1958?
9 Which controversial US artist was popularly dubbed Jack the Dripper?
10 Which New York art gallery designed by Frank Lloyd Wright was opened in 1959?

Half-time teaser

David Morgan of Burford has the world's largest collection of traffic cones –
how many different cones does he have?

Round 3: Whiter than White

1 Who had a number one hit in the UK in 1967 with 'A whiter shade of pale'?
2 What is a WASP?
3 How is Maurice Micklewhite better known?
4 Which king is the subject of T. H. White's book *The Once and Future King*?
5 Which English naturalist wrote *The Natural History and Antiquities of Selborne*?
6 By what name did Priscilla White become famous?
7 What was the name of the ship in which the heir of Henry I drowned in 1120?
8 Which snooker player has been (to date) runner-up in the World Championship no less than six times?
9 Which soul singer noted for his deep, gravelly voice died in 2003?
10 From which pop song comes the line 'some man comes on and tells me how white my shirts could be but he can't be a man 'cos he doesn't smoke the same cigarettes as me'?

Round 4: Pot Luck

1 What is the name of the world's second-highest mountain?
2 Who invented dynamite? ✴
3 What do the initials AWAC stand for?
4 What is the name of the monument to the dead of the two world wars that stands in Whitehall, London?
5 Who played Terry, a former boxer, in the 1954 film *On the Waterfront*?
6 Who was known as Satchmo?
7 The Mansion House in London is the official residence of whom?
8 Who had trouble getting past Sylvia's mother in 1972?
9 Who fought Muhammad Ali in the 1975 boxing match known as the Thriller in Manila?
10 Which hymn has been sung at FA Cup finals since 1927?

Jackpot

In which film did Sidney Poitier play a character called Virgil Tibbs?

✴ His father, incidentally, invented plywood.

Quiz 92

....

Round 1: Pot Luck

1 Coffee contains which stimulant?
2 Which state is ruled by members of the Grimaldi family?
3 What are the doldrums?
4 In the heptathlon, which event is contested first?
5 In the comic stories of Giovanni Guareschi, what is the job of Don Camillo?
6 What is a male swan called?
7 Who killed David Blakely?
8 How old was F. Scott Fitzgerald when he died – 44, 54 or 64?
9 In which sport do teams contest the Canada Cup?
10 Which youth organisation originally called its members 'Rosebuds'?

....

Round 2: Crime

1 Which presenter of television's *Crimewatch* became herself the subject of a crime featured on the programme in 1999?
2 Where did Sherlock Holmes and his arch-enemy Moriarty apparently fall to their deaths?
3 Who played the younger Vito Corleone in *The Godfather* series?
4 What name is given to a housebreaker who uses natural agility to gain entry to a building via a roof, window, chimney, etc.?
5 In the murder mystery by Dorothy L. Sayers, what are the Nine Tailors?
6 What was the name of the actor who assassinated Abraham Lincoln?
7 With which sensational crime was Ronnie Biggs intimately associated in 1963?
8 In which novel does Raskolnikov murder a much-hated pawnbroker?
9 Who played crime boss Tony Soprano in television's *The Sopranos*?
10 Who shot the sheriff in 1973?

....

Half-time teaser

In 2004, Edit Berces established a new world women's record for the distance travelled on a treadmill – how many miles did she cover?

....

Round 3: The 1940s

1 Who briefly succeeded Adolf Hitler as leader of Nazi Germany in 1945?
2 Where would the 1944 Olympic Games have been held if not cancelled?
3 Who replaced Winston Churchill as prime minister of the UK in 1945?
4 In which 1949 film does a part of London discover it is part of Burgundy and thus free from rationing? ✴
5 Which English cathedral was destroyed by bombs in November 1940?
6 What distinctive structure was invented by Richard Buckminster Fuller in 1945?
7 What mishap occurred during both the 1946 and 1947 FA Cup finals?
8 What first did Captain Charles Yeager achieve in 1947?
9 Who created the A-line, the H-line and the 'New Look' of 1947?
10 Under what slogan did Labour plan state assistance throughout a person's life?

Round 4: Pot Luck

1 What is a hurricane in the Pacific called?
2 Which is furthest north – Colorado, Montana or Utah?
3 In which year was the Cricket World Cup first contested – 1975, 1980 or 1985?
4 What was the name of the prefabricated outdoor air-raid shelters erected in British gardens during World War II?
5 Which British car company was founded by Lord Nuffield?
6 Which guitarist has the nickname Slowhand?
7 Which film company has a logo comprising a man striking a gong?
8 By what other name are antirrhinums popularly known?
9 Which French town lies at the heart of the claret-growing region?
10 How many general elections did Margaret Thatcher win?

Jackpot

Who is the only living US playwright to have a Broadway theatre named after him?

✴ The plot was apparently inspired by Canada's gift to Holland of the room in which Princess Juliana was about to bear a child, thus ensuring the child was born on Dutch territory.

Quiz 93

Round 1: Pot Luck
1 What was the Spice Girls' début single?
2 Who played Willy Wonka in the 1971 film *Willie Wonka and the Chocolate Factory*?
3 Which is the most popular tourist attraction in Britain?
4 The word gamelan refers to a species of alligator, a small game bird or a form of Indonesian music?
5 Who persuaded Shakespeare's Othello that his wife was being unfaithful?
6 What lamp with an innovative stand imitating the human arm was first marketed in 1933?
7 In which television comedy did Leonard Rossiter play the seedy landlord Rigsby?
8 What did Private Teruo Nakamura discover in December 1974?
9 What material did the jeweller René Lalique specialise in?
10 Where is the dong the main unit of currency?

Round 2: Executions
1 What has among its nicknames Old Smoky, Sizzling Sally and Gruesome Gerty?
2 In which year did Ruth Ellis become the last woman to be hanged in Britain?
3 What was the original career of Joseph Ignace Guillotin, inventor of the guillotine?
4 Who was the last official Chief Hangman for the United Kingdom?
5 In which film did Susan Sarandon win an Oscar as a nun who befriends a man on Death Row?
6 Who was known as 'the Hanging Judge'?
7 In eighteenth-century Britain the death penalty applied to 222 offences – true or false?
8 Which US murderer was the first to be executed when capital punishment was resumed in 1976?
9 Whose execution in 1918 brought about the end of the Russian monarchy?
10 Which character goes to the guillotine in *A Tale of Two Cities* saying 'It is a far, far better thing that I do, than I have ever done. It is a far, far better rest that I go to, than I have ever known'?

Half-time teaser

The world's largest millipede is an African giant black millipede owned by Jim Klinger of Coppell, Texas – how many legs does it have?

Round 3: Sport and Leisure

1 From which sport comes the saying 'three strikes and you're out'?
2 Which BBC commentator delivered the immortal line 'They think it's all over' during the 1966 Wembley World Cup final?
3 Which country was admitted to rugby union's Five Nations Championship in 2000, making it the Six Nations Championship?
4 By what name did the Jules Rimet Trophy become better known?
5 The English cricketer C. B. Fry was once offered the throne of which country?
6 Which US football club did David Beckham leave Real Madrid for in 2007?
7 Which British Formula One driver was killed at Hockenheim in 1968?
8 What innovation in dress did Bunny Austin introduce to Wimbledon in 1933?
9 In three-day eventing, what is the first day devoted to?
10 Which sportsperson was the first BBC Sports Personality of the Year?

Round 4: Pot Luck

1 'Leopard' and 'panther' are different names for the same animal – true or false?
2 In which country did the Ayatollah Khomeini seize control in 1979?
3 What was the name of the character played by Frankie Howerd in *Up Pompeii*?
4 Who was prime minister at the time of the 'I'm backing Britain' campaign?
5 Which Buddy Holly single was named after the girlfriend of the drummer with the Crickets?
6 Who was worried about her pussy in the sitcom *Are You Being Served*?
7 What was the political and military organisation founded in 1958 by Yasser Arafat?
8 Members of which branch of the British army are known as the Red Devils?
9 Which long-running children's story programme was revived on television in 2006?
10 Who wrote the book on which Steven Spielberg based *Jurassic Park*?

Jackpot

What musical instrument was patented by Anthony Faas of Philadelphia in 1854?

⁎ He actually belonged to a family of official executioners and as early as 11 years old, when asked in a school exercise what he wanted to be when he grew up, wrote 'When I leave school I should like to be the Official Executioner.'

Quiz 94

Round 1: Pot Luck

1 On which mountain is Noah's Ark traditionally supposed to have come to rest?

2 What does the acronym CAMRA stand for?

3 What does an aeroplane's altimeter measure?

4 Who was Marie Antoinette's husband?

5 Joseph Stalin was once a trainee priest – true or false?

6 Which British Olympic medal-winner famously received his gold medal by post?

7 Which guidebook was allegedly used to direct German air raids on historic British cities in World War II?

8 Where does the Buran wind blow?

9 Which actress married both Frank Sinatra and André Previn?

10 Who was run down by a tram in *Coronation Street*?

Round 2: Animals

1 Which animal comes in grey and timber varieties?

2 What is the world's largest venomous snake?

3 Cobb, Kerry Hill and Scottish Blackface are all breeds of what?

4 What kind of animal is a miller's thumb?

5 How many horns does an Indian rhinoceros have?

6 What is a beaver's home called?

7 What kind of animal is a bobolink?

8 What is a black and white horse called?

9 Apart from humans, which is the only animal to suffer from sunburn?

10 What kind of animal comes in hairstreak and meadow brown varieties?

Half-time teaser

William Henry 'Fatty' Foulke holds the record as the heaviest footballer to play for England – how heavy (in kilograms) was he?

Round 3: Nicknames

1 Which British monarch was nicknamed 'Farmer George'?
2 Which snooker player earned the nickname 'Interesting' for his dull public persona?
3 What is the nickname of the third battalion of the Royal Regiment of Scotland?
4 What was the nickname of General H. Norman Schwarzkopf, commander of Operation Desert Storm in 1991?
5 Who was Brandy Nan?
6 Which English monarch had the nickname 'Old Rowley'?
7 What is the nickname of the Scottish football club Celtic?
8 Which US general was nicknamed 'Old Blood and Guts'?
9 What is the nickname of the New Zealand rugby league team?
10 Which British footballer was known as 'the White Ghost' or 'the Preston Plumber'?

Round 4: Pot Luck

1 In which city was there an Easter Rising in 1916?
2 A Persian Blue is a variety of what?
3 Who helped Bonnie Prince Charlie escape Scotland disguised as her maid?
4 Which country includes among its rivers the Arno and the Po?
5 Who was the lead singer of INXS who apparently killed himself in Sydney in 1997?
6 Which flying insect spreads sleeping sickness?
7 In which country was Greenpeace founded – France, Germany or Canada?
8 From 1982 to 1993 only two women claimed the Women's Singles title at Wimbledon – Martina Navratilova and who else?
9 Which footballer became, in 2002, the subject of the first thirty-million-pound transfer?
10 What was the title of the book by Bob Woodward and Carl Bernstein about Watergate?

Jackpot

Which military force was founded by David Stirling?

✳ The hunt for the remains of the Ark continues today, with various locations being identified and bits of wood being presented as fragments of the biblical boat. The favoured site on the mountain in question suggests a vessel 309 metres in width, equivalent to the largest modern aircraft carrier.

Quiz 95

Round 1: Pot Luck
1 In which war did the Battle of the Atlantic take place?
2 What did US writer Elbert Hubbard summarise as 'one damned thing after another'?
3 Which evangelical and charitable organisation was founded by William Booth in 1865?
4 On which earlier tune was the song 'Danny Boy' based?
5 Who had the nickname 'Old Groaner'?
6 Which battle on British soil claimed the most lives?
7 How many balls do you need to play a game of snooker?
8 What was the name of the spinster witch played by Angela Lansbury in the Walt Disney film *Bedknobs and Broomsticks*?
9 What do the initials ECT stand for?
10 To which historical figure did Beethoven dedicate his third symphony?

Round 2: British Television
1 Which television sitcom written by Jimmy Perry was set in India and Burma during World War II?
2 What nickname of the BBC reflects what many people have seen as its cautious, conservative nature?
3 Who wrote the music that is used as a theme tune for television's *The Sky at Night*?
4 Which cult television programme starred a motley band of resistance fighters opposed to the Terran Foundation?
5 On which long-running television talent show did such stars as Mary Hopkin, Bonnie Langford and Freddie Starr get their big break?
6 For what television programme is 'Barnacle Bill the Sailor' the theme tune?
7 What is the name of the Yorkshire village in which the television drama series *Heartbeat* is set?
8 Who for many years presented the television pop music programme *Old Grey Whistle Test*?
9 Which television programme of the 1960s had the slogan 'The weekend starts here'?
10 What was the name of the fictional village in which the television comedy series *The League of Gentlemen* was set?

Half-time teaser
How far is it in miles from Birmingham, England to Birmingham, Alabama?

Round 3: Shopping

1 Which street in Soho, London, became a focus for fashionable youth in the 1960s?
2 What phrase describes the activity of looking at things for sale without planning to buy them?
3 Which British businessman lost his job after publicly scorning the products of his own leading high-street company?
4 Which brand of soup was immortalised in paintings by Andy Warhol? ✳
5 According to a VAT tribunal ruling of 1991, is a Jaffa cake a cake or a biscuit?
6 In which year did Smarties first go on sale – 1927, 1937 or 1947?
7 What product is sold with the help of the biblical slogan 'Out of the strong came forth sweetness'?
8 Which is the world's largest hypermarket chain?
9 Which supermarket chain was created by the merger in 1965 of the Asquith chain of supermarkets and Associated Dairies?
10 Who provided a slogan for shoppers with her song 'A little of what you fancy does you good?'

Round 4: Pot Luck

1 Complete the following quotation: 'Are you sitting comfortably? . . .'
2 Which choral work written by Carl Orff during the Nazi period has become a popular standard of modern concert performances?
3 In which city is the famous al-Aqsa mosque?
4 Who wrote the 1951 play *The Rose Tattoo*?
5 Which Beatles album included the tracks 'Got to get you into my life', 'Taxman' and 'Here, there and everywhere'?
6 Which two countries fought the so-called Soccer War of 1969 after violence erupted following a football match between their national teams?
7 Which US president summarised his foreign policy in the phrase 'Speak softly and carry a big stick'?
8 Who created the concept of 'oneupmanship' in a 1952 book of that title?
9 Which town in Britain has the highest divorce rate?
10 What do golfers call the 'nineteenth hole'?

Jackpot

Who wrote the opera *Der Rosenkavalier*?

✳ He chose this subject after friends advised him to paint what he loved most: he had this soup most days for lunch for some 20 years.

Quiz 96

Round 1: Pot Luck

1 From which country does retsina come?
2 Which three South American countries does the equator go through?
3 Which British writer became subject to an Iranian fatwa in 1989?
4 Which pop celebrity in 2004 had a marriage that lasted just 55 hours?
5 What colour is Sonic the Hedgehog?
6 Which English county has the heaviest rainfall?
7 Which board game started life as Lexico?
8 What kind of meat is used to make Bombay duck?
9 Where did Boddington's brewery close in 2005?
10 In which sport was Charles McCoy, the original 'real McCoy', a world champion?

Round 2: Europe

1 Which bay lies off northern Spain and south-western France?
2 What is the Latin name for Switzerland?
3 In which country do Ajax play domestic football?
4 In which country is the westernmost point of mainland Europe?
5 Of which European country is Vaduz the capital?
6 Who is 'the Muscles from Brussels'?
7 How many times has a British football side won football's European Nations Championship?
8 Latvia and Lithuania are two of the Baltic states – which is the third?
9 On which river does Budapest stand?
10 Which country has finished last most times in the Eurovision Song Contest?

Half-time teaser

How many hours did the longest competitive tennis match on record last?

Round 3: Minority Sports

1 The Stanley Cup is contested in which sport?
2 In which sport do teams play chukkas lasting seven and a half minutes?
3 In which sport might one use a besom?
4 Which sport is James Gibb credited with inventing in 1890 – table-tennis, billiards or ski-jumping?
5 Essendon, Port Adelaide, Collingwood and West Coast Eagles are all leading teams in which sport?
6 Who is the only cyclist to have won the Tour de France seven times?
7 From which sport comes the phrase 'the moment of truth'?
8 Which sport is associated with the Circus Tavern, Purfleet?
9 In which sport do teams contest the Iroquois Cup?
10 What term describes a surfer falling off his board?

Round 4: Pot Luck

1 Which ingredient is present in beer but missing in ale?
2 The death of which iconic figure occurred five days after that of Princess Diana?
3 Which is furthest south – Bhutan, Cambodia or Thailand?
4 Which US general was known by his detractors as 'the American Caesar'?
5 What was the name given to the temporary steel bridges put up by the Allies during World War II?
6 Who is the only person to have won the PFA Player of the Year two years running?
7 Which Caribbean island was devastated by hurricane Hugo in 1989?
8 What object stands in the middle of the Place de la Concorde in Paris?
9 Which writer was played by Anthony Hopkins in the film *Shadowlands*?
10 Which singer had a hit in 2001 with 'It's raining men'?

Jackpot

Which public statement of 1917 made clear British policy on Palestine?

✳ The phrase alludes to the fact that on some occasions he turned in lacklustre performances, while on others he fulfilled expectations and provided 'the real McCoy'.

Quiz 97

Round 1: Pot Luck

1 In which big country house does much of Daphne du Maurier's novel *Rebecca* take place?
2 The equator does not go through India – true or false?
3 Where did the first Butlin's holiday camp open in 1936?
4 In which county is the village of Adlestrop, made famous as the setting of a poem by Edward Thomas?
5 Which US town was the scene of a notorious witchcraft trial in 1692?
6 What was Cliff Clavin's job in the US television series *Cheers*?
7 Which country emerged victorious in the Six Day War of 1967?
8 Which Russian city was known as Leningrad from 1924 to 1991?
9 Which sports stadium is informally known as Billy Williams' Cabbage Patch after the man who first developed it?
10 Who succeeded Peter Sellers in the role of Inspector Clouseau in 2006?

Round 2: Music of the Seventies

1 Who went 'Kung fu fighting' in the singles charts in 1974?
2 What nationality were the 1970s band Tangerine Dream?
3 Who were 'calling occupants of interplanetary craft' in 1977?
4 According to the Buggles, who killed the radio star?
5 Who warned Billy against being a hero in 1974?
6 Who replaced Peter Gabriel as lead singer of Genesis in 1975?
7 In 1978, who wanted to know if you thought he was sexy?
8 Which member of Abba was from Norway?
9 With which band did Les McKeown sing lead vocals?
10 Who had their only chart hit in 1977 with 'The Floral Dance'?

Half-time teaser

How many years did Matt Busby serve as manager of Manchester United?

Round 3: Food and Drink

1 Which variety of pasta comes in long flat ribbons?
2 In cockney rhyming slang, what is the 'currant bun'?
3 On which day are pancakes traditionally eaten?
4 With what wine does Hannibal Lecter admit to having consumed the liver of one of his victims in the film *The Silence of the Lambs*?
5 Who released an album called *Meaty, Beaty, Big and Bouncy*?
6 Which variety of drink was allegedly invented on 4 August 1693 by a Benedictine monk called Dom Perignon? ✳
7 What name is given to a roasted fillet of beef baked in a pastry crust?
8 Which popular foodstuff was supposedly created on 24 August 1853 by one George Crum, chef at Moon's Lake House near Saratoga Springs, New York?
9 Which cocktail is made with vodka and tomato juice?
10 Who released the album *Breakfast in America*?

Round 4: Pot Luck

1 Who had a number one hit in the UK in 1970 with 'I hear you knocking'?
2 What is the name of the hero in J. R. R. Tolkien's *The Hobbit*?
3 Which architect is famous for his observation that 'the house is a machine for living in'?
4 By what name is Siddhartha Gautama better known?
5 Near which English port is Hellfire Corner, the scene of fierce fighting during the Battle of Britain?
6 Under what name did Gordon Sumner become famous?
7 What was the popular name of the flintlock musket carried by British soldiers in the eighteenth and nineteenth centuries?
8 Which pop group comprised Rob Manzoli and the Fairbrass brothers?
9 What was the name of Doctor Finlay's older colleague?
10 Which actor provides the voice of Bob the Builder?

Jackpot

Who wrote *Out of Africa*?

✳ Such was his delight that he immediately ushered a fellow-monk over to share the concoction with the words, 'Come quickly, brother. I am tasting the stars!'

Quiz 98

Round 1: Pot Luck

1 Where is opera singer Kiri Te Kanawa from?
2 Charlie Fairhead was a character in which hospital drama series?
3 How many minutes are there in four-and-a-half hours?
4 Which Tom Stopped play was based on characters from Shakespeare's *Hamlet*?
5 Who is the only tennis player to have won two complete Grand Slams?
6 Who was head of the Argentine government during the Falklands War?
7 At which London station do rail travellers from Aberdeen arrive?
8 Which historical leader had a name that translated as 'very mighty ruler'?
9 Which planet became the third to be visited by spacecraft from Earth?
10 Which English football league club plays at the Madejski Stadium?

Round 2: Art and Artists

1 Which art gallery stands on the north side of Trafalgar Square?
2 Which artist included among his masterpieces *Les Demoiselles d'Avignon*?
3 What name do artists give the point on the horizon at which various parallel lines within a painting converge?
4 After the *Mona Lisa* was stolen from the Louvre in Paris in 1911, visitor numbers fell by half – true or false?
5 Which Spanish artist famously depicted the horrors of the Peninsular War?
6 Which German artist served as court painter to Henry VIII and painted prominent figures of the day?
7 What word is used to describe the thickness of paint on a canvas or panel?
8 Which Italian artist became known by his nickname, meaning 'little dyer'?
9 Which French artist worked as a tax collector in Paris before establishing a reputation as a painter?
10 Which of his ears did Vincent Van Gogh cut off in 1888?

Half-time teaser

Ashrita Furman holds the record for pogo-stick jumping – how many miles did he go?

Round 3: British Royalty

1 Which king founded the Royal Navy?
2 Which British monarch wrote a tract against smoking?
3 What did Elizabeth II celebrate in 2002?
4 Who was the first Tudor king?
5 Which king of England died with the words 'Monk! Monks! Monks!'?
6 Who was the last Roman Catholic monarch of Britain?
7 To the memory of which queen were 12 crosses erected between Lincoln and London?
8 Which king of England was the fattest?
9 At which castle in Northamptonshire was Mary, Queen of Scots beheaded?
10 Who comes next in the Order of Succession after Prince Charles, Prince William and Prince Harry?

Round 4: Pot Luck

1 Which country includes among its cities Sheffield, Nelson and Wanganui?
2 In wrestling, what name is given to the hold in which one fighter sits on the back of another, with the other's legs tucked under his arms?
3 What did Burma officially change its name to in 1989?
4 Which influential religious publication was compiled by Thomas Cranmer?
5 Which English football league club originally played as St Domingo FC?
6 Lambic and faro beers are drunk in which European country?
7 Which former member of a classic pop duo died in a skiing accident in 1998?
8 In cricket, what name is given to a lower-order batsman sent in to protect a key player late in the day?
9 In which year was the National Trust founded – 1895, 1945 or 1975?
10 Which country lies between Nicaragua and Panama?

Jackpot

How old did recruits to the Home Guard in World War II have to be?

∗ Vincent carefully wrapped the severed ear in newspaper and sent it to a local prostitute called Rachel, asking her to keep it safe.

Quiz 99

....

Round 1: Pot Luck

1 What scale is used to measure the strength of earthquakes?
2 Who created the Muppets?
3 Who was an 'innocent man' in 1984?
4 In Rudyard Kipling's *The Jungle Book*, what kind of animal is Bagheera?
5 Who directed the 1940 film *The Grapes of Wrath*?
6 In which athletic event was Sergei Bubka a star?
7 Where is the US Military Academy based?
8 Who played Captain Queeg in the 1953 film *The Caine Mutiny*?
9 Which country has sovereignty over Easter Island?
10 In advertising, what is recommended 'for hands that do dishes'?

....

Round 2: Films

1 Which film director made the silent classic *The Birth of a Nation*?
2 Whose death in police custody inspired Richard Attenborough's 1987 film *Cry Freedom*?
3 The films *You Only Live Once*, *They Live by Night*, *Gun Crazy* and *Thieves Like Us* were all about which pair of notorious US bank robbers?
4 In which country did the action depicted in the 1974 film *A Bridge Too Far* take place?
5 In which film did Audrey Hepburn appear as Holly Golightly?
6 In which 1957 film did Alec Guinness play the part of Colonel Nicholson?
7 Which other Hollywood star was due to play the lead in the classic 1942 film *Casablanca* until he became unavailable and the part passed to Humphrey Bogart?
8 Who won successive Oscars for Best Actor in 1993 and 1994?
9 On which middleweight boxer's life was the 1980 film *Raging Bull* based?
10 What was the role for which Philip Seymour Hoffman won an Oscar for Best Actor in 2006?

....

Half-time teaser

How many people were executed by the authorities in the USA in 2005?

....

Round 3: Beside the Sea

1 Who got to number two in the UK charts with 'Stranger on the shore'?
2 For what radio programme is 'By the sleepy lagoon' the theme tune?
3 Who proclaimed the virtues of Echo Beach in 1980?
4 What kind of sea animal is a crown-of-thorns? *
5 Who, in 1947, crossed the Pacific in a balsa wood raft called the *Kon-Tiki*?
6 What title were transatlantic liners formerly awarded for the fastest crossing of the Atlantic?
7 What do the initials ASDIC stand for?
8 In which ocean are the Mariana Islands?
9 'Leviathan Rising', 'A Silence in the Water' and 'Great White' were all considered as alternative titles for which 1975 film?
10 Who died in 2006 when attacked by a stingray?

Round 4: Pot Luck

1 What name is given to a person who smokes one cigarette after another, without taking a break between?
2 Who spent his childhood in Smallville, USA?
3 Who played television's *Six-Million Dollar Man*?
4 How was the Japanese city of Yeda or Edo renamed in 1868?
5 Which famous cellist was married to conductor Daniel Barenboim?
6 Who took the place of Judas Iscariot?
7 Only two novelists have won the annual Man Booker literary prize more than once – name one of them.
8 Which Shakespeare play includes characters called Trinculo, Alonso, Stephano and Sebastian?
9 Who had a number one hit in the UK in 1983 with 'True'?
10 Who finished last in the 2003 Eurovision Song Contest, representing the UK?

Jackpot

Which novel ends with the words: 'Until we have wiped the last one of them from the face of the land they have usurped'?

* It is held partly responsible for the continuing destruction of the Great Barrier Reef.

Quiz 100

Round 1: Pot Luck

1 Which country was called East Pakistan until 1972?

2 How may actor Joss Ackland and motor-racing driver Mario Andretti claim to be younger than they appear to be?

3 In 1952, who won Olympic gold in the 5,000 metres, 10,000 metres and marathon events?

4 Which rock band took its name from World War II slang for mystery aircraft?

5 Which northern rambler wrote a series of books detailing routes for walkers?

6 How many points does a snooker player get for potting the black ball?

7 Which style of twentieth-century architecture favoured unfinished moulded concrete and monumental designs?

8 In which sport do players aim for a goal called a hail?

9 What camera did artists use long before the invention of photography?

10 Which shredded vegetable is a main ingredient of sauerkraut?

Round 2: The 1930s

1 Who broke five world records in one day in the 1935 Olympics?

2 In which English county was the Sutton Hoo ship burial unearthed in 1939?

3 Gillespie Road underground station was renamed in honour of which football team in 1932?

4 Which word described the placatory policy of Britain and France towards the Fascist powers in the 1930s?

5 Which pressure group was founded in 1935 to promote enjoyment of the countryside and public access to it?

6 How, in 1933, was the death of Henry Royce of Rolls-Royce Ltd commemorated in the company's cars?

7 Driving tests were introduced in Britain in which year – 1934, 1936 or 1939?

8 The bombing of which Spanish town in 1937 inspired a painting by Picasso?

9 What happened to end Huey Long's presidential campaign in 1935?

10 What was the name of the airship destroyed by fire in New Jersey in 1937 with the loss of 36 lives?

Half-time teaser

In 2005, a new record was set for the number of horses taking part in the same race – how many were there?

Round 3: Endings

1 Under which sign of the zodiac does the year end on 31 December?
2 In which play does William Shakespeare appear to bid a final farewell to the stage?
3 At one minute before midnight on 1 January 1949 a UN ceasefire ended war between which two Commonwealth members?
4 With which song did television's *The Good Old Days* always end?
5 What did Lenin describe as 'a weapon with a worker at both ends'?
6 Which is the only word in the English language that ends in the letters 'mt'?
7 In which city did Jimi Hendrix die in 1970?
8 What was the title of the Charles Dickens novel left unfinished at the author's death?
9 In which film did Noël Coward make his final screen appearance?
10 Which novel ends with the words 'After all, tomorrow is another day'?

Round 4: Pot Luck

1 Which river is spanned by the Clifton Suspension Bridge? *
2 What is a trug?
3 Which city has the nickname 'Auld Reekie'?
4 Which artist had a garden at Giverny in Normandy?
5 Which company made the Camel fighter used in World War I?
6 Alongside Ronaldo, who is only person to have won the FIFA World Footballer of the Year three times?
7 Which is the longest bone in the human body?
8 In which sport was the Gordon Bennett Trophy formerly a major prize?
9 Which Cornish town was devastated by a flash flood in 2004?
10 Who painted *The Last of England*?

Jackpot

Which record company was set up by Berry Gordy in Detroit in 1959?

---

* The bridge has a notorious reputation for the number of people who have committed suicide by throwing themselves off it. The story is still told of one young woman who hurled herself from the parapet in 1885, only to float gracefully to the ground on her billowing skirts.

New Year Quiz

Round 1: Pot Luck

1 What is the name given to New Year celebrations in Scotland?
2 What ceremony performed by a tall dark-haired man at midnight on New Year's Eve is supposed to promote the luck of the household?
3 Who wrote the words of 'Auld Lang Syne'?
4 What is the gemstone for January?
5 What is the Jewish New Year called?
6 The sixth of January, which marks the end of Christmas, is sometimes referred to by what name?
7 Which of these is not the name of a Chinese year – dog, eel or rat?
8 Who, on New Year's Day 1985, made the first mobile phone call in the UK?
9 On 1 January in which year did the UK become a member of the European Community?
10 What event signalled the start of the New Year in ancient Egypt?

Round 2: In with the New

1 Babies born on New Year's Day share which star sign?
2 Which US silversmith born on New Year's Day 1735 is remembered for telling his neighbours 'The British are coming'?
3 Which Frenchman born on New Year's Day 1863 went on to become the founder of the modern Olympic Games?
4 Which British novelist who went on a passage to India was born on New Year's Day 1879?
5 On New Year's Day 1925 the Norwegian city of Christiania changed its name to what?
6 Which reclusive US author born on New Year's Day 1919 created the fictional Holden Caulfield?
7 Who was the FBI chief in the years 1924 to 1972 who was born on New Year's Day 1895?
8 What currency was introduced on 1 January 1999?
9 Which major US sporting event first took place on New Year's Day 1902?
10 Which two central European countries came into being on 1 January 1993?

Half-time teaser

On New Year's Day 1907 President Theodore Roosevelt established a new record for the number of hands shaken in one day – how many did he shake?

Round 3: Out with the Old

1 Which notorious British serial killer committed suicide on 1 January 1995, aged 53?

2 In 1953 which country singer died in the back of a car on his way to a New Year's Day concert in Ohio, aged 29?

3 On New Year's Day 1788 which British newspaper changed its name from the *Daily Universal Register*?

4 Name the creator of private eye Sam Spade who died on New Year's Day 1961.

5 US actor Cesar Romero died on New Year's Day 1994 – which part in the long-running US television series *Batman* did he play?

6 The end of French rule on 1 January 1804 led to the establishment of the first independent country in the West Indies, under what name?

7 What name did Turkish president Mustafa Kemal adopt on New Year's Day 1935?

8 What kind of advertising was banned on US television from 1 January 1971?

9 On 1 January 1797 which city replaced New York City as the capital of New York state?

10 The importation of what into the USA was banned on 1 January 1808?

Round 4: Pot Luck

1 What bug failed to materialise on 1 January 2000?

2 What title was bestowed upon Queen Victoria on New Year's Day 1877?

3 Who had a hit with 'New Year's Day' in 1983?

4 All racehorses become a year older on New Year's Day – true or false?

5 Who did Sherlock Holmes meet for the first time on New Year's Day 1881?

6 What announcement did the Japanese emperor Hirohito make on New Year's Day 1946?

7 Which British pop group auditioned for Decca on New Year's Day 1962?

8 Who began a famous diary on 1 January 1660?

9 On New Year's Day 1896 what did Wilhelm Roentgen announce he had discovered?

10 What hit single about a melancholy guesthouse did Elvis Presley record on New Year's Day 1956?

Jackpot

What gifts did ancient Persians exchange at New Year: fish, coins, eggs or swords?

✻ It was made in front of the press from St Katharine's Dock, London, to Vodafone's headquarters, then housed above a curry shop in Newbury, Berkshire.

St Valentine's Day Quiz

Round 1: Pot Luck

1 What is the date of St Valentine's Day?
2 Which Roman emperor had the original St Valentine put to death for defying the rule forbidding young soldiers from marrying?
3 St Valentine's Day was an official church holiday until 1969 – true or false?
4 From which Roman festival did the modern feast of St Valentine develop?
5 According to the proverb, what makes the heart grow fonder?
6 What St Valentine's custom did Charles, Duke of Orleans supposedly begin in 1415?
7 In which US city did the St Valentine Day's massacre of 1929 take place?
8 Who played the star-crossed lover Romeo in the 1996 film version of Shakespeare's *Romeo and Juliet*?
9 Which celebrity couple named their son Romeo in 2002?
10 How many calories can a person burn off in one minute's snogging – 26, 106 or 326?

Round 2: Loving Couples

1 What family relationship already existed between Queen Victoria and her husband Prince Albert?
2 To whom was Courtney Love married until his suicide?
3 How many husbands has Elizabeth Taylor been married to?
4 Whom did Sir Elton John marry in a civil partnership in December 2005?
5 Who shared 'endless love' with Luther Vandross in 1994?
6 With whom did Lancelot enjoy an illicit relationship?
7 For whom did Grace Kelly abandon Hollywood in 1956?
8 Who played Lord Alfred Douglas opposite Stephen Fry's Oscar Wilde in the 1997 film *Wilde*?
9 What is the name of Ozzy Osbourne wife?
10 Which pair of popular daytime television presenters married in 1986 and have since co-hosted chat shows on both ITV and Channel Four?

Half-time teaser

How many millions of pounds are spent on flowers for St Valentine's Day each year in the UK?

Round 3: Fictional Romances

1 Who played Leonardo DiCaprio's lover in the blockbuster film *Titanic*?
2 Who marries Edgar Linton in Emily Brontë's *Wuthering Heights*?
3 Who kissed Burt Lancaster in the surf in the 1953 film *From Here to Eternity*?
4 Which US actress was pursued by a tongue-tied Hugh Grant in *Four Weddings and a Funeral*?
5 Which US actress was romantically entangled with Hugh Grant in *Bridget Jones's Diary*?
6 Who, in the role of Mr Darcy, made a dripping entrance in the 1995 television adaptation of Jane Austen's *Pride and Prejudice*?
7 Which romantic 1970 film was advertised with the slogan 'Love means never having to say you're sorry'?
8 In which 1989 film did Tom Conti and Pauline Collins play lovers against the backdrop of a Greek island resort?
9 What is the name of Scarlett O'Hara's roguish admirer in *Gone With the Wind*?
10 What is the name of the enigmatic employer with whom the heroine falls in love in *Jane Eyre*?

Round 4: Pot Luck

1 Which is generally considered to be the most romantic city in the world?
2 Which English monarch declared St Valentine's Day to be a holiday?
3 By what name was British actor Valentine Dyall well known?
4 What is the name of the son of the goddess Venus, who plays a prominent role in St Valentine mythology?
5 Allied soldiers writing to their lovers during World War II were prohibited from writing Xs for kisses in case they conveyed secret information – true or false?
6 Which group, according to recent surveys, receive the most Valentine cards – secretaries, teachers or politicians?
7 Who wrote the novel *Women in Love*?
8 Which of the following does not have a reputation as an aphrodisiac – oysters, oranges or tomatoes? ✳
9 From a prison in which Italian city did the romantic adventurer Casanova escape in 1756?
10 Which songwriting partnership composed the jazz standard 'My funny Valentine'?

Jackpot

Who wrote the novels *The Pursuit of Love* and *Love in a Cold Climate*?

✳ Less well-known aphrodisiac foods over the centuries have included cabbage, leeks, lettuce and potatoes.

St David's Day Quiz

Round 1: Pot Luck

1 On which date is St David's Day celebrated?
2 Which flower is worn by many people on St David's Day?
3 What is regarded as the Welsh national anthem?
4 What is the principal ingredient of laverbread?
5 Which three colours appear on the Welsh flag?
6 Which ancient earthwork roughly marks the border between Wales and England?
7 Who, in 1216, became the first Prince of Wales?
8 What is the name of the main Welsh nationalist party?
9 There are five cities in Wales – Cardiff, Newport, Swansea, St David's and which other?
10 What should you do with bara brith – drink it, wear it or eat it?

Round 2: The Land of Song

1 What is the name of the leading annual Welsh festival of poetry and music?
2 Which Welsh baritone was knighted in 1969 in recognition of his performances in such roles as Figaro, Falstaff and Wozzeck?
3 Which Welsh composer wrote such songs as 'Keep the home fires burning' and 'We'll gather lilacs'?
4 Who, in 1968, lamented the carryings-on of one Delilah?
5 Which popular Welsh singer was born Charlotte Maria Reed in 1986?
6 Which Cardiff-born singer had 15 top ten hits in the 1980s, among them 'You drive me crazy' and 'A love worth waiting for'?
7 Welsh singer Bonnie Tyler topped the singles charts for four weeks in 1982 with which song?
8 Which Welsh singer is the only artist to have recorded two theme tunes for the James Bond films?
9 Which Welsh rock band has remained in business despite the mysterious and still unsolved disappearance of its drummer in 1995?
10 Which Welsh singer and entertainer achieved fame in the 1950s in such roles as Neddie Seagoon?

Half-time teaser

How long, in miles, is the coastline of Wales?

Round 3: The Sporting Welsh

1 Which other team, alongside Cardiff City and Swansea City, plays in the English Football League?
2 Welsh sportsmen Terry Griffiths, Mark Williams and Matthew Stevens are all top contestants in which sport?
3 What is the nickname of the Welsh national rugby union team?
4 Which is the only first-class cricket club in Wales?
5 What is the nickname of Cardiff City football club?
6 In which year did the Welsh national rugby union team achieve a grand slam in the Six Nations Championship?
7 Which Welsh athlete won gold medals in the 1993 and 1999 World Championship 110 metres hurdles events?
8 Alan Rees and Tom Pryce reached the highest level in which sport?
9 Who holds the record for most tries scored for the Welsh national rugby union team?
10 Which Welsh boxer, variously nicknamed 'the pride of Wales' and 'the Italian Dragon', won his first Super Middleweight Championship in 1997?

Round 4: Pot Luck

1 What is the Welsh language name for Wales?
2 Which English king conquered Wales in the thirteenth century?
3 Who led a rebellion against English rule early in the fifteenth century?
4 Which is the highest mountain in Wales?
5 What is the English name for the Welsh island of Ynys Mon?
6 What two colours appear on the flag of St David, sometimes used as an alternative to the dragon flag?
7 Which Welsh comedian is best known for his television appearances in the role of Keith Barret?
8 Which member of the *Monty Python* team was born in Colwyn Bay, Wales?
9 Where in Wales can be found the best-preserved Roman amphitheatre in Britain?
10 Which actor and champion of Welsh nationalism disappointed Welsh fans when he took dual US–Welsh nationality in 2000?

Jackpot

What does the name Wales mean?

✴ There used to be a sixth city in Wales, the cathedral town of St Asaph, but this lost its city status during the twentieth century. With a population of around 3,500, it failed in attempts to have its city status restored in 2000 and 2002, but as host of the North Wales International Music Festival still advertises itself as 'the city of music'.

St Patrick's Day Quiz

Round 1: Pot Luck

1 On which date is St Patrick's Day celebrated?
2 What is the emblem of St Patrick?
3 How did St Patrick first come to Ireland?
4 Where is St Patrick believed to lie buried?
5 Ireland has no snakes or reptiles – true or false?
6 By what name did the Romans usually refer to Ireland?
7 Which three colours make up the Irish Tricolour flag?
8 On which river does Dublin stand?
9 What is the Irish name for Ireland?
10 In which year was the Kingdom of Ireland merged with the Kingdom of Great Britain to form the United Kingdom of Great Britain and Ireland?

Round 2: The Emerald Isle

1 Ireland is divided into four provinces – Ulster, Connacht, Leinster and which other?
2 How many counties are there in Northern Ireland?
3 Which Irish town lent its name to a form of comic verse?
4 Which is the only inland city in southern Ireland?
5 What is the northernmost tip of Ireland called?
6 In which county is Ireland's highest mountain, Carrantuohill?
7 What is Newgrange in County Meath famous for?
8 Which breed of animal is County Kildare famous for?
9 What are Macgillicuddy's Reeks?
10 Which part of the Irish coastline is a renowned venue for surfing?

Half-time teaser

How many species of mammal are native to Ireland?

Round 3: Famous Irish Folk

1 James Joyce was the first Irishman to win the Nobel Prize for Literature – true or false?
2 With which family group did Irish singer Enya first enjoy success?
3 Which character was played by Ardal O'Hanlon in *Father Ted*?
4 Which Irish singer created a furore when she tore up a picture of the pope on US television?
5 Which Irish actor played Albus Dumbledore in the first Harry Potter films?
6 Which Belfast-born star was variously nicknamed 'the Belfast Boy' and 'the fifth Beatle'? *
7 Who became president of the newly declared Irish Republic in 1919?
8 Which Irish writer suggested in a famous satirical pamphlet that one way to solve the problem of the poor in Ireland was for them to sell their children to be eaten?
9 Which Irish actor played the lead role in such films as *Michael Collins* and *Rob Roy*?
10 Which playwright wrote *The Playboy of the Western World*?

Round 4: Pot Luck

1 In which decade did the Great Famine devastate the population of Ireland?
2 Which musical instrument appears in the Guinness logo?
3 Which traditional Irish band, led by Paddy Moloney, has played with the likes of Van Morrison, Mick Jagger, the Corrs and Sting?
4 What is the main ingredient of the traditional dish colcannon?
5 What term has been applied to the resurgent Irish economy in recent years?
6 How many players are there in a Gaelic football team?
7 In which year did the Republic of Ireland football team reach the quarter-finals of the World Cup?
8 What would you do with a bodhran – feed it, play it or have it exorcised?
9 What was the name of the agreement under which the restoration of self-government in Northern Ireland was started?
10 Which hill in County Meath is traditionally believed to have been the seat of the High Kings of Ireland?

Jackpot

In which Irish sport are the *caman* and the *sliotar* essential pieces of kit?

---

* Other figures who have been known as 'the fifth Beatle' have included drummer Pete Best, manager Brian Epstein and boxer Muhammad Ali. Charles Manson also claimed the title.

Mother's Day Quiz

Round 1: Pot Luck
1 Which mother appears in the title of a popular pantomime?
2 Which mother famously ministered to the poor of Calcutta?
3 Which comedian's catchphrases included 'Can you hear me, mother?'
4 Who released an album called *Atom Heart Mother*?
5 Which flower is traditionally associated with Mother's Day in France?
6 Which actor played a man dominated by his mother in the television sitcom *Sorry*?
7 Who, in 1991, promised 'the mother of all battles'?
8 Who, in a 1987 film, was tempted to throw his momma from the train?
9 Which Scottish football club plays at Fir Park?
10 Which mother featured in the title of a play by Bertolt Brecht?

Round 2: Famous Mothers
1 Who was Liza Minnelli's ill-fated mother?
2 Who was Queen Mother during the reign of George VI?
3 Which ex-royal is mother to Beatrice and Eugenie?
4 Which mother's controversial attitude to her children was exposed in *Mommie Dearest*?
5 Which actress is mother of Carrie Fisher?
6 Who is the celebrity mother of Brooklyn, Romeo and Cruz?
7 Who was the mother of Helen of Troy?
8 What was the birth name of Elizabeth II's mother?
9 The biblical Elisabeth gave birth to which character by Zacharias?
10 Who is the celebrity mother of Apple and Moses?

Half-time teaser
What is the highest number of children recorded as having been borne by one woman?

Round 3: Mother's Day Gifts

1 What kind of cake was traditionally given by daughters to their mothers on Mothering Sunday?
2 Which transparent soap was first sold commercially in London in 1789?
3 What mother-related substance connected with shellfish is used to make jewellery and craft goods?
4 What treat has a name that meant 'bitter water' in the language from which it came?
5 Which brand of soap and toiletries is made by Cussons?
6 Which form of jewellery comprises solidified pine resin?
7 Which type of perfume was originally obtained from Asian deer?
8 Which popular pot plant has leaves that turn red around the end of the year?
9 Which company, founded in Sheffield in 1911, is now Britain's largest manufacturer and retailer of specialist chocolates?
10 Which company makes Poison perfume?

Round 4: Pot Luck

1 Who, in 1927, sang about his 'dear old mammy'?
2 Who had a hit in 1972 with the single 'Mother and child reunion'? ✳
3 Which fairy-tale character is forced to do all the housework by her wicked stepmother?
4 Which pop group sang about 'Mamma mia' in 1975?
5 What was the mummy's name in the 1999 film *The Mummy*?
6 What mother-related name is given to folk plays depicting Saint George, the Quack Doctor and other traditional characters?
7 Whose mummy, found in 1923, has been admired by millions of people around the world?
8 Which pop group had a hit with 'California dreamin''?
9 What did Old Mother Hubbard go to her cupboard for?
10 Which mother-linked sitcom included among the characters Gunner/Bombardier 'Gloria' Beaumont and Battery Sergeant-Major Williams?

Jackpot

Which headland on Swansea Bay has a mother-related name?

✳ Legend has it that the song was inspired by an item on a Chinese menu given this name because it combined chicken and egg.

St George's Day Quiz

Round 1: Pot Luck

1 Upon what date does St George's Day fall?
2 What colour is the cross on the flag of St George?
3 In which year is St George usually said to have died – 303, 903 or 1203?
4 Of which of the following countries is St George not the patron saint – England, Georgia, Canada, Portugal or Hungary?
5 St George's Day is a public holiday in England – true or false?
6 In years gone by, what flower did people wear in their lapel on St George's Day?
7 Which hymn is often sung in English churches on or around St George's Day?
8 The Queen traditionally announces new appointments to which royal order on St George's Day?
9 In which army is St George said to have served?
10 Which famous English playwright's life began and ended on St George's Day?

Round 2: England and the English

1 Which castle on the Cornish coast is identified as the birthplace of King Arthur?
2 Which folkloric hero is supposedly buried at Kirklees Priory in West Yorkshire?
3 Which English composer is particularly associated with Malvern, Worcestershire?
4 During World War II, fish and chips were one of the few foodstuffs not subject to rationing – true or false?
5 How many years passed between the England cricket team's victory in the Ashes in 2005 and their previous victory?
6 The original sixth verse of the national anthem begged God for assistance against which enemy?
7 Who is supposed to have dismissed the English as 'a nation of shopkeepers'?
8 Who expected to see a non-indigenous species of bird over English cliffs in 1940?
9 In which play did Shakespeare extol the virtues of England as 'this sceptred isle'?
10 According to the song, there will always be an England while there's a – what?

Half-time teaser

For how many years has Britain been ruled by a George?

Round 3: Famous Georges

1 Which George had a notorious conversation with an oak tree?
2 Which famous George was created by John Le Carré?
3 Which George was a boyhood idol of Diego Maradona?
4 What was George on *Blue Peter*?
5 Which George has appeared in television adverts for Martini?
6 Who starred as George of the Jungle in 1997?
7 By what name did George O'Dowd become better known?
8 Which George was linked romantically with Alfred de Musset, Franz Liszt and Frédéric Chopin?
9 Which George starred opposite Dustin Hoffman in *Straw Dogs*?
10 Which George wrote 'Rhapsody in blue'?

Round 4: Pot Luck

1 Which country honours St George in its name?
2 What did St George kill the dragon with?
3 Who fought in the Holy Land with the cross of St George on their tunics?
4 According to Christian tradition, how was St George martyred for his faith?
5 Who was considered the patron saint of England before St George?
6 Of which royal complex is St George's Chapel a feature?
7 Which Shakespearean figure rallies his men with the words 'Cry God for Harry, England and St George!'?
8 Which Spanish playwright died on St George's Day in 1616?
9 Which one of the following organisations does not consider St George its patron saint – the Scouts, the Royal Automobile Club or the Freemasons?
10 Who, in 1893, was proclaimed patron saint of England by Pope Leo XIII in preference to St George? *

Jackpot

During the reign of which Edward was St George recognised as the patron saint of England?

* St George was removed altogether from the calendar of the Roman Catholic Church in 1963, although he could still be honoured locally. Although Pope John Paul II restored St George to the calendar in 2000, he remains a minor second-class saint in the eyes of Rome.

Father's Day Quiz

Round 1: Pot Luck

1 In which month is Father's Day celebrated in the UK?
2 On which saint's day is Father's Day celebrated in many Roman Catholic countries?
3 According to William Wordsworth, what is the father of the man?
4 Who wrote 'My heart belongs to Daddy'?
5 From which Shakespeare play comes the line 'Full fathom five thy father lies'?
6 Who, in 1986, told her papa not to preach?
7 The famous painting 'And when did you last see your father?' depicts an event during which war?
8 Who, in a remake of 1991, was cinema's father of the bride?
9 With what kind of music was Fatha Hines associated?
10 Of which country was Papa Doc the ruler?

Round 2: Famous Fathers

1 Who was 'the Father of Medicine'?
2 Of what is Charles Babbage considered the father?
3 Who is the famous father of actor Emilio Estevez?
4 Who was 'the Father of Ragtime'?
5 Who was 'the Father of Television'?
6 Who became known as 'the Father of Angling'?
7 Which British racing driver had a son who followed him to the Formula One championship?
8 Who is identified as 'the Father of Nuclear Physics'?
9 Who was 'the Father of the Helicopter'?
10 Who is remembered as 'the Father of History'?

Half-time teaser

Wei-yi and Wei-ning have the longest family tree in the world and can trace their lineage through their fathers all the way back to their direct ancestor Confucius – how many generations of fathers does their tree include?

Round 3: Daddy's Toys

1 Which car manufacturer has a prancing black stallion as its badge?
2 Which beer has been sold under the slogan 'It looks good, tastes good and, by golly, it does you good'?
3 Which all-male pop group has been rocking all over the world since 1977?
4 How did Eric Morley please men around the world in 1951?
5 What do the initials TVR stand for?
6 The terms 'four-in-hand', 'half-Windsor' and 'kipper' all relate to what?
7 Which British actress disappointed her male admirers at Sudeley Castle in 2007 by getting married to someone else?
8 What does LCD stand for in 'LCD television'?
9 *The Legend of Bagger Vance* and *Caddyshack II* were films about which sport?
10 Which English football club found itself in 2005 owned by Americans, managed by a Scotsman and captained by an Irishman?

Round 4: Pot Luck

1 In which year was Father's Day first marked in the USA – 1908, 1938 or 1958?
2 Under which US president was Father's Day recognised as an official holiday in 1972?
3 Which US river is known as 'the Father of the Waters'?
4 What implement is Father Time usually depicted holding?
5 Which member of Dad's Army worked as an undertaker?
6 Which father in Shakespeare goes mad after falling out with the sweetest of his three daughters?
7 In which county does 'Father Thames' have its source?
8 What was the name of the ship in which the Pilgrim Fathers sailed?
9 As which father did Dermot Morgan become well known?
10 Which infamous African dictator had the nickname Dada?

Jackpot

Who is revered as 'the Father of English History'?

⚹ Wags have noted that Father's Day falls roughly nine months before Mothering Sunday, suggesting that if Father gets his present on Father's Day, Mother gets hers nine months later.

Hallowe'en Quiz

Round 1: Pot Luck

1 Which Hallowe'en custom of US origin has resulted in British children going from door to door in recent years?

2 In which part of the British Isles is Hallowe'en sometimes called 'Pooky Night'?

3 Hallowe'en was influenced by which Celtic festival?

4 What is a group of witches called?

5 In which county did the Pendle witches terrify their neighbours?

6 At which school of witchcraft does Harry Potter learn the magic arts?

7 Who wrote 'The Fall of the House of Usher'?

8 The ghost of which US president has reportedly been seen at the White House?

9 What is Audrey II in the *Little Shop of Horrors*?

10 Who was England's Witchfinder-General?

Round 2: Horror Films

1 In which horror film does Jack Nicholson pursue Shelley Duval with an axe?

2 What is the name of the bloodthirsty murderer in the *Hallowe'en* films?

3 In *Gremlins*, what are the two essentials that have to be remembered to prevent the adorable creatures becoming monsters?

4 In which 1939 comedy thriller is Bob Hope among guests menaced by a maniac in an old dark house?

5 Which horror actor was billed as 'the Man of a Thousand Faces'?

6 In which film do three student film-makers film events leading to their own deaths?

7 Who was 'the abominable Dr Phibes'?

8 In which 1968 film are five people trapped in a farmhouse by rampaging zombies?

9 What fate befalls Sergeant Howie in *The Wicker Man*?

10 In which film does Kenneth Williams proclaim 'Frying tonight!' as he descends into a vat of boiling wax?

Half-time teaser

How many episodes were made of the *Munsters* television comedy?

Round 3: Vampires

1 Who wrote the original Dracula story?
2 Which Hungarian leader is said to have inspired the character of Dracula?
3 Which horror film star was buried in the cape he wore as Count Dracula?
4 Which snooker player was nicknamed 'Dracula'?
5 Who starred as television's Buffy the Vampire-Slayer?
6 Which 1922 horror film introduced the vampire on the silver screen?
7 What is the name of the lawyer who visits Dracula's castle at the beginning of the original tale?
8 Which vegetable is said to ward off vampires?
9 At which British port does Dracula's ship put in?
10 Dracula actor Bela Lugosi was born in Transylvania – true or false?

Round 4: Pot Luck

1 Who wrote the 1818 novel *Frankenstein*?
2 What is an arachnophobe scared of?
3 Over which land does the White Witch rule in *The Lion, the Witch and the Wardrobe*?
4 Who terrified the world as the Mummy in 1932?
5 Which hit television documentary on the supernatural is presented by Yvette Fielding and Derek Acorah?
6 How many witches confront Macbeth in the opening scene of Shakespeare's play?
7 What name is given to a ghost which confines itself to making noises and moving things?
8 From which direction did the wicked witch of *The Wizard of Oz* come?
9 Which supernatural creature has been linked with the medical condition lycanthropy?
10 Why didn't the skeleton go to the ball?

Jackpot

Who wrote the classic 1764 horror novel *The Castle of Otranto*?

✴ The modern custom is an echo of a much older tradition, in which householders left offerings of food and drink to appease the dead if they chose to revisit their own homes.

St Andrew's Day Quiz

Round 1: Pot Luck

1 On which date is St Andrew's Day celebrated?
2 What is the colour of the cross on the flag of St Andrew?
3 By what name is the Order of St Andrew also known?
4 St Andrew was the brother of which other disciple?
5 What was the biblical St Andrew's trade?
6 Of which is St Andrew not a patron saint – Russia, Sicily, Romania or Italy?
7 When did St Andrew become the patron saint of Scotland – the fifth century AD, the tenth century or the fifteenth century?
8 Whereabouts in eastern Scotland is St Rule said to have brought the bones of St Andrew?
9 For whom is St Andrew a patron saint – candlemakers, fishmongers or waiters?
10 In the 1960s the Vatican returned relics of St Andrew to Scotland – in which city are these now?

Round 2: Scotland and the Scottish

1 Where is Arthur's seat?
2 Whereabouts in Scotland is Skara Brae?
3 What was the name of the wall built by the Romans north of Hadrian's Wall?
4 What were the supporters of Bonnie Prince Charlie called?
5 Which rocky outcrop is claimed by Scotland, Denmark, Iceland and Ireland?
6 The Royal Bank of Scotland still produces a £1 note – true or false?
7 Which novel by Irvine Welsh illuminated the lives of Scottish heroin addicts?
8 Scotland has four major international airports, at Aberdeen, Edinburgh, Glasgow – and where else?
9 Who took Dr Samuel Johnson on a tour of the Hebrides in 1773?
10 What is Sean Connery's first name?

Half-time teaser

Andy Roddick has the fastest recorded serve in professional tennis – how fast is it in miles per hour?

Round 3: Famous Andrews

1 Which Andrews provided the voice of the queen in *Shrek II*?
2 Which Scottish tennis player was a pupil at Dunblane Primary School at the time of the tragic 1996 shootings?
3 Which US president carried scars from a beating he received for refusing to clean the boots of a British officer?
4 Which Andrew topped the UK charts with 'Flava', 'I feel you' and 'Mysterious girl'?
5 What colour were Andy Pandy's pyjamas?
6 Which Andrews starred in *The Ox-Bow Incident*, *Laura* and *The Best Years of Our Lives*?
7 Which Andrews presented his guests with a big red book?
8 The Andrews Sisters were not sisters – true or false?
9 Which Andrew became famous for the products of his New York Factory?
10 Which British broadcaster born in Rochdale is a noted champion of world music?

Round 4: Pot Luck

1 Which heraldic term is also an alternative name for the flag of St Andrew?
2 Which branch of the armed services is sometimes nicknamed 'the Andrew'?
3 Which notable aircraft is kept at Andrews Air Base near Washington, DC?
4 Which leading Scottish politician is chancellor of St Andrews University?
5 Who wrote the novel *Joseph Andrews*?
6 Which dummy Andrews had a successful partnership with Peter Brough?
7 What is the name of the royal palace in Edinburgh?
8 What is Scotland's national football stadium?
9 Which motorway connects Glasgow and Edinburgh?
10 In which year, to within two years, did the Scottish parliament agree to make St Andrew's Day an official bank holiday?

Jackpot

On which ship did Prince Andrew serve during the Falklands War?

⁎ When Boswell asked Dr Samuel Johnson what he considered the finest view in Scotland, the venerable writer replied 'The high road to England.'

Christmas Quiz

Round 1: Pot Luck

1 What were the names of the Three Wise Men?
2 Where did St Nicholas live?
3 In *A Christmas Carol*, what was the name of Ebenezer Scrooge's partner?
4 Which saint's feast falls on 26 December?
5 Which country annually donates the Christmas tree to be erected in Trafalgar Square?
6 At Christmas 2006, whose lifeless body was found near the Christmas tree in Albert Square gardens?
7 In the Christian calendar, what is the name of the season leading up to Christmas?
8 In which year did opposing troops in the trenches during World War I leave their posts at Christmas and fraternise in no-man's-land?
9 Which feast falls on 6 January?
10 Who wrote *The Snowman*?

Round 2: Christmas Music

1 Who wrote the song 'White Christmas'?
2 Which tenth-century ruler of Bohemia appears today in a popular carol?
3 With what song did Cliff Richard top the Christmas charts in 1988?
4 For what festival was the song 'Jingle Bells' originally written?
5 How many gifts are given in total in the song 'The Twelve Days of Christmas'?
6 Who topped the 1980 Christmas charts with 'There's no one quite like Grandma'?
7 In the 'Twelve days of Christmas', what is a 'colly bird'?
8 What did Frosty the Snowman have for a nose?
9 According to the song, what is the only thing the singer wants for Christmas?
10 In the Christmas song by Slade, who is having fun?

Half-time teaser

In which year were electric lights first used to decorate Christmas trees?

Round 3: Christmas Traditions

1 What innovation of 1843 became a standard feature of Christmas?
2 Which plant used in Christmas decorations was sacred to Druids?
3 Which modern Christmas tradition was borrowed from the Moravian Church?
4 Who introduced the idea of the decorated Christmas tree to Great Britain?
5 Which Christmas pantomime features Widow Twankey?
6 What is the name of the little boy left behind at Christmas in *Home Alone*?
7 Which plant widely used as a Christmas decoration has the Latin name *ilex aquifolium*?
8 Which British monarch made the first royal Christmas broadcast?
9 What Christmas essential was introduced by Tom Smith in 1847?
10 By what name is the large place of wood traditionally burnt in the hearth at Christmas known?

Round 4: Pot Luck

1 In the poem by A. A. Milne, what was it that King John wanted for Christmas?
2 Which of the following is not the name of one of Father Christmas's reindeer – Blitzen, Lancer or Comet?
3 What is the name of the town that is the setting for *It's a Wonderful Life*?
4 Which plant with red and green foliage makes a popular Christmas gift? ✳
5 If you were given frumenty at Christmas, would you drink it, eat it or spray it on yourself?
6 Who wrote *The Father Christmas Letters*?
7 Where does Father Christmas live?
8 What did Harry Potter receive for his first Christmas at Hogwarts?
9 Which New York department store features prominently in the film *Miracle on 34th Street*?
10 In *A Christmas Carol*, who is Tiny Tim's father?

Jackpot

For which popular Christmas poem is Clement Clarke Moore remembered?

✳ According to Mexican legend, a penniless child who had nothing else to bring to church on Christmas Eve uprooted a handful of weeds and took them instead: once inside the church the humble weeds miraculously bloomed into magnificent red and green flowers.

Answers

Quiz 1 answers

Round 1

1 The Nile. 2 The maple leaf. 3 A murder. 4 Splatt (which is in Devon in the UK). 5 Not in my back yard. 6 Chesterfield. 7 Better on lips than on paper. 8 Sunderland. 9 A massive tree, otherwise known as the giant redwood. 10 A cappuccino.

Round 2

1 Charlotte, Emily and Anne. 2 Raymond Chandler. 3 Pelham Grenville. 4 The Three Musketeers. 5 Chingachgook. 6 *King Solomon's Mines* (1885) by H. Rider Haggard. 7 Frances Eliza Hodgson Burnett. 8 Sir Percy Blakeney. 9 Captain Ahab. 10 Ian Fleming.

Half-time teaser   72.

Round 3

1 Eddie. 2 False (but he did have one called Elvis). 3 Sir Isaac Newton. 4 1930. 5 An ostrich (Theodore Roosevelt had a hyena, while John Quincy Adams had an alligator). 6 Long John Silver. 7 China (possibly as early as the fourth century AD). 8 A jill. 9 His pet rat. 10 True.

Round 4

1 Greenland. 2 Bats. 3 An ice-pick. 4 Charles Barry. 5 The Blarney Stone. 6 Half a crown (two shillings and sixpence). 7 The rowan. 8 Rhythm. 9 Special Weapons and Tactics. 10 Brian.

Jackpot   A prison.

Quiz 2 answers

Round 1

1 The blue whale. **2** The Renaissance. **3** The Slovak Republic (or Slovakia).
4 With its stare. **5** Children's Laureate. **6** Pitcairn Island. **7** Manchester.
8 A carnivorous marsupial. **9** Antonín Dvořák. **10** Destiny's Child.

Round 2

1 Cochineal. **2** The butterfly effect. **3** Honey bees. **4** The Goliath beetle.
5 The daddy-longlegs (or cranefly). **6** Potatoes. **7** A spider. **8** Five.
9 Giacomo Puccini. **10** Alexander Pope.

Half-time teaser 23.

Round 3

1 The London Eye. **2** Tower Bridge. **3** Mayfair. **4** Admiralty Arch.
5 Billingsgate Market. **6** Charing Cross. **7** Fulham. **8** Marylebone Road.
9 The Palace of Westminster (the Houses of Parliament). **10** Highgate Hill.

Round 4

1 The Enigma code. **2** Kingsley Amis. **3** Paris. **4** *Dawson's Creek*.
5 The bicycle shot. **6** To cool your porridge. **7** Lord Louis Mountbatten.
8 Todd Woodbridge. **9** Brotherhood of Man. **10** Eminem.

Jackpot Richard Krajicek.

Quiz 3 answers

Round 1

1 Bart Simpson. 2 Australian and New Zealand Army Corps. 3 The English Civil War. 4 *The Winter's Tale*. 5 St Jude. 6 *EastEnders*. 7 A shark. 8 A dozen. 9 The Caspian Sea. 10 The Atlantic and Pacific oceans.

Round 2

1 Albert. 2 Leo Sayer. 3 *Fidelio*. 4 Radio Caroline. 5 Cliff Richard. 6 In a plane crash in 1967. 7 All Saints. 8 Empty orchestra. 9 Arthur Sullivan. 10 Peter Maxwell Davies.

Half-time teaser   4,500 miles.

Round 3

1 Barbara Cartland. 2 Everton. 3 Detroit. 4 Bill Clinton. 5 'Chemical Ali'. 6 Margaret Thatcher (abbreviation of 'there is no alternative'). 7 'The Thunderer'. 8 Robert Maxwell. 9 Jane Fonda. 10 Doctor Harold Shipman.

Round 4

1 950. 2 Lyon. 3 Symphony No. 6. 4 *The Cider House Rules*. 5 Berkeley Castle. 6 From the oven. 7 Narcissus. 8 Virginia. 9 Copper. 10 William Randolph Hearst.

Jackpot   A parabola.

Quiz 4 answers

Round 1

1 They were cousins. 2 12 August. 3 14. 4 The Windmill Theatre. 5 Under the Arc de Triomphe. 6 Alan Garner. 7 Loki. 8 The abominable snowman. 9 The Black Eyed Peas. 10 Green.

Round 2

1 Mont Blanc. 2 Mexico. 3 Dartmoor. 4 The Grampians. 5 The Matterhorn. 6 The Golan Heights. 7 Kinder Scout. 8 Switzerland and Italy. 9 The Carpathians. 10 Nepal.

Half-time teaser 12 seconds.

Round 3

1 Doctor Foster. 2 He ran away. 3 Under a haystack, fast asleep. 4 Lucy Locket. 5 Lean. 6 Little Tommy Stout. 7 Wednesday. 8 The sparrow. 9 'Ring a ring o' roses'. 10 School.

Round 4

1 The D-Day landings. 2 Frank Sinatra (in the single 'My Way'). 3 Sweden. 4 An ant. 5 Dr Aziz. 6 Nostradamus. 7 Terry Pratchett. 8 The British film industry. 9 The Penguin. 10 The US Civil War.

Jackpot In the prison.

Quiz 5 answers

Round 1

1 George Mallory. **2** Germany's. **3** They kept the lights on throughout the show. **4** A ghost. **5** The Rosetta Stone. **6** Kate Bush. **7** King John. **8** Jack Straw (then British foreign secretary). **9** MI5. **10** *The Scream*.

Round 2

1 Reading. **2** He ran barefoot. **3** Bobby Riggs (1939). **4** Rowing (or skulling). **5** Mike Tyson. **6** Drag-racing (referring to the parachute deployed to reduce speed). **7** 88. **8** Lewis Hamilton. **9** Zara Phillips. **10** Gold.

Half-time Teaser

Eight minutes and 20 seconds.

Round 3

1 Charles I. **2** George I. **3** Mary, Queen of Scots. **4** The Black Prince. **5** The name Mary. **6** Twice. **7** Richard III. **8** Alexandrina. **9** Louis XIV of France. **10** They were all born with teeth.

Round 4

1 Art. **2** Times Square. **3** A biscuit. **4** Edward VIII. **5** *Friends*. **6** The halfpenny. **7** Scott Tracy. **8** Eric Idle. **9** Gin. **10** False.

Jackpot Nikita Khruschev.

Quiz 6 answers

Round 1

1 London. 2 Solidarity. 3 Nirvana. 4 The railways. 5 Johnny Haynes. 6 Jihad. 7 Robert the Bruce. 8 Ayr. 9 Elizabeth I. 10 Alanis Morissette.

Round 2

1 Spiders. 2 Seven. 3 Alice Cooper. 4 Betty Grable's. 5 True. 6 Howard Hughes. 7 Venezuela. 8 George Washington. 9 1983. 10 Vietnam.

Half-time teaser   35 m.p.h.

Round 3

1 15. 2 Card games. 3 44. 4 Bobby Fischer. 5 A spanner. 6 28. 7 Mah-jong. 8 Monopoly. 9 Spear Games. 10 A deck of tarot cards.

Round 4

1 *The Merchant of Venice*. 2 False (they are white). 3 Vitamin C. 4 Soupçon. 5 Kieren Fallon. 6 Depression. 7 Joe Cocker. 8 Clwyd. 9 Take That. 10 Noël Coward.

Jackpot   *The Grapes of Wrath*.

Quiz 7 answers

Round 1

1 Louis XVIII. 2 Casper. 3 100. 4 Olivia Newton-John. 5 Caesar salad.
6 Omaha and Utah. 7 The Himalayas. 8 Charlene Mitchell. 9 Miniatures.
10 Loving and giving.

Round 2

1 Earth. 2 Bronze. 3 *Eagle*. 4 Joseph Priestley. 5 Green. 6 Betamax.
7 Heavy water. 8 The machine-gun. 9 False. 10 The invention of the
telephone.

Half-time teaser   13,386.

Round 3

1 The Jolly Roger. 2 Henry Morgan. 3 Davy Jones. 4 Captain Flint's.
5 The *Black Pig*. 6 Blackbeard. 7 Fifteen. 8 Sir Francis Drake. 9 A cutlass.
10 It was eaten by a crocodile.

Round 4

1 Dr Black. 2 *The Threepenny Opera*. 3 The Mogul Empire. 4 Lyndon B.
Johnson. 5 Atomic Kitten. 6 The Drones. 7 Barbie. 8 Dwight D.
Eisenhower. 9 Little Miss Muffet. 10 Salome.

Jackpot   Aphrodite.

Quiz 8 answers

Round 1

1 Barrels. 2 A drey. 3 Augusta, Georgia. 4 Cholera. 5 1960. 6 They all became MPs. 7 Toyota. 8 Duran Duran. 9 Polo. 10 Sir Gordon Richards.

Round 2

1 The Dead Sea. 2 Tunisia. 3 Venezuela (the Angel Falls). 4 Monaco. 5 South America (the Atacama desert in Chile). 6 Egypt. 7 The mantle. 8 Winds. 9 The Pacific. 10 The Red Sea.

Half-time teaser   26.

Round 3

1 Oysters. 2 Firm to the teeth. 3 Squid or cuttlefish. 4 Hungary. 5 Herring. 6 Cabbage. 7 False (there is no difference). 8 Cheese. 9 In Scotland. 10 Angels on horseback.

Round 4

1 The Roman god of doorways, Janus. 2 Chick peas. 3 Plato. 4 Edward Heath. 5 Pink Floyd. 6 February. 7 Hercules. 8 *Goldie*. 9 World War II. 10 *Baywatch*.

Jackpot   Ray Milland.

Quiz 9 answers

Round 1

1 Diane Keaton. 2 Austria. 3 Marc Bolan. 4 Alec Issigonis. 5 The foxtrot.
6 A dress. 7 *The Royle Family.* 8 Georges Bizet. 9 Ludwig Mies Van Der Rohe.
10 The Boston Strangler.

Round 2

1 Oliver Mellors. 2 Shadowfax. 3 George Orwell's *Nineteen Eighty-four*
(1949). 4 Patrick Harper. 5 *The African Queen.* 6 Evelyn Waugh. 7 *Beau
Geste.* 8 Death. 9 Brendan Behan. 10 Cephalonia.

Half-time teaser 45,000.

Round 3

1 *EastEnders.* 2 Nelson Gabriel. 3 *Emmerdale.* 4 Ramsay Street. 5 1960.
6 *Eldorado.* 7 *Home and Away.* 8 Benny (Hawkins). 9 Tamsin Greig.
10 Status Quo.

Round 4

1 13. 2 Cotopaxi (in the Andes). 3 Michael Jackson. 4 On the Moon.
5 Hawker (later Hawker-Siddeley). 6 *The Rite of Spring.* 7 Animals.
8 Flags. 9 Jefferson City. 10 Monica Lewinsky.

Jackpot The Seychelles.

Quiz 10 answers

Round 1

1 The Alamo. 2 *Monty Python's Life of Brian*. 3 Finland. 4 Windscale (or Calder Hall). 5 The wire frame on a dartboard. 6 David Cassidy. 7 The UEFA Cup. 8 Orchid. 9 The Incas. 10 A hill.

Round 2

1 Hydrogen. 2 The willow. 3 One horsepower. 4 Vinegar. 5 Sodium chloride. 6 The Chemical Brothers. 7 Sir Humphry Davy. 8 Distance travelled. 9 *A Beautiful Mind*. 10 The ozone layer.

Half-time teaser 47.

Round 3

1 New Year's Day. 2 62. 3 Mothering Sunday. 4 Lady Day. 5 On Shrove Tuesday. 6 21 October. 7 Martin Luther King. 8 Orangeman's Day (known as 'the Twelfth' in Northern Ireland). 9 13. 10 They all have birthdays on 25 December.

Round 4

1 The landings at Gallipoli in the Dardanelles. 2 Chocolate. 3 Helmets were made compulsory. 4 *The Virginian*. 5 Durham. 6 Sapphire (or chrysolite). 7 *The Godfather Part II*. 8 Paris (in 1914). 9 Hawaii. 10 1932.

Jackpot Blue.

Quiz 11 answers

Round 1

1 Tchaikovsky. 2 He was shot dead by outraged fans. 3 The Phoney War.
4 The Stereophonics. 5 *The Rocky Horror (Picture) Show*. 6 New Orleans.
7 A platform on which a dead body is placed. 8 The pH scale. 9 Punishment.
10 The House of Lancaster and the House of York.

Round 2

1 Athens. 2 Damon Hill. 3 Scrabble. 4 William Webb Ellis. 5 An olive
wreath. 6 False (England and France – the only teams that entered –
played cricket in the Olympic Games of 1900: England won). 7 Tennis.
8 Babe Ruth. 9 Paul Ince. 10 He had only one arm.

Half-time teaser   34 years old.

Round 3

1 Heineken. 2 KFC (Kentucky Fried Chicken). 3 John Lewis stores. 4 Audi.
5 Ronseal wood varnish. 6 Playtex Wonderbra. 7 Hamlet. 8 Bovril.
9 Martini. 10 Johnnie Walker whisky.

Round 4

1 Patina. 2 Nobby Styles. 3 The Labour Party. 4 Columbo. 5 The League
of Nations. 6 Rembrandt. 7 The Aga cooker. 8 Lieutenant Commander
'Scotty' Scott. 9 Santa's Little Helper. 10 Yellow.

Jackpot   O (recorded in the Semitic alphabet as early as 1300 BC)

Quiz 12 answers

Round 1

1 Nine. 2 Sarah Bernhardt. 3 Dwight D. Eisenhower. 4 Sauron the Great.
5 Brno (in the Czech Republic, where it was first made) and Enfield (in
Birmingham, where production continued). 6 Hampshire. 7 Ryan Giggs.
8 Blondie. 9 She throws herself off a parapet. 10 Swiss.

Round 2

1 The boa. 2 Shoes. 3 A short jacket. 4 A bustle. 5 The Emanuels. 6 Calvin
Klein. 7 Leather bags. 8 Pink. 9 The miniskirt. 10 Jean Shrimpton.

Half-time teaser 71.

Round 3

1 Holy Island. 2 The Shetlands. 3 The George Cross. 4 Hispaniola.
5 Oahu. 6 Robben Island. 7 Sicily. 8 Capri. 9 Ellis Island. 10 Dogs (their
name in Latin is *Insulae Canariae*, meaning 'Island of the Dogs').

Round 4

1 Australian. 2 Silver. 3 Greenland. 4 André Agassi. 5 Four. 6 *The Battleship
Potemkin*. 7 False (he sold one, entitled *Red Vineyard*). 8 Lewis Carroll.
9 The kneecap. 10 George VI.

Jackpot 36.

Quiz 13 answers

....

Round 1

1 Robbie Williams. 2 Harley Street. 3 John F. Kennedy. 4 A gargoyle. 5 *The Jungle Book*. 6 Gatcombe Park, Gloucestershire. 7 Oswald Mosley. 8 The Old Contemptibles. 9 24. 10 David Icke.

....

Round 2

1 The Czech Republic (they drink more than 35 gallons of beer per year each). 2 Pepsi-Cola. 3 The koala. 4 Absinthe. 5 Alcopops. 6 Ginger ale. 7 Coca-Cola. 8 CAMRA (Campaign for Real Ale). 9 Carlsberg. 10 Stella Artois beer.

....

Half-time teaser 340,000.

....

Round 3

1 Dylan Thomas. 2 Captain Lawrence Oates. 3 George V. 4 Edith Cavell (shot by a German firing squad in 1915). 5 Beethoven. 6 Hamlet. 7 Charles II. 8 Elizabeth I. 9 'Kiss me, Hardy' (or, possibly, 'Kismet, Hardy', acknowledging the power of fate over life and death). 10 Sir Walter Raleigh.

....

Round 4

1 Billy the Kid. 2 Timothy Leary. 3 The Royal Ulster Constabulary. 4 Southfork. 5 Clare Short. 6 Michael Caine. 7 The House of Stuart. 8 The Mississippi. 9 Green Day. 10 Attila the Hun.

....

Jackpot St Clare.

....

Quiz 14 answers

Round 1

1 The Great Barrier Reef. 2 The pine. 3 The two-pound coin. 4 30.
5 Cleveland. 6 Genesis. 7 Alan Bennett. 8 The *Sun*. 9 Cricket. 10 Suzi
Quatro.

Round 2

1 The *Mary Rose*. 2 The *Titanic*. 3 The *Bowbelle*. 4 Grace Darling.
5 The *Queen Elizabeth*. 6 The *Arizona*. 7 The *Herald of Free Enterprise*.
8 The *Graf Spee*. 9 The *Sea Empress*. 10 Four.

Half-time teaser 1,070.

Round 3

1 Dreamtime. 2 A pool. 3 'Waltzing Matilda'. 4 New South Wales. 5 Gold.
6 *Endeavour*. 7 Bondi Beach. 8 Brisbane. 9 The Liberal Party. 10 The
Tasman Sea.

Round 4

1 Gary Sobers. 2 The Colorado. 3 R. A. ('Rab') Butler. 4 *Lemony Snicket: A
Series of Unfortunate Events*. 5 Green. 6 Charles Trenet. 7 Psalms. 8 Barry
Humphries. 9 Switzerland. 10 The Central Intelligence Agency (CIA).

Jackpot Mongolia.

Quiz 15 answers

....

Round 1

1 11 November, 1918. **2** Curling. **3** The Bonzo Dog Doo Dah Band.
4 Ronaldinho. **5** Terence. **6** 'Spirit in the sky'. **7** Ross Kemp (her husband).
8 *Alien*. **9** Marie Curie. **10** Sue Ellen.

....

Round 2

1 *Stagecoach* (1939). **2** Lauren. **3** *Monty Python's Flying Circus*. **4** Corporal
Jones. **5** George Formby. **6** Greta Garbo. **7** Buzz Lightyear. **8** Vicky Pollard
(in the television series *Little Britain*). **9** True. **10** David Dickinson.

....

Half-time teaser   17 feet, 6 inches.

....

Round 3

1 King John. **2** The Battle of Crécy in 1346 (by the English). **3** Overlord.
4 He played his fiddle (more accurately, his lyre). **5** The Falklands War
(1982). **6** General Patton. **7** Spain. **8** Attila the Hun. **9** The defence of
Rorke's Drift against the Zulus in 1879. **10** The Scots (because of their
kilts).

....

Round 4

1 A monkey. **2** William Blake. **3** A rabbit. **4** *Red Dwarf*. **5** Scafell Pike.
6 *The Browning Version*. **7** The Cavern Club. **8** Garibaldi. **9** *Ballykissangel*.
10 Earl's Court, London.

....

Jackpot   1,125 miles (1,800 km).

....

Quiz 16 answers

Round 1

1 Cerberus. 2 Nine. 3 Clive Dunn. 4 Pomeroy's. 5 False (the Ashmolean is the oldest). 6 Sound. 7 1783. 8 Jarndyce and Jarndyce. 9 An épée. 10 Sebastian Coe.

Round 2

1 The North Sea. 2 Windermere. 3 The Caribbean. 4 The Sargasso Sea. 5 Superior. 6 Self-Contained Underwater Breathing Apparatus. 7 Garrison Keillor. 8 Africa. 9 Between Wales and Ireland. 10 Finisterre.

Half-time teaser 17,508.

Round 3

1 Jon Voight. 2 Carrie Fisher. 3 False (she was the daughter of India's first prime minister Jawaharlal Nehru). 4 They are mother and daughter. 5 He was Wagner's son-in-law. 6 Ravi Shankar. 7 They are sisters. 8 Vanessa Redgrave. 9 Mia Farrow. 10 Horatio Nelson and Emma Hamilton.

Round 4

1 Dauphin. 2 The trombone. 3 Dunkirk. 4 A compass. 5 14. 6 Neil Diamond. 7 Tokyo Rose. 8 Ayr. 9 The Samaritans. 10 They are all dances.

Jackpot The house.

Quiz 17 answers

Round 1

1 Kenya. 2 Cruella De Vil. 3 Charlie Parker. 4 Percy Bysshe Shelley.
5 Barbarella. 6 *Oklahoma!* 7 Richard Rogers. 8 In the country. 9 Three
Mile Island. 10 A one-armed bandit.

Round 2

1 Bucephalus. 2 Dick Turpin. 3 Copenhagen. 4 George Stubbs. 5 Roger
Lloyd Pack. 6 Arkle. 7 Rosinante. 8 Silver. 9 America. 10 A beetle.

Half-time teaser   3,212 feet.

Round 3

1 Charlie Chaplin. 2 David Lean. 3 *They Shoot Horses, Don't They?* 4 *The
Third Man.* 5 Robert Powell. 6 John Wayne. 7 Fred Astaire. 8 *Master and
Commander.* 9 Peter Finch. 10 *Heaven's Gate.*

Round 4

1 Concorde. 2 The Louvre, in Paris. 3 The Synod of Whitby. 4 Captain
Marvel. 5 Roseanne Barr. 6 Kenny Dalgleish. 7 Madagascar. 8 Rose.
9 False (but she was one-eighth Iroquois Indian). 10 Get a life.

Jackpot   Bakelite.

Quiz 18 answers

Round 1

1 Androcles. 2 Sri Lanka. 3 Slavery. 4 Its tail. 5 Rab C. Nesbitt. 6 Thin Lizzy. 7 Boris Yeltsin. 8 Two. 9 Ten. 10 Cape Horn.

Round 2

1 Buddhism. 2 The Koran. 3 Hinduism. 4 White smoke from the Vatican chimney. 5 Confucianism. 6 Shari'a. 7 The Christian Scientists. 8 'Blood and fire'. 9 Judaism. 10 The Unification Church.

Half-time teaser   18.

Round 3

1 The skunk. 2 False. 3 Stink. 4 Yves St Laurent. 5 A fungus. 6 Imperial Leather. 7 Rotten eggs. 8 A rose. 9 Decaying flesh (or corpses). 10 Miss You Nights.

Round 4

1 Watling Street. 2 Jilly Cooper. 3 Vesuvius. 4 The Mason–Dixon Line. 5 Elizabeth Montgomery. 6 A hedgehog. 7 Real Madrid. 8 Frances McDormand. 9 They were both posthumous champions. 10 *The Comedy of Errors.*

Jackpot   Patsy Stone.

Quiz 19 answers

....

Round 1

1 George Harrison. **2** Guantanamo Bay, Cuba. **3** Michael Foot. **4** On Jupiter. **5** Six. **6** Football. **7** The Atlantic and Pacific oceans. **8** Norway. **9** Menachem Begin. **10** Gerald Ford.

....

Round 2

1 Mercury. **2** Sputnik 1. **3** Pluto. **4** *Beagle* 2. **5** Stephen Hawking's *A Brief History of Time*. **6** HAL. **7** Apollo 13. **8** Laika. **9** *Challenger*. **10** Mars.

....

Half-time teaser   36,220 feet.

....

Round 3

1 Gilbert O'Sullivan. **2** Maurice. **3** 'Bitter sweet symphony'. **4** The Wurzels (who topped the charts with 'Combine harvester'). **5** The Police. **6** Pat Boone. **7** 'My perfect cousin'. **8** Bananarama. **9** Rod Stewart. **10** Scottish.

....

Round 4

1 Paraguay. **2** Catherine Parr. **3** *Ring of Bright Water*. **4** Joan Bakewell. **5** Iron oxide. **6** They were all battles in the American War of Independence. **7** Matthew. **8** 15. **9** The Isle of Man (in 1880). **10** 1988.

....

Jackpot   Naples.

....

Quiz 20 answers

Round 1

1 Good Friday. **2** Phoenix. **3** Andrew. **4** Apartheid. **5** Sheep's milk.
6 New Zealand. **7** Romanian. **8** *Great Expectations*. **9** Bangor. **10** A sofa.

Round 2

1 Evander Holyfield. **2** Prometheus. **3** Queen Elizabeth II. **4** Polonius (an
arras is a curtain). **5** Thomas Becket. **6** Anakin Skywalker. **7** Lady Godiva.
8 Luddites. **9** Ronald Reagan. **10** Jansher Khan.

Half-time teaser 6,779 metres.

Round 3

1 Pi. **2** Her right hand. **3** An elephant. **4** A goat. **5** Yellow lines. **6** Dublin.
7 A donkey. **8** Ireland. **9** Libra. **10** E.

Round 4

1 Hyde Park. **2** Ice-skating. **3** Dad's Army. **4** Frozen carbon dioxide.
5 Westminster Abbey. **6** 1970. **7** Hermann Goering. **8** Sean Bean.
9 *Thriller*. **10** A diamond.

Jackpot 'Spirit of Ecstasy'.

Quiz 21 answers

Round 1

1 Donald Duck. **2** Royal. **3** A kangaroo and an emu. **4** The *Altmark*.
5 Birmingham. **6** Baldrick. **7** Vangelis. **8** James Dean. **9** Gryffindor.
10 Cassandra.

Round 2

1 True. **2** False (they never snore). **3** A marlin. **4** The crows. **5** True (they
are closer to raccoons). **6** A baby oyster. **7** An albatross. **8** Ants.
9 Antelope. **10** A mule.

Half-time teaser 51,696.

Round 3

1 Fear of strangers. **2** Genoa (where they were first made). **3** Hair grip.
4 Horses. **5** Bell-ringing. **6** Serendipity. **7** A net. **8** Pub signs. **9** An
eight-year-old girl murdered in Alton, Hampshire in 1867. **10** Copper
(called Cyprian metal by the Romans).

Round 4

1 Celtic and Rangers. **2** Buy one, get one free. **3** John Constable. **4** Jethro
Tull. **5** The centrefold. **6** Amy Johnson. **7** Francis Matthews. **8** Prawns.
9 Pakistan. **10** Her husband Bruce Willis.

Jackpot   Creedence Clearwater Revival.

Quiz 22 answers

Round 1

1 Spain. **2** *A Midsummer Night's Dream*. **3** Seven. **4** Charles II. **5** The galley. **6** Ian Dury and the Blockheads. **7** Wine. **8** *Warrior*. **9** Malin. **10** Doncaster.

Round 2

1 *Top of the Pops*. **2** Two. **3** W. H. Auden. **4** Their sapphire anniversary. **5** Stanley Kubrick (in *Eyes Wide Shut*). **6** Sibyl. **7** Walter Raleigh's. **8** Princess Alexandra of Kent (cousin of Elizabeth II). **9** Julie Andrews. **10** Charlotte.

Half-time teaser   186,000.

Round 3

1 The slave trade. **2** Maypoles. **3** She was shot by a firing squad. **4** The British Army. **5** Horatio Nelson. **6** Chatsworth House. **7** George IV. **8** Henry VIII. **9** Charles II. **10** Sir Barnes Wallis.

Round 4

1 Spaghetti Junction. **2** *The Railway Children*. **3** A strike. **4** The Pacific. **5** Methodism. **6** A dig. **7** Pillars (or columns). **8** The World's Strongest Man. **9** The Witan. **10** A harp.

Jackpot   A bird.

Quiz 23 answers

Round 1

1 The bikini (after the Bikini atoll where atom-bomb testing took place).
2 Cheese. **3** Shakespear's Sister. **4** The sinking of the *Titanic*. **5** *Trumpton*.
6 He was a doctor. **7** Walter Matthau. **8** Beverly Hills. **9** David Bowie.
10 Fish and chips.

Round 2

1 Alice Cooper. **2** Boz. **3** Boris Karloff. **4** Saki. **5** Judy Garland.
6 A Mississippi pilots' cry (meaning 'two fathoms deep'). **7** Tarzan. **8** The
sabre-toothed tiger. **9** Sirius. **10** Ayers Rock.

Half-time teaser   594.

Round 3

1 Cheese and onion. **2** Spinach. **3** Chewing-gum. **4** Tinned food. **5** True.
6 Manna. **7** False (it ended in 1954). **8** Australian soprano Dame Nellie
Melba. **9** Vincent Van Gogh. **10** The Australians.

Round 4

1 By drinking hemlock. **2** 666. **3** Hamlet. **4** The Brat Pack. **5** *A Hard Day's
Night*. **6** A tree. **7** Polo. **8** *Beyond the Fringe*. **9** A type of rose. **10** *Oz*.

Jackpot   David Hempleman-Adams.

Quiz 24 answers

Round 1

1 The diamond. 2 Deadly nightshade. 3 Show-jumping. 4 T. Rex. 5 1801.
6 The stoat. 7 Cambridge and London. 8 A squint. 9 Mercutio. 10 Welsh.

Round 2

1 Jellystone Park. 2 Charlie Chaplin. 3 Arnhem. 4 Peter Pan's. 5 The
Cairngorms. 6 The Isle of Wight. 7 Neil Simon. 8 Princess Anne.
9 Kenneth Williams. 10 Kenny.

Half-time teaser   70.

Round 3

1 Gloucester, Hereford and Worcester. 2 *Monty Python's Flying Circus*.
3 Britney Spears. 4 Manchester. 5 *Evita*. 6 An organ. 7 *Pictures at an
Exhibition*. 8 The violin. 9 George Michael. 10 From characters in the
Tintin cartoons.

Round 4

1 Wine. 2 Japan. 3 Birmingham. 4 Caligula. 5 Michael. 6 The British
Empire Games. 7 Joseph Goebbels. 8 K2. 9 Antarctica. 10 *The Handmaid's
Tale*.

Jackpot   The Heffalump.

Quiz 25 answers

Round 1

1 Krakatoa (volcanic explosion and tidal wave). 2 The Impressionists.
3 The nape of the neck. 4 Ireland. 5 'Banzai!' 6 Keith Moon. 7 Enoch
Powell. 8 Cliff Richard. 9 Jack Charlton. 10 Geoff Hurst.

Round 2

1 Wilkie Collins. 2 Mrs Hudson. 3 Father Brown. 4 Ngaio Marsh.
5 Robert Ironside. 6 Brother Cadfael. 7 Endeavour. 8 Dick Tracy. 9 Albert
Campion. 10 Jim Bergerac.

Half-time teaser 91 feet 10 inches.

Round 3

1 The hovercraft. 2 True (he was Adolphe Sax). 3 Anthony Trollope.
4 Mary Quant. 5 Frank Zappa. 6 The sewing-machine. 7 Phil Spector.
8 Lewis Carroll (in *Through the Looking-Glass*). 9 Barnes Wallis. 10 Tarmac
(originally Tarmacadam).

Round 4

1 Daphne du Maurier. 2 Vicious. 3 George Bernard Shaw. 4 Black
September. 5 Pete Best. 6 David Brent. 7 Iron Maiden. 8 TASS. 9 Michael
Heseltine. 10 *Pride and Prejudice*.

Jackpot Donald Duck.

Quiz 26 answers

Round 1

1 Elvis Presley. 2 Crocus. 3 Kentucky. 4 Motor-racing. 5 Richard Nixon.
6 Bevin Boys. 7 Oliver Reed. 8 The guitar. 9 Rail. 10 Flamingos.

Round 2

1 Y. 2 A leopard. 3 A handbag. 4 She was the first test-tube baby (born by
in vitro fertilisation). 5 *A.I.* 6 Pudsey Bear. 7 Baby-boomers. 8 Loving and
giving. 9 Sporty. 10 *Million Dollar Baby*.

Half-time teaser   211.

Round 3

1 True. 2 Harry Hill. 3 Frank Spencer. 4 Sydney. 5 Ben Elton. 6 Lenny
Henry. 7 'I'm the only gay in the village.' 8 *Shameless.* 9 Steve Coogan.
10 *The Navy Lark.*

Round 4

1 Philadelphia. 2 Getting softer. 3 23.50. 4 Cricket (in Australia). 5 The
crab. 6 617 Squadron. 7 Book. 8 A swan. 9 Basketball. 10 Jack Nicholson.

Jackpot   The becquerel.

Quiz 27 answers

....

Round 1

1 Mars. 2 *All Quiet on the Western Front.* 3 *A Hard Day's Night.* 4 32. 5 The River Dee. 6 *Auf Widersehen, Pet.* 7 The Bastille. 8 The Bermuda Triangle. 9 Tottenham Hotspur. 10 The Ryder Cup.

....

Round 2

1 The crocodile. 2 The Ford Zephyr. 3 The *Victory*. 4 Cary Grant. 5 New Amsterdam. 6 True. 7 The Malvinas. 8 Nosey Parker. 9 Stuart. 10 Vidkun Quisling.

....

Half-time teaser   2,639.

....

Round 3

1 The *Queen Mary*. 2 Four miles per hour (6.4 km/h). 3 The *Spirit of St Louis*. 4 Because US bottoms had got bigger. 5 A beltway. 6 *Duel*. 7 Christopher Eccleston. 8 Charon. 9 *The Lady Vanishes*. 10 Roscoe Tanner.

....

Round 4

1 The Theatre Museum. 2 Lindisfarne. 3 Rwanda. 4 Income tax. 5 The Sugarbabes. 6 Worcester cathedral. 7 Gerald Ford. 8 They were joined for the first time by ballgirls. 9 Richard II. 10 *Minder*.

....

Jackpot   Mauritius.

....

Quiz 28 answers

Round 1

1 Bamboo (at a rate of 38 cm a day). 2 Barbara Castle. 3 The 20 pence coin. 4 Ohms. 5 Archaeology. 6 A table. 7 'Don't go breaking my heart'. 8 Swans. 9 True. 10 *Under Milk Wood*.

Round 2

1 The Olympic Games. 2 The United Nations. 3 Roy Jenkins. 4 Switzerland. 5 The Society of Friends (the Quakers). 6 A giant panda. 7 Thrush. 8 False (Austria joined in 1995, 22 years after the UK). 9 The Red Cross. 10 The Jehovah's Witnesses.

Half-time teaser 69.

Round 3

1 Cardiff. 2 Richard Rogers. 3 Cheese and bread (toast). 4 The leek. 5 Richard Burton. 6 Laura Ashley. 7 Chepstow. 8 Emlyn Williams. 9 Fashion. 10 Shirley Bassey.

Round 4

1 Madrid. 2 *Revenge*. 3 Parma. 4 The US Civil War. 5 Trinity College. 6 *The Rivals*. 7 Pan's People. 8 The Archbishop of Westminster. 9 Sikhism. 10 A form of massage.

Jackpot Robespierre.

Quiz 29 answers

Round 1

1 Graceland. **2** *Desperate Housewives*. **3** *Cider with Rosie*. **4** David Essex.
5 A marine. **6** A urinal. **7** On a fingertip. **8** Raquel Welch. **9** Peanuts.
10 The Green Rifles.

Round 2

1 St Patrick. **2** St Andrew. **3** True. **4** St Peter. **5** St Bernard (of Montjoux).
6 Edward the Confessor. **7** St James (St James's Park). **8** All Saints.
9 St Andrews. **10** As a tent-maker.

Half-time teaser   98,721.

Round 3

1 Richard Greene. **2** *M.A.S.H.* **3** *As Time Goes By.* **4** Toothpaste (Gibbs SR).
5 Holby. **6** Jacob Bronowski. **7** Tony Robinson. **8** *Absolutely Fabulous.*
9 Uncle Fester. **10** Teddy.

Round 4

1 The Jackal. **2** 1914. **3** Ravel's *Boléro*. **4** Flatfishes. **5** The Eagles. **6** Dundee.
7 Seasonal affective disorder. **8** Woody Allen. **9** Op(tical) art. **10** A Belisha
beacon.

Jackpot   Lieutenant Pigeon.

Quiz 30 answers

Round 1

1 Joseph. 2 U2. 3 General Douglas MacArthur (referring to the Philippines).
4 Good intentions. 5 Eugene Ionesco. 6 A cap. 7 Finchley (and Barnet,
Finchley). 8 Father. 9 Ernie Els. 10 Peninsular and Oriental.

Round 2

1 What you see is what you get. 2 A. 3 Computer-generated imagery.
4 The at sign (@). 5 Apple Macintosh. 6 Keep it simple, stupid. 7 Charles
Babbage. 8 Frequently Asked Questions. 9 A central processing unit.
10 Rolling on floor laughing.

Half-time teaser 227.

Round 3

1 Emily Davison. 2 The River Ouse. 3 Led Zeppelin. 4 In a plane crash.
5 Gianni Versace. 6 Anton von Webern. 7 Jesse James. 8 Clark Gable.
9 Olof Palme. 10 *Gladiator*.

Round 4

1 Maundy Thursday. 2 Bluebird. 3 Oasis. 4 Newfoundland. 5 Axis.
6 *Groundhog Day*. 7 Samoa. 8 George. 9 *Dreadnought*. 10 Athens.

Jackpot Six.

Quiz 31 answers

Round 1

1 Sealed with a loving kiss. 2 Pepper. 3 Pentangle. 4 *The Onedin Line*.
5 Edward VII. 6 *University Challenge*. 7 A Volkswagen Beetle. 8 Malaysia.
9 Apollo. 10 John Le Carré.

Round 2

1 Professor Moriarty. 2 Taking (a vehicle) without the owner's consent.
3 For trying to steal the Crown Jewels. 4 Interpol. 5 *Police 5*. 6 Dick
Barton. 7 Sun Hill. 8 The Black Panther. 9 The Costa del Crime.
10 The hoodie.

Half-time teaser

Eleven feet one inch.

Round 3

1 Cubism. 2 Dutch. 3 Salvador Dali. 4 Venice. 5 Art Deco. 6 The Pre-
Raphaelite Brotherhood (or Pre-Raphaelites). 7 Charles I. 8 Tracey Emin.
9 Tahiti. 10 You can't – it was destroyed after Churchill's death by his
widow, who hated it.

Round 4

1 Malta. 2 Eleven (from their shape). 3 Lara Croft. 4 Gregory Peck.
5 Sweden. 6 Katrina and the Waves. 7 Jupiter. 8 Synchronised swimming.
9 Chicago. 10 The Circle line.

Jackpot   George I.

Quiz 32 answer

Round 1

1 Discretion. 2 Chester. 3 She became the first woman cox in the Boat Race. 4 Earl Grey. 5 The five inhabited continents. 6 The Dave Clark Five. 7 A friend. 8 The Caledonian Canal. 9 Al Gore. 10 Eye.

Round 2

1 Eldorado. 2 Venice. 3 Captain Cook. 4 Ferdinand Magellan. 5 Alan Shepard. 6 Christopher Columbus. 7 Roald Amundsen. 8 Robert Falcon. 9 *Santa Maria*. 10 Ranulph Fiennes.

Half-time Teaser   4,862.

Round 3

1 Justin Timberlake. 2 Mariah Carey. 3 Avril Lavigne. 4 Nelly Furtado. 5 Joe Strummer. 6 Kelly Clarkson. 7 'Crazy frog'. 8 Legal downloads from the internet. 9 Leeds. 10 The Arctic Monkeys (*Whatever People Say I Am, That's What I'm Not*).

Round 4

1 The high jump. 2 San Francisco (in the single 'Let's go to San Francisco'). 3 The Fifth Amendment. 4 Woody Allen. 5 Beatrix Potter. 6 Harold Wilson. 7 A crossbar. 8 Celia Johnson. 9 Arthur Hailey. 10 *Nautilus*.

Jackpot   James Garfield.

Quiz 33 answers

....

Round 1

1 Arthur Wellesley, Duke of Wellington. **2** *The Borrowers* by Mary Norton.
3 Gary Cooper. **4** Mogadishu. **5** As an ambulance driver (with the Red
Cross). **6** 1964. **7** James Abbott McNeill Whistler. **8** Alexis Colby.
9 T. Rex. **10** Friends of the Earth.

....

Round 2

1 The Mount of Olives. **2** Lesotho. **3** The Rialto. **4** The Vatican. **5** Oxford.
6 Rio de Janeiro. **7** Wellington (the capital of New Zealand). **8** Slough.
9 Florence. **10** Nicaragua.

....

Half-time teaser   1,811 times.

....

Round 3

1 William Shakespeare. **2** John Keats. **3** Charles II. **4** Sir Christopher Wren
(in St Paul's Cathedral, which he designed). **5** Karl Marx. **6** Dorothy Parker.
7 Mel Blanc (US cartoon voice artist). **8** W. B. Yeats. **9** Spike Milligan.
10 Edgar Allan Poe.

....

Round 4

1 The Bullet Train. **2** *Whistler's Mother*. **3** *The African Queen*. **4** Lord Haw-
Haw. **5** Bobby Moore. **6** A doe. **7** The Rovers Return. **8** Yorick.
9 Dana International. **10** Houdini.

....

Jackpot   Antonio Gaudí.

....

Quiz 34 answers

Round 1

1 Mandarin Chinese. 2 Halley's Comet. 3 Percussion. 4 Portugal.
5 *Anything Goes*. 6 January. 7 'Chattanooga choo choo'. 8 Egg-shaped.
9 Jesse. 10 The British Expeditionary Force.

Round 2

1 Cul-de-sac. 2 Hoi polloi. 3 Hindi. 4 Non sequitur. 5 Afrikaans.
6 Chutzpah. 7 Faux pas. 8 Ombudsman. 9 Kitsch. 10 Prêt-à-porter.

Half-time teaser 365 feet.

Round 3

1 *The Lord of the Rings*. 2 Angel Clare. 3 *Three Men in a Boat*. 4 Edward.
5 *David Copperfield*. 6 Bunbury. 7 Eton. 8 *The Lost World*. 9 Mr Funny.
10 Leo McKern.

Round 4

1 Across, or beyond. 2 The Open University. 3 Football. 4 The Battle of
the Bulge. 5 The farthing. 6 Rowan. 7 The orchid. 8 William IV.
9 Wagner. 10 Kelly Holmes.

Jackpot The press.

Quiz 35 answers

Round 1

1 The Pyramids of Egypt. **2** The Red Arrows. **3** The Arndale Centre.
4 *Mastermind*. **5** Portmeirion, Gwynedd. **6** True. **7** Sirhan Sirhan. **8** He
was a gardener (more precisely, head gardener to Charles II). **9** Benjamin
Britten's. **10** William Shakespeare (in 1964).

Round 2

1 To stop perspiration from the forehead running down into the eyes.
2 Twenty-four. **3** False (it takes 12 to smile and just 11 to frown).
4 Elle Macpherson. **5** The bodyline tour. **6** Body-popping. **7** The Body
Shop. **8** The leg. **9** False (there are 206). **10** Kevin Costner.

Half-time Teaser 1,680 hours.

Round 3

1 *I'm a Celebrity, Get Me Out of Here!* **2** The Netherlands. **3** Mustique.
4 Brad Pitt. **5** The Church of Scientology. **6** Patsy Kensit. **7** Kate Winslet.
8 Sean Penn. **9** Lisa Marie Presley. **10** Beckham.

Round 4

1 L. S. Lowry. **2** Reggae. **3** Sudan. **4** Potatoes. **5** Céleste. **6** Queensland
(where bananas are widely grown). **7** Portugal. **8** Brothel-creepers.
9 Little Jimmy Osmond. **10** Rin Tin Tin.

Jackpot Ramsay MacDonald.

Quiz 36 answers

Round 1

1 Rome. **2** The gridiron. **3** The Sweet. **4** Stalin. **5** The French Open (tennis). **6** *Hotel du Lac*. **7** Said Aouita. **8** Victory. **9** The sweet chestnut. **10** *The Archers*.

Round 2

1 *A Tale of Two Cities* by Charles Dickens. **2** *Rawhide*. **3** Reveille. **4** 'Da capo'. **5** *Twelfth Night*. **6** Green. **7** Julio Iglesias. **8** Distant. **9** C. **10** *The Lion, the Witch and the Wardrobe* by C. S. Lewis.

Half-time teaser   14.

Round 3

1 The Jordan. **2** The Zambesi. **3** The Test. **4** The Hudson. **5** Tchaikovsky. **6** The Yangtse. **7** The Danube. **8** The Nene. **9** The Rhine. **10** The Rio Grande.

Round 4

1 Casterbridge. **2** Formula One motor-racing. **3** The Plimsoll line. **4** Aaron. **5** True. **6** Smokey Robinson. **7** Nottinghamshire. **8** Frank Zappa. **9** Bobby Riggs. **10** Alec Douglas-Home.

Jackpot   Charles Laughton (for *The Private Life of Henry VIII*).

Quiz 37 answers

....

Round 1

1 Mount Kilimanjaro. 2 Blair Babes. 3 Melanie B. 4 Constantinople.
5 The America's Cup. 6 Judy Garland. 7 True. 8 Gerard Manley Hopkins
(the poem was 'The Wreck of the Deutschland'). 9 The Red Duster.
10 E. H. Shepherd.

....

Round 2

1 Sam Peckinpah. 2 Ben Murphy and Pete Duel. 3 Billy the Kid. 4 The
Searchers. 5 'Apache' (by the Shadows). 6 The Sioux. 7 *The Lone Ranger*.
8 Wounded Knee. 9 *The High Chaparral*. 10 Gene Wilder.

....

Half-time Teaser   132.

....

Round 3

1 The *News of the World*. 2 The marriage of playwright Arthur Miller and
actress Marilyn Monroe. 3 *Private Eye*. 4 A crossword (in *The Daily
Express*). 5 The *Beano*. 6 The marriage of Prince Charles and Camilla
Parker Bowles. 7 The *Daily Express*. 8 Argentina's *General Belgrano*.
9 The *Dandy*. 10 *OK!*

....

Round 4

1 Elvis Presley's. 2 *Catch-22*. 3 Obi-Wan Kenobi. 4 Adolf Hitler. 5 Canberra.
6 Walter Winterbottom. 7 Ingrid Bergman. 8 *The Fly*. 9 Madame Tussaud's.
10 General Patton.

....

Jackpot   The Hays Code.

....

Quiz 38 answers

Round 1

1 Wimbledon. 2 An umbrella. 3 Earthworms. 4 Paris. 5 An Oscar (Academy Award). 6 Baseball. 7 In Milan. 8 Wizzard. 9 False. 10 The Royal Horticultural Society.

Round 2

1 Charles Lindbergh. 2 The Hebrides. 3 A fruit bat. 4 Canada. 5 Harrison Ford. 6 New Hampshire. 7 Derbyshire. 8 She became the first air hostess. 9 Boston, Massachusetts. 10 Squadron Leader.

Half-time Teaser 1,513.

Round 3

1 The Chancellor of the Exchequer. 2 Sexton Blake. 3 A pub. 4 The Archbishop of Canterbury. 5 George Washington. 6 Arsenal Stadium, Highbury. 7 The Royal Air Force. 8 Wall Street. 9 Queen Victoria. 10 Blue.

Round 4

1 Impatience. 2 Road rage. 3 Maya Angelou. 4 Los Angeles. 5 *Madame Butterfly*. 6 Australia. 7 Adam Smith. 8 Beethoven. 9 Wind speed. 10 Cycling (tiredness caused by lack of food).

Jackpot The decimal halfpenny.

Quiz 39 answers

Round 1

1 The Lady of the Lamp. 2 Dolly. 3 The Pipkins. 4 Real Madrid. 5 J. R. Ewing (in television's *Dallas*). 6 Jack Nicholson. 7 Liberty's. 8 London and Portsmouth. 9 Highgrove. 10 Iain Duncan Smith.

Round 2

1 The Battle of Marston Moor. 2 *Peter Pan*. 3 Pickles. 4 True. 5 John Wayne (who had a dog called Duke). 6 Max. 7 Dog licences were abolished. 8 They do not bark. 9 Vivian Stanshall. 10 Nipper.

Half-time Teaser   3,106 carats.

Round 3

1 In his bath. 2 Colombia. 3 He dissolved them in a bath of acid. 4 John Nettles. 5 The A6. 6 Norman Bates. 7 Doctor Crippen. 8 True. 9 Saddleworth. 10 10 Rillington Place.

Round 4

1 A detective. 2 Jimmy Durante. 3 Lillie Langtry. 4 False (it lasted 116 years). 5 Minimalism. 6 Midge Ure. 7 Thermal underwear. 8 Roald Amundsen. 9 Coventry. 10 The Severn.

Jackpot   Mannerism.

Quiz 40 answers

Round 1

1 Belgium. 2 Five. 3 *Henry VIII*. 4 Tin Pan Alley. 5 Lourdes, in southern France. 6 Trinity House. 7 Ecuador. 8 A. 9 Charles II. 10 George Bush Senior.

Round 2

1 Thomas De Quincey. 2 Pelé. 3 Adolf Hitler. 4 Laurie Lee. 5 Wayne Sleep. 6 Flora Thompson. 7 Tammy Wynette. 8 Roald Dahl. 9 Henry Thoreau. 10 Gertrude Stein.

Half-time teaser   1,189.

Round 3

1 A pear. 2 Apples. 3 Broccoli. 4 A clementine. 5 True. 6 A beetroot. 7 A loganberry. 8 Mushrooms. 9 Vitamin C. 10 A peach.

Round 4

1 Shergar. 2 The *Ark Royal*. 3 Arsenal. 4 *Peter Pan*. 5 Glandular fever. 6 Spain. 7 'Mad world'. 8 Tasmanian wolf. 9 The men's discus. 10 Frans Hals.

Jackpot   Richmond, Virginia.

Quiz 41 answers

Round 1

1 Yuri Gagarin. 2 Ralph McTell. 3 Nicole Kidman. 4 Arthur Askey.
5 Rudolph Valentino. 6 John Dryden. 7 The spring term. 8 Hungarian.
9 Stanley Matthews. 10 The Kaiser Chiefs.

Round 2

1 The Mediterranean and the Red Sea. 2 England. 3 A pedalo. 4 Jack
Hawkins. 5 Albatross. 6 False (it is the real thing). 7 The Battle of
Copenhagen. 8 Australia (Harold Holt). 9 Madagascar. 10 Lord Horatio
Kitchener.

Half-time teaser 10,570 miles.

Round 3

1 Toto. 2 Damon Runyon. 3 *Annie Get Your Gun* (based on the life of
Annie Oakley). 4 Sally Bowles. 5 *Brigadoon.* 6 *Calamity Jane.* 7 Billy
Bigelow. 8 *Oh, What a Lovely War!* 9 *The Philadelphia Story.* 10 *Bugsy
Malone.*

Round 4

1 *The Wild One.* 2 Arthur Negus. 3 New Zealand. 4 Red. 5 Boris Johnson.
6 *Miami Vice.* 7 David Jacobs. 8 *The Tempest.* 9 The Three Stooges.
10 Eddie 'The Eagle' Edwards.

Jackpot Friday.

Quiz 42 answers

Round 1

1 New Zealand. 2 *101 Dalmatians*. 3 Russia. 4 *Bend It Like Beckham*.
5 Edward VIII (on the day that he acceded to the throne, in 1936).
6 Chiaroscuro. 7 *The Taming of the Shrew*. 8 Anne of Cleves. 9 George
Carey. 10 Alzheimer's.

Round 2

1 Gilbert and Sullivan. 2 False. 3 Nelson Mandela and F. W. de Klerk.
4 Barbed wire. 5 Lord Peter Wimsey. 6 George Bush Senior. 7 Jerry Mouse.
8 Edinburgh. 9 William Rodgers. 10 They were transatlantic aviators.

Half-time teaser 66.

Round 3

1 Polaris. 2 Galaxies. 3 The Hubble Space Telescope. 4 Douglas Adams.
5 The solar system. 6 Uranus. 7 Five years. 8 Nebula. 9 The USSR (in
1959). 10 77.

Round 4

1 Procrastination. 2 Charles De Gaulle. 3 Lester Piggott (30). 4 12.
5 Theatre critic Alexander Woollcott. 6 The haka. 7 Fox-hunting. 8 Jeffrey
Bernard (*Jeffrey Bernard is Unwell*). 9 Tesco. 10 Mayfair.

Jackpot Shelta.

Quiz 43 answers

Round 1

1 Thomas Jefferson. 2 *Yellow Submarine*. 3 Marcel Proust. 4 Guitar.
5 Canada. 6 *All About Eve*. 7 Roland Rat. 8 Samuel Beckett. 9 False.
10 Joe DiMaggio.

Round 2

1 Karl Benz. 2 The bonnet. 3 The VW Beetle. 4 The Brighton Run.
5 Tracy Chapman. 6 Chappaquiddick. 7 Madness. 8 The Reliant Robin.
9 Kraftwerk (with the single 'Autobahn'). 10 *The Highway Code*.

Half-time teaser   12.

Round 3

1 Gavrilo Princip (who assassinated the Austrian Archduke Ferdinand in
Sarajevo and thus helped precipitate World War I). 2 The Boston Tea
Party. 3 U2. 4 The Angels of Mons. 5 The Crimean War. 6 Agent Orange.
7 The Desert Rats. 8 Kuwait. 9 The German invasion of Russia in 1941.
10 The (Second) Boer War.

Round 4

1 *Abbey Road*. 2 *Rosemary's Baby*. 3 He was killed when an eagle dropped
a tortoise on his head. 4 Britpop. 5 False (it was in the USA). 6 Coventry.
7 Mexico (Quetzalcoatl). 8 US president Franklin D. Roosevelt. 9 The
British Library. 10 Ink-blots.

Jackpot   *Anne of Green Gables* (and its sequels, including *Anne of Avonlea*).

Quiz 44 answers

Round 1

1 The Roundheads (or Parliamentarians). 2 John Constable. 3 *The Beggar's Opera*. 4 Ontario. 5 November. 6 The *Mona Lisa*. 7 Margaret Thatcher. 8 *Brookside* 9 A daisycutter. 10 Greece.

Round 2

1 Fred Astaire. 2 John Ravenscroft. 3 Sting. 4 Captain Black. 5 Uncle Remus. 6 Bill Wyman. 7 Tony Bennett. 8 Anthony. 9 Charles Bronson. 10 Pelé.

Half-time teaser 5,801.

Round 3

1 John F. Kennedy. 2 François Mitterand. 3 President Gamal Abdel Nasser. 4 Abraham Lincoln. 5 Paul von Hindenburg. 6 *The West Wing*. 7 The Elysée Palace. 8 True. 9 'Hail to the chief'. 10 Mount Rushmore.

Round 4

1 Dance. 2 Kodak. 3 Led Zeppelin. 4 Boris Becker. 5 The South Downs Way. 6 Ash Wednesday. 7 Palm trees. 8 Alabama. 9 Wormwood Scrubs. 10 Sir Edwin Landseer.

Jackpot An ice-pick.

Quiz 45 answers

Round 1

1 The discovery of penicillin. 2 The Mekon. 3 Pinkie. 4 Dario Fo.
5 To measure eyesight. 6 Steak tartare. 7 Yellow. 8 Berni Inns. 9 Arnold
Wesker. 10 Imelda Marcos.

Round 2

1 York. 2 The Scilly Isles. 3 Aylesbury. 4 Glasgow. 5 The Golden Mile.
6 The congestion charge. 7 Walmington-on-Sea. 8 Birmingham.
9 Caernarvon. 10 Newlyn.

Half-time teaser   14.

Round 3

1 Broadway. 2 *Waiting for Godot.* 3 The World Snooker Championship.
4 The Old Vic. 5 Aunt Edna. 6 Method. 7 Gertrude Lawrence. 8 Angry
Young Men. 9 *Arsenic and Old Lace.* 10 *Hamlet.*

Round 4

1 Eight (Belgium, Luxembourg, Germany, Switzerland, Italy, Monaco,
Andorra and Spain). 2 The Boers. 3 Four. 4 George Bernard Shaw.
5 The Cat. 6 Wham! 7 Dorset. 8 The Hippocratic Oath. 9 Ally Pally
(Alexandra Palace, London). 10 Sheep.

Jackpot   Aldo Moro.

Quiz 46 answers

Round 1

1 'Bigfoot'. 2 Andrew Jackson. 3 The ordination of women. 4 Ben Gunn.
5 Schubert. 6 The membrane between the nostrils. 7 Chuck Berry. 8 Isaac
Newton. 9 Plover. 10 Paul Ince.

Round 2

1 The introduction of antiseptics in surgery. 2 Vitamin D. 3 Shortsightedness.
4 Rubella. 5 The ambulance. 6 The first sex-change operation. 7 High blood
pressure. 8 Tourette's syndrome. 9 Sputum. 10 Heart surgery.

Half-time teaser   34 centimetres.

Round 3

1 George Dixon (of Dock Green). 2 Ray Reardon. 3 *Tosca*. 4 New Scotland
Yard. 5 Richard Hannay. 6 True. 7 Chief Wiggum. 8 The Kray Twins.
9 Buzzer. 10 Because of their black-and-white markings.

Round 4

1 King Kong. 2 Decibels. 3 The top row. 4 Australian. 5 St Paul. 6 They
were all deaf. 7 Essex. 8 Detroit. 9 Greg Norman. 10 The Scaffold.

Jackpot   Reptiles.

Quiz 47 answers

Round 1

1 Tripoli. 2 True. 3 Cher. 4 Lake Victoria. 5 Harold Pinter. 6 Thalidomide.
7 Sri Lanka (1960). 8 Orcs. 9 He was a doctor. 10 Belshazzar.

Round 2

1 New York City. 2 California. 3 Enrico Caruso. 4 Big Ears. 5 The US state
of Georgia (which is twice the size of the republic). 6 Maine. 7 Fort Knox.
8 True (since 2003). 9 Rip Van Winkle. 10 Veterans Day.

Half-time teaser David (it appears over 1,000 times).

Round 3

1 They both faked famous works of art. 2 Myra Hindley. 3 41. 4 William
Joyce ('Lord Haw-Haw', hanged in 1946). 5 Sweeney Todd. 6 Al-Qaida.
7 R. D. Blackmore's *Lorna Doone* (1869). 8 Scarface. 9 Phil Silvers.
10 The Butcher of Lyon.

Round 4

1 Coconut ice. 2 'Macarena'. 3 Milky Way. 4 The boat owned by Charlie
Allnutt (played in the film by Humphrey Bogart). 5 The Tour de France.
6 The hardness of materials. 7 The Duke of Buckingham. 8 Dartmoor.
9 Mezzanine. 10 Sarah Michelle Gellar.

Jackpot The Hermitage in St Petersburg.

Quiz 48 answers

Round 1

1 Garrard. **2** Bros. **3** Road tunnels. **4** *Death of a Salesman.* **5** Leslie Howard. **6** The Potomac. **7** Harry S. Truman. **8** Graham Kerr. **9** Three. **10** His right heel.

Round 2

1 Bath. **2** Waterloo. **3** W. H. Smith. **4** Amtrak. **5** Anna Karenina. **6** 1843. **7** Casey Jones. **8** Grand Central station in New York. **9** Dublin. **10** A dragon.

Half-time teaser   1,852.

Round 3

1 Canada. **2** The US PGA. **3** 86 kg. **4** Red. **5** Skiing and shooting. **6** Meccano. **7** Eight. **8** Betty Stove. **9** Fencing. **10** The Kaiser.

Round 4

1 Wales. **2** Captain Hastings. **3** False (it is Welsh). **4** Field-Marshal Montgomery. **5** Dwight D. Eisenhower. **6** The English throne. **7** Tasmania. **8** Israel. **9** Violins. **10** Liquorice.

Jackpot   Seaweed.

Quiz 49 answers

Round 1

1 Australia. 2 Anti-social behaviour order. 3 The Drifters. 4 Typhoid Mary. 5 Catherine Zeta-Jones. 6 Eddie Merckx. 7 Amman. 8 Catseyes. 9 Airships (it was the site of the hangar in which R101 was kept). 10 Mother Shipton.

Round 2

1 The bikini. 2 Nîmes, in France. 3 Vivienne Westwood. 4 Bra Wars. 5 Ecuador. 6 Men's bathing-trunks. 7 Blue. 8 Madness. 9 Bobby socks. 10 Ian Dury and the Blockheads.

Half-time teaser 25.

Round 3

1 Chairman Mao. 2 Marshal Ney. 3 Robert Catesby (Guy Fawkes was in charge of the gunpowder). 4 George II (at Dettingen in 1743). 5 David Steel. 6 Akela. 7 Arthur Scargill. 8 Mussolini. 9 Genghis Khan. 10 Screaming Lord Sutch.

Round 4

1 Six. 2 Henry Ford. 3 *The Brittas Empire*. 4 Queen Victoria. 5 Tom Sharpe. 6 False (it is getting bigger due to overgrazing of surrounding areas). 7 The Rubicon. 8 Q. 9 Prince Harry. 10 *A Town Like Alice*.

Jackpot   Heraldry.

Quiz 50 answers

Round 1

1 Jamboree. **2** John Paul II. **3** Four. **4** They were brothers. **5** Nova Scotia.
6 A fox. **7** The apex. **8** Two. **9** Romulus. **10** The Singing Nun.

Round 2

1 Rome. **2** Seattle. **3** Istanbul. **4** False (it is in Morocco). **5** Sydney. **6** Venice.
7 Edinburgh. **8** Washington DC. **9** Sheffield. **10** Glasgow.

Half-time teaser   30 hours, 45 minutes.

Round 3

1 Women's hats. **2** A butcher. **3** Mining. **4** Gerald Ford. **5** Carts and
wagons. **6** He is a weaver. **7** Clark Gable. **8** Television weather presenters.
9 Christopher Dean. **10** Assistant to the chief electrician.

Round 4

1 Samuel Morse. **2** A brownfield site. **3** Coconut. **4** David Bowie. **5** Leeds
and London. **6** Haemophilia. **7** Oasis. **8** Tom Wolfe. **9** Photography.
10 The Ming Dynasty.

Jackpot   Volleyball.

Quiz 51 answers

Round 1

1 Australia. 2 A rat. 3 Siam. 4 Chrissie Hynde. 5 Derek Jacobi. 6 Eric the Red. 7 The platypus. 8 1961. 9 The number 13. 10 Elba.

Round 2

1 Captain Matthew Webb. 2 Uruguay. 3 The 1920s. 4 Ernest Rutherford. 5 *Trial by Jury*. 6 *Snow White and the Seven Dwarfs* (1937). 7 Tobacco. 8 Lancelot. 9 Diana, Princess of Wales. 10 A getaway car.

Half-time teaser 21.

Round 3

1 The shopping trolley. 2 Allinson wholemeal bread. 3 Poison. 4 '. . . not in your hand' (slogan for Treets confectionery). 5 The *Big Issue*. 6 The escalator. 7 Grace Brothers. 8 The Pet Shop Boys. 9 Selfridge's. 10 Granville.

Round 4

1 Greece. 2 Ragtime. 3 Tiananmen Square. 4 Kurt Cobain. 5 Stevie Smith. 6 Lake Superior. 7 Athlete's foot. 8 Coventry. 9 Quakers. 10 Golf.

Jackpot Thabo Mbeki.

Quiz 52 answers

Round 1

1 Bastille Day. 2 Fiat. 3 Leopold Bloom. 4 Pope. 5 A gigantic aircraft built by Howard Hughes. 6 David Cameron. 7 A human shield. 8 Yemen. 9 Cliff. 10 Italy.

Round 2

1 Kenya. 2 Queen Anne. 3 Belgium. 4 Cnut. 5 Italy. 6 10. 7 Sweden. 8 Worcester. 9 Benny Goodman. 10 King Midas.

Half-time teaser 40.

Round 3

1 Geraint Evans (Evans was a bass, the others were tenors). 2 Irving Berlin. 3 The Doors. 4 Dave Dee, Dozy, Beaky, Mick and Tich. 5 *The Sound of Music*. 6 True. 7 *Summer Holiday*. 8 Because little girls get bigger every day. 9 The sitar. 10 The *1812 Overture*.

Round 4

1 Captain Cook. 2 Crown green bowls. 3 The Seychelles. 4 In a castle (they are parts of the battlements). 5 Hara-kiri (the other two are foods). 6 Hatfield. 7 Henry Irving. 8 Rutland. 9 The Atlantic Wall. 10 London clubs.

Jackpot Gossip (or rumours).

Quiz 53 answers

Round 1

1 Omega. 2 Read only memory. 3 Bollywood. 4 Gordonstoun. 5 Heathrow airport. 6 An early bicycle. 7 Nigeria. 8 Frank Capra. 9 Jean-Marie Le Pen. 10 Brian Jones.

Round 2

1 Michael Collins. 2 L'Oréal hair and beauty products. 3 Andy Warhol. 4 Celtic. 5 *All Gas and Gaiters*. 6 Harold Macmillan. 7 *The Avengers*. 8 'Back in the USSR'. 9 The Bay of Pigs. 10 John F. Kennedy (quoted as saying '*Ich bin ein Berliner*', a *berliner* being German for a type of doughnut).

Half-time teaser   30.3 per cent.

Round 3

1 Pablo Picasso. 2 Green. 3 Chris De Burgh. 4 Black (in the single 'Paint it black'). 5 Marlene Dietrich. 6 Audie Murphy. 7 The Incredible Hulk. 8 Yellow. 9 Rugby. 10 Green.

Round 4

1 Advisory, Conciliation and Arbitration Service. 2 A police procedural. 3 Renee and Renato. 4 Ian Rankin. 5 The CIA. 6 Leeds United. 7 Beavers. 8 Saudi Arabia. 9 Pointillism. 10 Bow.

Jackpot   Melchester Rovers.

Quiz 54 answers

Round 1

1 American football. **2** The United Arab Emirates. **3** Iron. **4** Greek.
5 Oxfam. **6** Poland. **7** The Japanese empire. **8** Sugar Ray Leonard.
9 *Pal Joey*. **10** Czechoslovakia.

Round 2

1 John Logie Baird. **2** Six. **3** £2. **4** William Tell. **5** False (the presenters were
Leila Williams and Christopher Trace). **6** *Dr Finlay's Casebook*. **7** Slade.
8 Psoriasis. **9** *University Challenge*. **10** Hercules.

Half-time teaser 175,000.

Round 3

1 Seaweed. **2** True. **3** The oyster. **4** A clownfish. **5** Amity. **6** A calf. **7** Terns.
8 *A Fish Called Wanda*. **9** The herring family. **10** The puffin.

Round 4

1 Rome. **2** 25 January. **3** James I. **4** Gloucestershire. **5** Akihito. **6** Bob
Hope. **7** Flushing Meadows, New York. **8** Alexander the Great (he cut it
with his sword). **9** A breed of dog. **10** Drunk.

Jackpot A caryatid.

Quiz 55 answers

Round 1

1 Three. **2** George and Ira Gershwin. **3** *When Harry Met Sally*. **4** Will Carling. **5** Galaxies. **6** The New Seekers. **7** The Bering Strait. **8** Cecil Beaton. **9** Jack London. **10** Rice.

Round 2

1 Ham. **2** Henry I (with at least 20). **3** *Children's Hour*. **4** Destiny's Child. **5** *His Dark Materials* (by Philip Pullman). **6** Davy Jones. **7** False (it was his grandson). **8** *Bagpuss*. **9** A cow (and calf). **10** Jenny Agutter.

Half-time teaser   771 feet.

Round 3

1 Gladys Knight and the Pips. **2** Dr Richard Beeching. **3** Carnforth (in Lancashire). **4** He was run down by Stephenson's *Rocket*, thus becoming the first person to die in a rail accident. **5** Tony Hancock (in *Hancock's Half-Hour*). **6** Gordon. **7** The Flying Scotsman. **8** The O'Jays. **9** Waterloo. **10** The Tay Bridge Disaster of 1879.

Round 4

1 Elton John. **2** *The Benny Hill Show*. **3** Captain W. E. Johns. **4** (South) America. **5** Alton Towers. **6** Haiti. **7** Mark Spitz. **8** Richard Chamberlain. **9** Pink Floyd. **10** 1992.

Jackpot   Carmel.

Quiz 56 answers

Round 1

1 Red, white and green. 2 Arrows. 3 Jacqueline Wilson. 4 Football.
5 Lapwing. 6 Hair (especially on the scalp). 7 Persia. 8 Joe Orton.
9 Eurythmics. 10 Kashmir.

Round 2

1 Shirley Conran. 2 The violin. 3 1937. 4 She invented the automatic
dishwasher. 5 Bath. 6 1945. 7 Rolex. 8 Terence Conran. 9 1936. 10 They
introduced the first home computer.

Half-time teaser   80.

Round 3

1 Exodus. 2 13¾. 3 Raymond Briggs. 4 *The Lord of the Rings*. 5 Anita
Loos. 6 *Lolita*. 7 Fay Weldon. 8 *Bleak House*. 9 *Moby-Dick*. 10 *Harry Potter
and the Philosopher's Stone*.

Round 4

1 Westminster Abbey. 2 Super-heavyweight. 3 Potassium. 4 Birds. 5 Airey
Neave. 6 The Elgin Marbles. 7 Victoria. 8 Alexander Kerensky. 9 *Macbeth*.
10 Little Richard.

Jackpot   Hawaii.

Quiz 57 answers

Round 1

1 Hercules. **2** Aretha Franklin. **3** Buddy Holly. **4** Hammer Films. **5** Mexico.
6 'The Ride of the Valkyries' by Richard Wagner. **7** Bob Beamon. **8** Meryl
Streep. **9** Morecambe and Wise. **10** A light-emitting diode.

Round 2

1 The Catholic Church (strictly speaking, the Anglo-Catholic Church).
2 He was the only English pope (born Nicholas Breakspear). **3** The Great
Schism. **4** John (23 so far). **5** *Ben-Hur*. **6** Rex Harrison. **7** John Paul I.
8 Opus Dei. **9** Londonderry (Derry). **10** Under Blackfriars Bridge in
London.

Half-time teaser 88.

Round 3

1 *Birds of a Feather*. **2** An albatross. **3** 14 February (St Valentine's Day).
4 Bird flu. **5** The Tweets. **6** The Birdman of Alcatraz. **7** The Byrds. **8** True.
9 The Magpies. **10** Edith Piaf.

Round 4

1 Macduff. **2** Fletcher Christian. **3** Westlife. **4** Alan Sugar (the name
Amstrad was arrived at from the initials of Alan Michael Sugar combined
with Trading). **5** False (he hated it). **6** Bernie Taupin. **7** True. **8** Oedipus.
9 The Royal British Legion. **10** Sir Galahad.

Jackpot Elbrus.

Quiz 58 answers

Round 1

1 Global Positioning System. **2** Seven. **3** He is Nicolas Cage's uncle.
4 Dexy's Midnight Runners (in their single 'Come on Eileen'). **5** It is the
rearmost mast. **6** Epsom. **7** George Bernard Shaw. **8** The aubergine.
9 The Comet. **10** Trevor Francis.

Round 2

1 30. **2** The Tarpeian Rock. **3** Charles II. **4** Mata Hari. **5** Queen Victoria.
6 Benedict Arnold. **7** The Spanish Civil War. **8** The Tower of London.
9 Elizabeth I. **10** Marshal Philippe Pétain.

Half-time teaser   28.1 metres.

Round 3

1 *Today*. **2** William Golding. **3** Princess Royal. **4** He became the first player
to be sent off in an FA Cup final. **5** Bob Champion. **6** The sixpence. **7** The
Soviet invasion of Afghanistan. **8** Lionel Richie. **9** Greenland won
independence from Denmark and left the community. **10** Bobby Robson.

Round 4

1 Ben Jonson. **2** Amontillado. **3** The Great Bear. **4** True. **5** Triangular.
6 Astronomer Royal. **7** The BBC. **8** Golf. **9** South African. **10** *EastEnders*.

Jackpot   Stan Laurel.

Quiz 59 answers

Round 1

1 Pudding Lane. 2 Belgian. 3 George Eliot. 4 Robert Palmer. 5 L. Ron Hubbard. 6 Kazakhstan. 7 The Turner Prize. 8 *Taxi Driver*. 9 Hot Chocolate. 10 Sodor.

Round 2

1 Au. 2 Benson and Hedges. 3 Ethel Merman. 4 The Crazy Gang. 5 The Referendum Party. 6 *Rowan and Martin's Laugh-In*. 7 *The Treasure of the Sierra Madre*. 8 The Berlin Film Festival. 9 Fool's gold. 10 Tina Turner.

Half-time teaser   122.

Round 3

1 Max Miller. 2 Stephen Fry and Hugh Laurie. 3 *Life of Brian*. 4 Norman Wisdom. 5 Hattie Jacques. 6 Barcelona. 7 Harpo. 8 On Craggy Island. 9 The Algonquin Round Table. 10 Billy Connolly.

Round 4

1 Beatrix Potter. 2 Kiss. 3 C. S. Lewis. 4 Camelot. 5 Doodlebugs. 6 Savannah. 7 Six (Donny, Alan, Jimmy, Wayne, Jay and Merrill). 8 Maplin's. 9 Ethiopia. 10 *Any Which Way You Can*.

Jackpot   Nepal (the flag consists of two triangles, one above the other).

Quiz 60 answers

Round 1

1 180. 2 An elephant. 3 Lotus. 4 *Don Giovanni*. 5 Yellow. 6 Queen's Park Rangers. 7 *The Riddle of the Sands*. 8 Sleep. 9 A butler. 10 Meteor showers.

Round 2

1 Clark Gable and Marilyn Monroe. 2 John. 3 Britney Spears. 4 Elvis Presley. 5 Pamela Anderson. 6 Sir Elton John. 7 Madonna. 8 Christina Aguilera. 9 Shilpa Shetty. 10 Pigs (who went on the run from an abattoir in Malmesbury in 1998).

Half-time teaser 75.

Round 3

1 'The Forces' Sweetheart'. 2 Alan Freeman. 3 Jack Nicklaus. 4 Cynthia Payne. 5 Jerry Lee Lewis. 6 'The Swedish Nightingale'. 7 Lord Longford. 8 Jesse Owens. 9 Princess Michael of Kent. 10 Mary Pickford.

Round 4

1 St Paul's Cathedral. 2 Weatherfield. 3 Area of Outstanding Natural Beauty. 4 Jean Borotra. 5 *The Canterbury Tales*. 6 Passover (or Pesach). 7 Richard Nixon. 8 Coniston. 9 *Far From the Madding Crowd*. 10 Cheese wrapped in nettles.

Jackpot Gymnastics.

Quiz 61 answers

....

Round 1

1 Victor Meldrew. 2 Cumbria. 3 Lady Jane Grey. 4 The Sex Pistols.
5 Azkaban. 6 4 July 1776 (date of the US declaration of independence).
7 True. 8 Pop art. 9 Santa Anna. 10 Jack Dempsey.

....

Round 2

1 *This Life*. 2 Six billion. 3 Emma Thompson. 4 *Schindler's List*. 5 Tommi
Mäkinen. 6 Benetton. 7 John Major's. 8 *Baywatch*. 9 Brit art. 10 Jarvis
Cocker.

....

Half-time Teaser   8,022 square miles.

....

Round 3

1 US president Theodore Roosevelt (apparently after he spared a young
bear tied up for him to shoot). 2 Housey-housey (or, going back to the
eighteenth century, lotto). 3 True (he used them to store gas). 4 Sandie
Shaw. 5 G. I. Joe. 6 The yo-yo. 7 Beanie Babies. 8 Bridge. 9 Sony. 10 Peter
Gabriel.

....

Round 4

1 Russell Crowe. 2 The Black Pearl. 3 Lindisfarne. 4 Jean-Paul Sartre.
5 The Solway Firth. 6 Bruce Wayne. 7 Jimmy Hoffa. 8 30. 9 The Beach
Boys. 10 Methuselah.

....

Jackpot   Ragnarok.

....

Quiz 62 answers

Round 1

1 A fawn. 2 Epilepsy. 3 *Bananaman*. 4 Argentina. 5 Midnight to 4 a.m.
6 Trowbridge. 7 Table-tennis. 8 Yes. 9 Order of the British Empire.
10 Cotton.

Round 2

1 *Gypsy Moth IV*. 2 Hajj. 3 The *Empire Windrush*. 4 Rome and Brindisi.
5 False. 6 Helen Sharman. 7 DeLorean. 8 It is within a human body (in a
mini-submarine). 9 *Starlight Express*. 10 St Christopher.

Half-time teaser 36.

Round 3

1 Ingrid Bergman. 2 *Carry On Sergeant*. 3 Renée Zellweger. 4 Stanley
Kubrick. 5 *The Boys from Brazil*. 6 Billy Wilder. 7 *Apocalypse Now*. 8
Harry Palmer. 9 *That'll Be the Day*. 10 *The Ten Commandments*.

Round 4

1 Vitamin C. 2 Crete. 3 Woodrow Wilson. 4 *West Side Story*. 5 Johnny
Cash. 6 The Benson and Hedges Cup. 7 *Under Milk Wood*. 8 Queen
Victoria. 9 The breastbone. 10 Los Angeles.

Jackpot Heart of Midlothian.

Quiz 63 answers

Round 1

1 A lavatory. **2** Tiger Woods. **3** *The Clangers*. **4** For what it's worth. **5** Dolly Parton. **6** The *Exxon Valdez*. **7** Jonestown. **8** False (there is more nitrogen than oxygen). **9** The Stratofortress. **10** The boxer Joe Louis.

Round 2

1 Zeus. **2** Hermes. **3** The Norse god Thor. **4** Haile Selassie. **5** Peter Shilton. **6** Kali. **7** Venus. **8** 'Life on Mars'. **9** Francis Ford Coppola. **10** A theatre.

Half-time teaser   Around 150,000.

Round 3

1 Sacha Distel's. **2** Cabin fever. **3** David Frost. **4** St Swithun's Day. **5** 'Telstar'. **6** *Gone With the Wind*. **7** Katrina. **8** Carole King. **9** Terry Jacks. **10** Travis.

Round 4

1 'Amazing Grace'. **2** *The Great Gatsby* by F. Scott Fitzgerald. **3** True. **4** A school. **5** 'All shook up'. **6** Red Rum. **7** José Carreras. **8** Oliver Cromwell. **9** Handwriting. **10** Chicken Kiev.

Jackpot   Ukraine.

Quiz 64 answers

Round 1

1 Havana. 2 Brooklands. 3 A sheriff. 4 Porsche. 5 Michael Winner. 6 The deep-fried Mars bar. 7 *Billy Elliot*. 8 48. 9 Speedway. 10 Cricket.

Round 2

1 Table Mountain. 2 Ethiopia. 3 The Springboks. 4 *The African Queen*. 5 Idi Amin. 6 Zimbabwe. 7 The hippo. 8 Eat it. 9 Tunisia. 10 True.

Half-time teaser   80.96.

Round 3

1 Pears. 2 Greece. 3 Kahlua. 4 Tequila. 5 Orange. 6 Drambuie. 7 Cherries. 8 Eight. 9 There is too much tannin in it. 10 A Harvey wallbanger.

Round 4

1 John Dunlop. 2 To the bottom of the sea. 3 Ethel Merman. 4 The Dardanelles (or Hellespont). 5 Margaret. 6 Nine. 7 David Walliams. 8 Julius Caesar. 9 The 19th century. 10 *Emmerdale Farm*.

Jackpot   The bluebell.

Quiz 65 answers

Round 1

1 Neverland. 2 Alice in Wonderland. 3 U2. 4 Regan. 5 'Ode to Joy' by Beethoven. 6 Canadian. 7 The Spencer family 8 A tower (usually part of a temple). 9 Baseball. 10 Napoleon did it himself.

Round 2

1 Calais. 2 The Quai d'Orsay. 3 Audrey Tautou. 4 Henri de Toulouse-Lautrec. 5 Jacques Tati. 6 Louis-Joseph de Montcalm. 7 Jane Birkin. 8 Big Bertha. 9 Renoir. 10 John Fowles.

Half-time teaser 49.

Round 3

1 They are third cousins. 2 Gerald Durrell. 3 Beetles. 4 The Grand Duchess Anastasia (posthumous DNA tests in 1991 proved she was not). 5 Alec Guinness. 6 Mrs Bridges. 7 *An Inspector Calls*. 8 Nepal. 9 Diana Rigg. 10 No (neither were they called Walker until they all adopted the name after forming the band).

Round 4

1 64. 2 Jan Vermeer. 3 Manfred Mann's Earth Band. 4 True. 5 Albanian. 6 *Last of the Summer Wine*. 7 Drunk. 8 The Battle of Hastings. 9 Rupert Bear. 10 The American Civil War.

Jackpot Terry Nation.

Quiz 66 answers

Round 1

1 The butterfly bush. 2 *The Wizard of Oz*. 3 The Globe Theatre. 4 Four.
5 The circulation of blood. 6 Oscar Wilde. 7 Pelota. 8 Orchestral
Manoeuvres in the Dark. 9 Nick Hornby. 10 Birmingham.

Round 2

1 At Niagara. 2 Cast iron. 3 Japan. 4 Belfast. 5 Majorca. 6 In the Louvre in
Paris. 7 To the Crystal Palace. 8 In the Tower of London. 9 The Victoria
Falls. 10 Cornwall.

Half-time teaser   1,072.

Round 3

1 Chaps. 2 A hat. 3 Tank tops. 4 On your face (they are long side-
whiskers). 5 Kilt. 6 A light scarf (worn over the head and shoulders).
7 Red. 8 Blue. 9 A hat. 10 Innuit (or Eskimo).

Round 4

1 An ape. 2 The yew. 3 Elvis Presley. 4 Pressure (or stress). 5 Evonne
Cawley. 6 Alan Shearer (with 260). 7 TV chefs. 8 Daniel Radcliffe.
9 Austrian. 10 Mauve (or light purple).

Jackpot   It's the dot above a letter i.

Quiz 67 answers

Round 1

1 Scooby Doo. 2 Tony Christie. 3 *Watership Down*. 4 Monday. 5 'Helter-skelter'. 6 Devon. 7 He was the first man to be convicted for driving a lawnmower while drunk. 8 Algeria. 9 Death. 10 St Helena.

Round 2

1 Breakfast and lunch. 2 At Easter. 3 Sirloin (though it more likely comes from the French *surlonge*, meaning 'above loin'). 4 Soya beans (curd). 5 Monosodium glutamate. 6 Molasses. 7 Two. 8 Ground almonds. 9 Henry I. 10 Two.

Half-time teaser   124.

Round 3

1 The Bash Street Kids. 2 Ofsted. 3 Darbishire. 4 Billy Bunter. 5 *The Blackboard Jungle*. 6 *The Prime of Miss Jean Brodie*. 7 Dotheboys Hall. 8 Jack Black. 9 Richard Brinsley Sheridan. 10 *Jane Eyre*.

Round 4

1 Baseball. 2 The keystone. 3 Shane MacGowan. 4 The clarinet. 5 Prince. 6 *Titanic*. 7 Lewis Carroll (he was over six feet tall, while Barrie stopped growing at the age of 15). 8 George Orwell, in his novel *Nineteen Eighty-Four*. 9 The dogs (in the single 'Who let the dogs out'). 10 Vlad the Impaler.

Jackpot   The Cheviots.

Quiz 68 answers

Round 1

1 Prima donna. **2** A diamond. **3** Hope. **4** Tony Curtis. **5** Portugal.
6 The Jam. **7** Italy. **8** Oven gloves. **9** True. **10** Augustus.

Round 2

1 Golf. **2** Princess Anne. **3** Denis Compton. **4** Joe Davis. **5** Nadia
Comaneci. **6** 1993 (the race was declared void). **7** None. **8** The eighteenth
century. **9** 300. **10** One hour.

Half-time teaser 84 hours.

Round 3

1 A venomous snake. **2** The alpaca. **3** Timmy. **4** A fish. **5** Mulberry leaves.
6 Two. **7** False (it is a large marine mammal). **8** Seals. **9** Otters. **10** 12.

Round 4

1 Draws maps. **2** Canoeing (or kayaking). **3** Lotus. **4** *Jaws*. **5** Rome. **6** The
Napoleonic War. **7** David Lloyd George. **8** Charles. **9** Live8. **10** Keith.

Jackpot Pound.

Quiz 69 answers

Round 1

1 Archimedes. **2** Sir George Gilbert Scott. **3** That the Earth revolves around the Sun. **4** Roy Lichtenstein. **5** Prince Charles. **6** *Queen Mary*. **7** Italy (1934 and 1938). **8** Artists. **9** Terry Waite. **10** Sir Henry Segrave.

Round 2

1 A glass ceiling. **2** Pretty damn quick. **3** Elvis Presley. **4** Asset stripping. **5** Remington (electric razors). **6** Young upwardly mobile professional person. **7** Carpetbaggers. **8** *Hobson's Choice* (by Harold Brighouse). **9** Doctor Robert Atkins. **10** The Big Bang.

Half-time teaser   27.87 square metres.

Round 3

1 Esmeralda. **2** J. B. Priestley. **3** Minnie Riperton. **4** 10. **5** 'God save the queen'. **6** Her dog bit him. **7** 1967. **8** Auguste Rodin. **9** The Housemartins. **10** Bromide.

Round 4

1 Little Big Horn. **2** Robinson Crusoe. **3** The Four Tops. **4** Margaret Thatcher. **5** Mike Myers. **6** Playing cards. **7** Aldwych farces. **8** American. **9** The Rolling Stones. **10** Cosa Nostra.

Jackpot   The Big Bopper.

Quiz 70 answers

Round 1

1 Oxford. 2 California. 3 Proton. 4 11. 5 P.T. Barnum. 6 They were cousins. 7 Badminton. 8 20. 9 Viv Anderson. 10 The Women's Institute.

Round 2

1 Iron. 2 The live wire. 3 Genetically modified. 4 10,000. 5 Four. 6 One kilogram. 7 7/100 (seven hundredths). 8 180. 9 The newton. 10 Six.

Half-time teaser 654.

Round 3

1 A joey. 2 The Order of the Thistle. 3 William Gladstone. 4 A rock stack in Orkney. 5 Wayne Rooney. 6 Theodore Roosevelt (aged 43). 7 Windsor Castle. 8 Mike Tyson. 9 Douglas MacArthur. 10 'Old Glory'.

Round 4

1 Margaret Thatcher. 2 Yellow. 3 *Grease*. 4 The Bahamas. 5 Scorpio. 6 200°C (400°F). 7 *Temeraire* 8 Turin. 9 The scooter. 10 Ruritania.

Jackpot It was the first warship made of (glass-reinforced) plastic.

Quiz 71 answers

Round 1

1 *Goldfinger*. 2 Robert Browning. 3 Maxwell House coffee. 4 Cream.
5 Darrell Hair. 6 Les Dawson. 7 Apples. 8 Gracie Fields. 9 The Democratic Republic of the Congo. 10 Knight of the Order of the Thistle.

Round 2

1 The Cultural Revolution. 2 The Gobi Desert. 3 New Zealand. 4 The Bamboo Curtain. 5 Chow mein. 6 The Boxer Rebellion. 7 T'Pau. 8 The Terracotta Army. 9 False (it depends on the lunar calendar). 10 The Huang He (or Yellow River).

Half-time teaser 31,173.

Round 3

1 Air Force One (when Tony Blair suggested he have one as well, it was dubbed 'Blair Force One'). 2 Enola Gay. 3 The jumbo jet. 4 Tail-End Charlie.
5 Hydrogen. 6 1,000 feet (300 metres). 7 A wind (the hot, dry Chinook wind melts snow and causes flash floods: in 1943 it raised the temperature in South Dakota from -20 degrees centigrade to 7 degrees centigrade in just two minutes). 8 Matt Busby. 9 Quidditch. 10 The Red Baron.

Round 4

1 Stormont, Belfast. 2 Elton John. 3 *Carry On Up the Khyber*. 4 Aunt Agatha. 5 Very Superior Old Pale. 6 17. 7 Dennis Skinner. 8 The Indianapolis 500 (Indy 500) motor race. 9 The Fates. 10 Roswell.

Jackpot Syd Barrett.

Quiz 72 answers

Round 1

1 The Mini (or the Morris Minor). 2 Ronald Reagan. 3 France. 4 Dartmouth. 5 Cricket. 6 Osmosis. 7 *Paper Moon*. 8 Benfica. 9 *Rebecca* by Daphne du Maurier. 10 *The Times*.

Round 2

1 William Hartnell. 2 *Stingray*. 3 Hector's (in *Hector's House*). 4 'Clementine'. 5 *Fireball XL 5*. 6 The Banana Splits. 7 Brains. 8 Honey. 9 Today Is Saturday, Watch And Smile (or Wear a Smile). 10 Newcastle upon Tyne.

Half-time teaser 8.91.

Round 3

1 Chicago. 2 Wyoming. 3 Mike Oldfield (*Tubular Bells*). 4 Acrylic paint. 5 Galileo's (referring to his theory concerning the movement of the Earth around the Sun). 6 Omdurman. 7 Betty Boothroyd. 8 1795. 9 Albania. 10 *The Jazz Singer*.

Round 4

1 Mr Spock. 2 Holy Innocents (or Childermass). 3 Goal nets were not invented until then. 4 The iris. 5 The Bloomsbury Group. 6 Cold calling. 7 The Corrs. 8 1919. 9 *Auf Wiedersehen Pet*. 10 West Ham United.

Jackpot Joachim von Ribbentrop.

Quiz 73 answers

Round 1

1 Chile. 2 The *Mona Lisa*. 3 Richard Cromwell. 4 Thomas Stearns. 5 Rocky Marciano. 6 Petrol. 7 Ray Stevens. 8 Juno. 9 Gnats. 10 Libya.

Round 2

1 Jacques Cousteau. 2 The *Mayflower*. 3 Portsmouth. 4 The *Hood*. 5 The quarterdeck. 6 The *Beagle*. 7 Aristotle Onassis. 8 *Rainbow Warrior*. 9 Admiral Jellicoe. 10 The *Torrey Canyon*.

Half-time teaser   16 years 129 days.

Round 3

1 June. 2 Aloysius. 3 *Citizen Kane*. 4 Annabel's. 5 Viscount Stansgate. 6 Rasputin. 7 Duchess of Cornwall. 8 *A Night at the Opera*. 9 Lord Alfred Douglas. 10 Two (Anne Boleyn and Catherine Howard).

Round 4

1 *Kidnapped*. 2 The Democratic Republic of the Congo. 3 Golf. 4 Welsh. 5 Mary McAleese. 6 Edward Elgar. 7 Gene Kelly. 8 The tie-breaker. 9 Chernobyl. 10 Barry Manilow.

Jackpot   The red card.

Quiz 74 answers

Round 1

1 At Versailles. 2 One year. 3 Archbishop of Canterbury. 4 Rugby. 5 'It's all over now'. 6 Devon Loch. 7 False. 8 A griffin. 9 Alaska and Hawaii. 10 Circular or ring-shaped.

Round 2

1 Thin Lizzy. 2 Avon. 3 George Foreman. 4 Gustav Mahler's. 5 David Fairclough. 6 The page three girl. 7 Canada. 8 Iran. 9 Boat people. 10 France (Brittany).

Half-time teaser 25,630.

Round 3

1 The Channel Islands. 2 Orkney. 3 Runnymede. 4 Paul Gascoigne (Gazza). 5 The Isle of Man. 6 The Falkland Islands. 7 Staffa. 8 The isle of Ely. 9 Jersey. 10 Skye.

Round 4

1 99. 2 Danger: no overtaking. 3 Peter Mandelson. 4 Portugal. 5 Isambard Kingdom Brunel. 6 Oracle. 7 Irish. 8 Erwin Rommel. 9 Denmark and Norway. 10 The Heimlich manoeuvre.

Jackpot Konard Adenauer.

Quiz 75 answers

Round 1

1 The Blitz. 2 Margaret Thatcher. 3 The Channel Tunnel. 4 Marni Nixon. 5 Monte Cassino. 6 False (Louis XIV of France reigned for 72 and Pepi II of Egypt for perhaps as long as 94 years). 7 The loose-fitting cap worn by players in the Australian cricket team. 8 They both suffered from poor eyesight. 9 Passepartout. 10 Cliff Richard.

Round 2

1 William Wallace. 2 The Campbells. 3 Jock Stein. 4 *The Wicker Man*. 5 Rudolf Hess. 6 AC/DC. 7 F. Scott Fitzgerald. 8 Idi Amin. 9 A large fifteenth-century cannon at Edinburgh Castle. 10 False (they continue to play even now, for instance in Basra in 2003).

Half-time teaser   60 (27 English and 33 French or Spanish).

Round 3

1 'Motor' and 'hotel'. 2 Yankee. 3 Underground. 4 Ecstasy. 5 A mole. 6 James Joyce's *Finnegans Wake*. 7 A spoon. 8 Cats. 9 Halcyon. 10 Czech.

Round 4

1 Red. 2 True. 3 The Chippendales. 4 Texas. 5 Bruce Springsteen. 6 Sylvia Plath. 7 Iron Maiden. 8 Anglesey. 9 *A Clockwork Orange*. 10 David Lloyd George.

Jackpot   White with red spots.

Quiz 76 answers

Round 1

1 The Korean War. 2 April. 3 Wear it (it is a form of dress material).
4 *Henry V*. 5 Shirley MacLaine. 6 Milan Kundera. 7 Karate. 8 True
(though women can be carriers). 9 False (it is Northumberland).
10 They show feathers.

Round 2

1 The Watergate Affair. 2 Lester Piggott. 3 The Profumo Affair. 4 Robert
Maxwell. 5 Günter Grass. 6 They raised their fists in black gloves (the
salute of the Black Panthers anti-racist movement) when receiving their
medals. 7 Marseille. 8 Edward Heath. 9 John Brown. 10 The Duke of
Wellington.

Half-time teaser 83 times.

Round 3

1 Thor. 2 The mistral. 3 10. 4 Jesus. 5 Snow Patrol. 6 An Aeolian harp.
7 *Butch Cassidy and the Sundance Kid*. 8 Cirrus. 9 Edward Heath.
10 Divine wind.

Round 4

1 Israel. 2 Puccini. 3 The Bridgewater Four. 4 False (it was Led Zeppelin).
5 Mike Hawthorn. 6 Edgbaston. 7 Tommy Lee Jones. 8 Munchausen's
Syndrome. 9 The *Monitor*. 10 The Khmer Rouge.

Jackpot July.

Quiz 77 answers

....

Round 1

1 Chequers. 2 The Desert Fox. 3 'Octopus's garden'. 4 Arachnophobia.
5 Connacht (also spelt Connaught). 6 True. 7 Egypt. 8 River Phoenix.
9 True. 10 Ronseal wood preservatives.

....

Round 2

1 Watergate. 2 Camp David (called Shangri-La until 1953). 3 Wilson
(Woodrow and Harold). 4 False (President John Quincy Adams was the
son of President John Adams). 5 Jack Nicholson. 6 Ronald Reagan.
7 Franklin D. Roosevelt. 8 The Gettysburg Address (1863). 9 Al Gore.
10 Nothing (his grandfathers both had surnames beginning with S, so this
was a way of honouring both).

....

Half-time teaser   3,605.

....

Round 3

1 Status Quo. 2 Nirvana. 3 The Quarry Men. 4 Björn Again (Abba tribute
band). 5 Bryan Ferry. 6 The Traveling Wilburys. 7 Malcolm McLaren.
8 Birmingham. 9 Slade. 10 Stephen Morrissey.

....

Round 4

1 Frank Sinatra. 2 Royal Academy of Dramatic Art. 3 George Headley.
4 *The X-Files*. 5 The boogie (in the single 'Blame it on the boogie').
6 A coelacanth. 7 Heroin. 8 Grace Kelly. 9 Quentin Tarantino.
10 Arthur Daley.

....

Jackpot   Ho Chi Minh City.

....

Quiz 78 answers

Round 1

1 James Brown. 2 Yew. 3 Canterbury cathedral. 4 Woodrow Wilson.
5 Ibrox stadium. 6 American football. 7 Richard Attenborough. 8 *The Barber of Seville*. 9 The Netherlands. 10 Breadfruit.

Round 2

1 An eyrie. 2 True. 3 A falcon. 4 Penguins. 5 The pheasant. 6 True.
7 Guano. 8 The goldcrest. 9 The gizzard. 10 Storm petrels.

Half-time teaser   637.

Round 3

1 True. 2 St Paul's Cathedral. 3 Colditz. 4 Liverpool. 5 False (Canterbury is the oldest). 6 Castle Howard. 7 Glasgow. 8 Salisbury. 9 Dorset.
10 The keep.

Round 4

1 Michael Jackson's. 2 Casino. 3 The Drifters. 4 Lancashire. 5 The North Sea.
6 Tatum O'Neal. 7 West Ham. 8 A mulligan. 9 Björk. 10 Bungee-jumping.

Jackpot

Pints and quarts (originally an innkeeper's phrase, referring to the chalked-up tally of drinks a person had to pay for).

Quiz 79 answers

Round 1

1 Benny Hill (in the hit single 'Ernie'). 2 Basin Street. 3 Saudi Arabia.
4 Dana. 5 Shredded Wheat. 6 Benito Mussolini. 7 The Tony awards.
8 The Jimi Hendrix Experience. 9 Great Britain. 10 John Ford.

Round 2

1 Oscar Wilde. 2 County Antrim. 3 Paul Hewson. 4 True (seven times up
to 2007). 5 Michael Collins. 6 The Shannon. 7 The Black and Tans.
8 Shergar. 9 Knock. 10 Seamus Heaney.

Half-time Teaser 594 days.

Round 3

1 Peter Shilton (with 125). 2 David Puttnam. 3 Sandy Lyle. 4 Andrew
'Freddie' Flintoff. 5 Swansea. 6 Sonny Liston. 7 The USA (four times).
8 The triple jump. 9 Sir Donald Bradman. 10 Silverstone.

Round 4

1 Scapa Flow. 2 Brian Epstein. 3 The aurora borealis. 4 Kathmandu. 5 The
love-apple. 6 Venus. 7 Alf Garnett. 8 John Steinbeck. 9 Hillary Clinton.
10 Johnny Nash.

Jackpot Haiti.

Quiz 80 answers

Round 1

1 *Macbeth*. 2 Base jumping. 3 Squeeze. 4 Manchester United. 5 Mystery fiction. 6 Honky-tonk. 7 Dean Martin. 8 *Carmen*. 9 Hull. 10 Lord's.

Round 2

1 The liver. 2 The collarbone. 3 The Sphinx. 4 Elizabeth I. 5 The big toe. 6 The retina. 7 The pancreas. 8 Canines. 9 30. 10 23.

Half-time teaser £33,230.

Round 3

1 Major. 2 The English Civil War. 3 The torpedo. 4 The Salvation Army. 5 Douglas Haig. 6 The Crimean War. 7 The Trojan War. 8 Iceland. 9 Tuberculosis. 10 Charles II.

Round 4

1 Gerald Ford. 2 Billy Bragg. 3 Tapping up. 4 The aardvark. 5 The Marx Brothers. 6 Table-tennis. 7 Richard Wagner's. 8 Lacrosse. 9 Bad Manners. 10 Bullfighting.

Jackpot Richard III.

Quiz 81 answers

Round 1

1 Twiggy. 2 Sir Edwin Landseer. 3 Magnus Magnusson. 4 Clara Bow.
5 Tommy Atkins. 6 Blur. 7 Culloden. 8 The dinar. 9 Mrs Robinson. 10 Big
Daddy.

Round 2

1 Spencer Perceval (in 1812). 2 He committed suicide. 3 *Twin Peaks*. 4 The
St Bartholomew's Day Massacre. 5 They all ate poisonous mushrooms.
6 Hungerford. 7 Marvin Gaye. 8 Reinhardt Heydrich. 9 He was stabbed
with a poisoned umbrella. 10 Polonium.

Half-time teaser   88.

Round 3

1 Mortimer Mouse. 2 Bambi. 3 Mel Blanc. 4 Betty Boop. 5 *Top Cat* (also
known in the UK as *Boss Cat*). 6 George Sanders. 7 Charles M. Schulz.
8 Fred Flintstone. 9 William Hanna and Joseph Barbera. 10 The Slag
Brothers.

Round 4

1 The Berlin Wall. 2 Route 66. 3 Sri Lanka. 4 Anita Dobson. 5 The water
closet (an early lavatory). 6 Benjamin Britten. 7 The French. 8 Noo Noo.
9 Al Pacino. 10 Alcatraz.

Jackpot   12.

Quiz 82 answers

Round 1

1 Rolf Harris. **2** Nero. **3** HMS *Belfast*. **4** A number five iron. **5** Iceland.
6 Sandro Botticelli. **7** Fox. **8** 15. **9** Beer and sandwiches. **10** A maiden.

Round 2

1 The town hall. **2** True. **3** Estonia. **4** Chile. **5** Zanzibar. **6** Montevideo.
7 Chicago. **8** Dionne Warwick. **9** Africa. **10** Jordan.

Half-time teaser 76 hours, 40 minutes.

Round 3

1 Mount St Helens. **2** Liverpool and Juventus. **3** Chernobyl. **4** France.
5 Superman. **6** Gareth Southgate. **7** True (as the result of an accidental
collision). **8** He was killed and put in a pie by Mrs MacGregor. **9** Exocet.
10 Schadenfreude.

Round 4

1 W. G. Grace. **2** The Republican Party. **3** Kent. **4** J. M. Barrie (in *Peter
Pan*). **5** Lincoln and the Grand National. **6** Junk. **7** Greg Lemond.
8 Earvin. **9** Commodore. **10** In the dungeon (it is a confined space where
prisoners could be conveniently 'forgotten').

Jackpot Dresden.

Quiz 83 answers

Round 1

1 Valhalla. 2 James Callaghan. 3 The theatre. 4 True. 5 William Hogarth.
6 Madonna. 7 The Ark of the Covenant. 8 Norman Tebbit. 9 False. 10 Six.

Round 2

1 William II (William Rufus). 2 Charles Laughton. 3 Elizabeth I.
4 Edward VII. 5 He was struck on the head by a cricket ball. 6 Anne
Boleyn. 7 Charles I. 8 Richard I (the Lionheart). 9 Martin Luther King.
10 Adam and the Ants.

Half-time teaser £1.57 million.

Round 3

1 Victor Mature. 2 Tony Curtis. 3 Arnold Schwarzenegger. 4 Sean
Connery. 5 George Clooney (nephew of Rosemary Clooney). 6 Bruce
Willis. 7 Johnny Depp. 8 Burt Lancaster. 9 Clint Eastwood. 10 Russell
Crowe.

Round 4

1 Andrex toilet tissue. 2 A red flag. 3 The Kinks. 4 The Long Range Desert
Group. 5 Ned Kelly. 6 Greying, leisured, affluent and married. 7 On a
sailing vessel. 8 Corporal. 9 False (drummer Frank Beard is clean-shaven).
10 Robbie Coltrane.

Jackpot Sergei Diaghilev.

Quiz 84 answers

Round 1

1 The Mersey. 2 Moe's. 3 False. 4 Nitrogen and sulphur. 5 Whitechapel.
6 A rabbit. 7 Daley Thompson. 8 Ronan Keating. 9 The US Civil War.
10 The Milk Cup.

Round 2

1 Fidel Castro. 2 A veteran car. 3 Rosa Parks. 4 *Playboy*. 5 Kenya.
6 The Beat Generation. 7 Stan Mortensen. 8 In a car crash. 9 Andy Capp.
10 Carl Perkins.

Half-time teaser   888.

Round 3

1 Freddie Mercury. 2 Birmingham City. 3 John F. Kennedy (who served on
torpedo boat PT 109). 4 Bill Wyman. 5 Paul Gauguin. 6 Andrew Jackson.
7 Charles Dickens. 8 Stan Laurel. 9 True. 10 Andy Warhol.

Round 4

1 Sand. 2 The Edinburgh Festival. 3 Rallying. 4 The Oklahoma bombing.
5 Hilda. 6 G. 7 1869. 8 Salisbury. 9 Stop playing (or be silent). 10 Monza.

Jackpot   *Nineteen Eighty-four* by George Orwell.

Quiz 85 answers

Round 1

1 Richard Nixon. 2 The Crucifixion. 3 Alan Shearer. 4 Charles Dickens.
5 Sir Henry Wood. 6 The Great Rift Valley. 7 The Chindits. 8 The Shadows.
9 John F. Kennedy International Airport (or JFK). 10 Massachusetts.

Round 2

1 The CIA (Central Intelligence Agency). 2 Q. 3 Sir John Vanbrugh.
4 *ITMA (It's That Man Again)*. 5 Karla. 6 George Blake. 7 Anthony Blunt.
8 Elizabeth I. 9 Timothy Dalton. 10 Alex Rider.

Half-time teaser 266.

Round 3

1 The hermit crab. 2 True. 3 Trigger. 4 T. S. Eliot. 5 The aspidistra (in her
song 'The biggest aspidistra in the world'). 6 False. 7 The Suffragettes.
8 Eric Burdon. 9 Jonah. 10 Stevie Wonder.

Round 4

1 A young child. 2 Tom Baker. 3 Des Lynam. 4 Rambo. 5 Mervyn Peake.
6 Audrey Hepburn. 7 The Colorado River. 8 Côte d'Ivoire (the Ivory Coast).
9 Donald Rumsfeld. 10 Cologne.

Jackpot Birmingham.

Quiz 86 answers

Round 1

1 Black. **2** Nigella Lawson. **3** Russia. **4** *The Yeomen of the Guard.* **5** Mario.
6 He was kidnapped. **7** Ferenc Puskas. **8** 168. **9** Playwright Joe Orton.
10 A holt.

Round 2

1 Greenland. **2** Brazil. **3** Peru. **4** Turkey. **5** Canada. **6** Australia. **7** Bahrain.
8 The UK. **9** Korea. **10** Russia.

Half-time teaser 13 hours, 25 minutes.

Round 3

1 Colour. **2** Jersey. **3** *The X-Files.* **4** Ally McBeal. **5** *Antiques Roadshow.*
6 *Big Brother* (he cheated). **7** Number 42. **8** Holmfirth (in Yorkshire).
9 Martin Clunes and Harry Enfield. **10** *Strictly Come Dancing.*

Round 4

1 Candles. **2** A wig. **3** Therefore. **4** Regent Street. **5** Auric. **6** Winter.
7 Britain. **8** Salisbury. **9** A touchdown. **10** Four.

Jackpot *Paddy Clarke Ha Ha Ha.*

Quiz 87 answers

Round 1

1 The Church of England. **2** The Home Service. **3** Björn Borg. **4** Edinburgh. **5** The Battle of the Somme. **6** Christopher Plummer. **7** *Pal Joey*. **8** An administrative organisation. **9** 'Lara's theme'. **10** None.

Round 2

1 Howard Carter. **2** Wiltshire. **3** Cartouches. **4** Constantine. **5** Corinthian. **6** Colchester. **7** Santorini (otherwise known as Thira). **8** Jason and the Argonauts. **9** The Titans. **10** With a blast of their trumpets.

Half-time teaser 2,467.5 kilograms.

Round 3

1 Del Shannon. **2** 'Back home'. **3** Celine Dion. **4** Telly Savalas. **5** The Boomtown Rats. **6** Luciano Pavarotti. **7** Girls Aloud. **8** Geri Halliwell. **9** Take That. **10** Jimmy Young.

Round 4

1 Sri Lanka. **2** The Grand Old Duke of York. **3** 1961. **4** C. S. Forester. **5** *Orlando*. **6** New York. **7** April. **8** Noël Coward (who also directed the film). **9** Its provenance. **10** Jasper Carrott.

Jackpot Nigel Bruce.

Quiz 88 answers

Round 1

1 Handel. **2** Spain. **3** Chad. **4** Rick Stein. **5** Graceland. **6** R. D. Wingfield.
7 The Isle of Wight. **8** Formic acid. **9** The M6. **10** The dead man's handle.

Round 2

1 Anne Hathaway. **2** Prince Edward (the Earl of Wessex). **3** Lilith.
4 Timothy Laurence. **5** Maryland. **6** Raisa. **7** Mel Brooks. **8** Anthony
Newley. **9** Jane Asher. **10** *The Mayor of Casterbridge*.

Half-time teaser   399.

Round 3

1 Sedgefield. **2** Gerry Adams. **3** The Conservative Party. **4** Donald Dewar.
5 Trident. **6** CND (Campaign for Nuclear Disarmament). **7** Norman
Lamont. **8** New Hampshire. **9** 35. **10** Vladimir Putin.

Round 4

1 Yellow. **2** A young salmon. **3** Pittsburgh. **4** 12. **5** Little Bighorn. **6** Finnish.
7 Alaska. **8** Leon Spinks. **9** Williams-Renault. **10** The Spanish Civil War.

Jackpot   James Earl Ray.

Quiz 89 answers

....

Round 1

1 King Arthur. **2** Iain Duncan Smith. **3** Italy. **4** Marengo. **5** Hawaii.
6 A bell-tower. **7** Baftas. **8** In front of the Louvre in Paris. **9** Johnny Haynes.
10 (Mary Beth) Lacey.

....

Round 2

1 'Rock around the clock'. **2** True. **3** The first international beauty contest.
4 Billiards. **5** Derby County (in 1946). **6** David Lloyd George. **7** 1893.
8 Len Hutton. **9** She became Britain's first woman to be elected as an MP.
10 Mark Twain.

....

Half-time teaser   5,034.

....

Round 3

1 True. **2** 13. **3** Room 101. **4** 1,000. **5** Four. **6** 42. **7** Public Enemy
Number One. **8** Number eights. **9** 99. **10** 666.

....

Round 4

1 Mr Micawber (in *David Copperfield*). **2** *Absolutely Fabulous*. **3** Bebop.
4 Carlsberg. **5** The Three Graces. **6** The Treaty of Versailles. **7** The Vietnam
War. **8** Newly-baked bread. **9** Jim Callaghan. **10** The Humber Bridge.

....

Jackpot   Borley Rectory.

....

Quiz 90 answers

Round 1

1 Australia. 2 Water. 3 The Super Bowl (in American football). 4 Senator Joseph McCarthy. 5 Liberace. 6 A supporting structure in buildings. 7 Female. 8 Mary I. 9 Rwanda. 10 An operetta has spoken dialogue.

Round 2

1 John. 2 Market place. 3 The Cinque Ports. 4 Bath. 5 The Crown. 6 HandMade Films. 7 Mr White. 8 Norbert. 9 Cambodia. 10 Reginald.

Half-time teaser 8 hours, 32 minutes.

Round 3

1 Pluto. 2 Diana Ross. 3 Richard Gere. 4 *Little Women*. 5 *Charley's Aunt*. 6 Russia. 7 Sullivan. 8 The Olivier. 9 Alfie. 10 *Carousel*.

Round 4

1 Insulin. 2 From oil. 3 Prince Charles. 4 Spanish. 5 Coral. 6 Alain Prost. 7 Angles. 8 Hollyhocks. 9 The England and Wales Cricket Board (ECB). 10 Rowing.

Jackpot Isambard Kingdom Brunel.

Quiz 91 answers

Round 1

1 Aslan. 2 *The Archers*. 3 Fred Perry. 4 Culture Club. 5 *The Ladykillers*.
6 Basra. 7 Jess. 8 Amnesty International. 9 Underwater. 10 Getafix.

Round 2

1 It was a power station. 2 *The Angel of the North*. 3 Collage. 4 David
Hockney. 5 Charles Saatchi. 6 Damien Hirst. 7 Francis Bacon. 8 Jacob
Epstein. 9 Jackson Pollock. 10 The Guggenheim Museum.

Half-time teaser   137.

Round 3

1 Procul Harum. 2 A White Anglo-Saxon Protestant. 3 Michael Caine.
4 King Arthur. 5 Gilbert White. 6 Cilla Black. 7 The White Ship. 8 Jimmy
White. 9 Barry White. 10 'Satisfaction' (by the Rolling Stones).

Round 4

1 K2. 2 Alfred Nobel. 3 Airborne warning and control. 4 The Cenotaph.
5 Marlon Brando. 6 Louis Armstrong. 7 The Lord Mayor of the City of
London. 8 Dr Hook. 9 Joe Frazier. 10 'Abide with me'.

Jackpot   *In the Heat of the Night.*

Quiz 92 answers

Round 1

1 Caffeine. 2 Monaco. 3 Light winds. 4 The 100 metres hurdles. 5 He is a Roman Catholic priest. 6 A cob. 7 Ruth Ellis. 8 44. 9 Golf. 10 The Brownies (younger female members of the Scouting Association).

Round 2

1 Jill Dando. 2 At the Reichenbach Falls. 3 Robert De Niro. 4 A cat burglar. 5 Church bells. 6 John Wilkes Booth. 7 The Great Train Robbery. 8 *Crime and Punishment*. 9 James Gandolfini. 10 Bob Marley.

Half-time teaser   153.6 miles.

Round 3

1 Karl Dönitz. 2 London. 3 Clement Attlee. 4 *Passport to Pimlico*. 5 Coventry cathedral. 6 The geodesic dome. 7 The ball burst. 8 He was the first man to break the sound barrier. 9 Christian Dior. 10 'From the cradle to the grave'.

Round 4

1 A typhoon. 2 Montana. 3 1975. 4 Anderson shelters. 5 Morris. 6 Eric Clapton. 7 The Rank Organisation. 8 Snapdragons. 9 Bordeaux. 10 Three.

Jackpot   Neil Simon.

Quiz 93 answers

Round 1

1 'Wannabe'. 2 Gene Wilder. 3 Alton Towers. 4 A form of Indonesian music. 5 Iago. 6 The anglepoise. 7 *Rising Damp*. 8 That World War II was over. 9 Glass. 10 Vietnam.

Round 2

1 The electric chair. 2 1955. 3 He was a doctor. 4 Albert Pierrepoint. 5 *Dead Man Walking*. 6 Judge Jeffreys. 7 True. 8 Gary Gilmore. 9 Tsar Nicholas II. 10 Sydney Carton.

Half-time teaser   256.

Round 3

1 Baseball. 2 Kenneth Wolstenholme. 3 Italy. 4 The World Cup. 5 Albania. 6 LA Galaxy. 7 Jim Clark. 8 Shorts. 9 Dressage. 10 Christopher Chataway.

Round 4

1 True. 2 Iran. 3 Lurcio. 4 Harold Wilson. 5 'Peggy Sue'. 6 Mrs Slocombe (played by Mollie Sugden). 7 Al Fatah. 8 The Parachute Regiment. 9 *Jackanory*. 10 Michael Crichton.

Jackpot   The accordion.

Quiz 94 answers

Round 1

1 Mount Ararat. 2 Campaign for Real Ale. 3 Its height. 4 Louis XVI. 5 True. 6 Harold Abrahams. 7 Baedeker. 8 Russia. 9 Mia Farrow. 10 Alan Bradley.

Round 2

1 Wolves. 2 The king cobra. 3 Sheep. 4 A fish. 5 One. 6 A lodge. 7 A bird. 8 A piebald. 9 Pigs. 10 Butterflies.

Half-time teaser   165 kilograms.

Round 3

1 George III. 2 Steve Davis. 3 The Black Watch. 4 Stormin' Norman. 5 Queen Anne. 6 Charles II. 7 The Bhoys. 8 General Patton. 9 The Kiwis. 10 Tom Finney.

Round 4

1 Dublin. 2 Cat. 3 Flora Macdonald. 4 Italy. 5 Michael Hutchence. 6 The tsetse fly. 7 Canada. 8 Steffi Graf. 9 Rio Ferdinand. 10 *All the President's Men.*

Jackpot   The SAS (Special Air Service).

Quiz 95 answers

Round 1

1 World War II. 2 Life. 3 The Salvation Army. 4 'The Londonderry Air'.
5 Bing Crosby. 6 The Battle of Towton (1461). 7 22. 8 Miss Price.
9 Electro-Convulsive Therapy. 10 Napoleon.

Round 2

1 *It Ain't Half Hot Mum.* 2 Auntie. 3 Sibelius. 4 *Blake's 7.* 5 *Opportunity Knocks.* 6 *Blue Peter.* 7 Aidensfield. 8 'Whispering' Bob Harris. 9 *Ready, Steady, Go!* 10 Royston Vasey.

Half-time teaser   4,320.

Round 3

1 Carnaby Street. 2 Window shopping. 3 Gerald Ratner. 4 Campbell's.
5 It is a cake (and thus taxed less heavily). 6 1937. 7 Lyle's Golden Syrup.
8 Wal-Mart. 9 ASDA. 10 Marie Lloyd.

Round 4

1 '. . . Then I'll begin' (the opening of the BBC radio programme *Listen with Mother*). 2 *Carmina Burana.* 3 Jerusalem. 4 Tennessee Williams. 5 *Revolver.*
6 Honduras and El Salvador. 7 Theodore Roosevelt. 8 Stephen Potter.
9 Blackpool. 10 The bar.

Jackpot   Richard Strauss.

Quiz 96 answers

Round 1

1 Greece. **2** Brazil, Colombia and Ecuador. **3** Salman Rushdie. **4** Britney Spears (to Jason Allen Alexander). **5** Blue. **6** Cumbria. **7** Scrabble. **8** Fish. **9** Manchester. **10** Boxing.

Round 2

1 The Bay of Biscay. **2** Helvetia. **3** The Netherlands. **4** Portugal. **5** Liechtenstein. **6** Jean-Claude Van Damme. **7** None. **8** Estonia. **9** The Danube. **10** Finland (last on eight occasions).

Half-time teaser 25 hours, 25 minutes.

Round 3

1 Ice hockey. **2** Polo. **3** Curling. **4** Table-tennis. **5** Australian Rules football. **6** Lance Armstrong. **7** Bullfighting. **8** Darts. **9** Lacrosse. **10** Wipe-out.

Round 4

1 Hops. **2** Mother Teresa. **3** Cambodia. **4** General Douglas MacArthur. **5** Bailey bridges. **6** Thierry Henry. **7** Montserrat. **8** An obelisk. **9** C. S. Lewis. **10** Geri Halliwell.

Jackpot The Balfour Declaration.

Quiz 97 answers

Round 1

1 Manderley. **2** True. **3** Skegness. **4** Gloucestershire. **5** Salem, Massachusetts. **6** He was a mailman. **7** Israel. **8** St Petersburg. **9** Twickenham rugby football ground. **10** Steve Martin.

Round 2

1 Carl Douglas. **2** (West) German. **3** The Carpenters. **4** Video (in the 1979 single 'Video killed the radio star'). **5** Paper Lace. **6** Phil Collins. **7** Rod Stewart. **8** Anni-Frid Lyngstad (the brunette). **9** Bay City Rollers. **10** The Brighouse and Rastrick Brass Band.

Half-time teaser 26.

Round 3

1 Tagliatelle. **2** The Sun. **3** Shrove Tuesday. **4** 'A nice Chianti'. **5** The Who. **6** Champagne. **7** Beef Wellington. **8** The potato crisp. **9** A Bloody Mary. **10** Supertramp.

Round 4

1 Dave Edmunds. **2** Bilbo Baggins. **3** Le Corbusier. **4** Buddha. **5** Dover. **6** Sting. **7** The Brown Bess. **8** Right Said Fred. **9** Doctor Cameron. **10** Neil Morrissey.

Jackpot Isak Dinesen (Karen Blixen).

Quiz 98 answers

Round 1

1 New Zealand. 2 *Casualty*. 3 270. 4 *Rosencrantz and Guildenstern Are Dead*. 5 Rod Laver. 6 General Galtieri. 7 King's Cross. 8 Genghis Khan. 9 Mars. 10 Reading.

Round 2

1 The National Gallery. 2 Pablo Picasso. 3 The vanishing point. 4 False (they actually went up). 5 Goya. 6 Hans Holbein. 7 Impasto. 8 Tintoretto. 9 Henri Rousseau. 10 His left ear.

Half-time teaser 23.11.

Round 3

1 Alfred the Great. 2 James I. 3 Her Golden Jubilee. 4 Henry VII. 5 Henry VIII. 6 James II. 7 Eleanor (of Castile). 8 George IV. 9 Fotheringhay. 10 Prince Andrew.

Round 4

1 New Zealand. 2 The Boston crab. 3 Myanmar. 4 The Book of Common Prayer. 5 Everton. 6 Belgium. 7 Sonny Bono (of Sonny and Cher). 8 Nightwatchman. 9 1895. 10 Costa Rica.

Jackpot 17.

Quiz 99 answers

Round 1

1 The Richter scale. **2** Jim Henson. **3** Billy Joel. **4** A panther. **5** John Ford. **6** The pole vault. **7** West Point. **8** Humphrey Bogart. **9** Chile. **10** Fairy Liquid.

Round 2

1 D. W. Griffith. **2** Steve Biko's. **3** Bonnie and Clyde (Bonnie Parker and Clyde Barrow). **4** The Netherlands. **5** *Breakfast at Tiffany's.* **6** *The Bridge on the River Kwai.* **7** George Raft. **8** Tom Hanks (for *Philadelphia* and *Forrest Gump*). **9** Jake LaMotta. **10** Truman Capote (in *Capote*).

Half-time teaser   60.

Round 3

1 Acker Bilk. **2** *Desert Island Discs.* **3** Martha and the Muffins. **4** A starfish. **5** Thor Heyerdahl. **6** The Blue Riband. **7** Anti-Submarine Detection Investigation Committee. **8** The Pacific. **9** *Jaws.* **10** Steve Irwin.

Round 4

1 Chain smoker. **2** Superman. **3** Lee Majors. **4** Tokyo. **5** Jacqueline du Pré. **6** Matthias. **7** J. M. Coetzee or Peter Carey. **8** *The Tempest.* **9** Spandau Ballet. **10** Jemini.

Jackpot   *The Day of the Triffids* by John Wyndham.

Quiz 100 answers

Round 1

1 Bangladesh. 2 They were both born on 29 February and thus have had fewer birthdays. 3 Emil Zatopek. 4 Foo Fighters. 5 Alfred Wainwright. 6 Seven. 7 Brutalism. 8 Shinty. 9 The camera obscura. 10 Cabbage.

Round 2

1 Jesse Owens. 2 Suffolk. 3 Arsenal. 4 Appeasement. 5 The Ramblers' Association. 6 The RR monogram on the bonnet was changed from red to black. 7 1934. 8 Guernica. 9 He was assassinated. 10 The *Hindenburg*.

Half-time teaser   228.

Round 3

1 Capricorn. 2 *The Tempest*. 3 India and Pakistan. 4 'Down at the Old Bull and Bush'. 5 A bayonet. 6 Dreamt. 7 London. 8 *The Mystery of Edwin Drood*. 9 *The Italian Job*. 10 *Gone With the Wind*.

Round 4

1 The Avon. 2 A shallow basket used by gardeners. 3 Edinburgh. 4 Claude Monet. 5 Sopwith. 6 Zinédine Zidane. 7 The thigh bone (femur). 8 Motor-racing. 9 Boscastle. 10 Ford Madox Brown.

Jackpot   Tamla Records (which became Tamla Motown).

New Year quiz answers

Round 1

1 Hogmanay. **2** First-footing. **3** Robert Burns. **4** Garnet. **5** Rosh Hashanah. **6** Twelfth Night (or Old Christmas Day or Epiphany). **7** Eel. **8** Ernie Wise. **9** 1973. **10** The flooding of the Nile.

Round 2

1 Capricorn. **2** Paul Revere. **3** Pierre de Coubertin. **4** E. M. Forster. **5** Oslo. **6** J. D. Salinger. **7** J. Edgar Hoover. **8** The euro. **9** The Rose Bowl (American football). **10** The Czech Republic and Slovakia.

Half-time teaser   8,513.

Round 3

1 Fred West. **2** Hank Williams. **3** *The Times*. **4** Dashiell Hammett. **5** The Joker. **6** Haiti. **7** Atatürk (Father of the Turks). **8** Cigarette advertising. **9** Albany. **10** Slaves.

Round 4

1 The millennium bug. **2** Empress of India. **3** U2. **4** True (in the northern hemisphere). **5** Dr Watson. **6** He announced that he was not a god. **7** The Beatles (they were turned down). **8** Samuel Pepys. **9** X-rays. **10** 'Heartbreak Hotel'.

Jackpot   Eggs.

St Valentine's Day quiz answers

Round 1

1 14 February. **2** Claudius II. **3** True. **4** The feast of Lupercalia. **5** Absence.
6 He sent the first Valentine's Day card. **7** Chicago. **8** Leonardo DiCaprio.
9 The Beckhams. **10** 26.

Round 2

1 They were first cousins. **2** Kurt Cobain. **3** Seven. **4** David Furnish.
5 Mariah Carey. **6** Guinevere. **7** Prince Rainier of Monaco. **8** Jude Law.
9 Sharon. **10** Richard Madeley and Judy Finnigan.

Half-time teaser £22 million.

Round 3

1 Kate Winslet. **2** Catherine Earnshaw. **3** Deborah Kerr. **4** Andie
MacDowell. **5** Renée Zellwegger. **6** Colin Firth. **7** *Love Story*. **8** *Shirley
Valentine*. **9** Rhett Butler. **10** Edward Rochester.

Round 4

1 Paris. **2** Henry VIII. **3** The Man in Black. **4** Cupid. **5** True. **6** Teachers.
7 D. H. Lawrence. **8** Oranges. **9** Venice. **10** Rodgers and Hart.

Jackpot Nancy Mitford.

St David's Day quiz answers

Round 1

1 1 March. **2** The daffodil. **3** 'Land of my fathers'. **4** Seaweed. **5** Red, white and green. **6** Offa's Dyke. **7** Llewelyn. **8** Plaid Cymru. **9** Bangor. **10** Eat it (it is a variety of fruit bread).

Round 2

1 The National Eisteddfod. **2** Sir Geraint Evans. **3** Ivor Novello. **4** Tom Jones. **5** Charlotte Church. **6** Shakin' Stevens. **7** 'Total eclipse of the heart'. **8** Shirley Bassey. **9** The Manic Street Preachers. **10** Harry Secombe.

Half-time teaser   750 miles.

Round 3

1 Wrexham. **2** Snooker. **3** The Dragons. **4** Glamorgan. **5** The Bluebirds. **6** 2005. **7** Colin Jackson. **8** Motor-racing (both were Formula One drivers). **9** Gareth Thomas (with 37). **10** Joe Calzaghe.

Round 4

1 Cymru. **2** Edward I. **3** Owen Glendower. **4** Snowdon. **5** Anglesey. **6** Black and gold. **7** Rob Brydon. **8** Terry Jones. **9** Caerleon. **10** Sir Anthony Hopkins.

Jackpot   'Stranger' or 'foreigner'.

St Patrick's Day quiz answers

Round 1

1 17 March. 2 The shamrock (three-leaved clover). 3 He was captured by raiders and sold as a slave. 4 In Downpatrick (under Down Cathedral). 5 False (it has one reptile, the common lizard). 6 Hibernia or Scotia. 7 Green, orange and white (or green, white and gold). 8 The Liffey. 9 Eire. 10 1801.

Round 2

1 Munster. 2 Six. 3 Limerick. 4 Kilkenny. 5 Malin Head. 6 County Kerry. 7 Its prehistoric remains. 8 Horses. 9 Mountains. 10 Donegal Bay.

Half-time teaser 31.

Round 3

1 False (he never won it). 2 Clannad. 3 Father Dougal McGuire. 4 Sinéad O'Connor. 5 Richard Harris. 6 George Best. 7 Eamon De Valera. 8 Jonathan Swift. 9 Liam Neeson. 10 J. M. Synge.

Round 4

1 The 1840s. 2 Harp. 3 The Chieftains. 4 Potatoes. 5 The Celtic Tiger. 6 15. 7 1990. 8 Play it (it is a drum). 9 The Good Friday Agreement. 10 Tara.

Jackpot Hurling (the *caman* is the hurling stick and the *sliotar* the ball).

Mother's Day quiz answers

Round 1

1 Mother Goose. 2 Mother Teresa. 3 George Formby. 4 Pink Floyd. 5 Lily of the valley. 6 Ronnie Corbett. 7 Saddam Hussein. 8 Danny DeVito (with the help of Billy Crystal). 9 Motherwell. 10 Mother Courage.

Round 2

1 Judy Garland. 2 Queen Mary. 3 Sarah Ferguson ('Fergie'). 4 Joan Crawford. 5 Debbie Reynolds. 6 Victoria Beckham. 7 Leda. 8 Elizabeth Bowes-Lyon. 9 John the Baptist. 10 Gwyneth Paltrow.

Half-time teaser   69 (borne by Mrs Feodor Vassilyev between 1725 and 1765).

Round 3

1 Simnel cake. 2 Pears soap. 3 Mother-of-pearl. 4 Chocolate. 5 Imperial Leather. 6 Amber. 7 Musk. 8 The poinsettia. 9 Thornton's. 10 Christian Dior.

Round 4

1 Al Jolson. 2 Paul Simon. 3 Cinderella. 4 Abba. 5 Imhotep. 6 Mummers' plays. 7 Tutankhamun. 8 The Mamas and the Papas. 9 A bone. 10 *It Ain't Half Hot Mum*

Jackpot   The Mumbles.

St George's Day quiz answers

Round 1

1 23 April. 2 Red. 3 303. 4 Hungary. 5 False. 6 A red rose. 7 'Jerusalem'. 8 The Order of the Garter. 9 The Roman army. 10 William Shakespeare.

Round 2

1 Tintagel. 2 Robin Hood. 3 Edward Elgar. 4 True. 5 16. 6 The Scots. 7 Napoleon. 8 Vera Lynn. 9 *Richard II*. 10 Country lane.

Half-time teaser   158.

Round 3

1 George III. 2 George Smiley. 3 George Best. 4 A tortoise. 5 George Clooney. 6 Brendan Fraser. 7 Boy George. 8 George Sand. 9 Susan George. 10 George Gershwin.

Round 4

1 Georgia. 2 A lance. 3 The Crusaders. 4 He was beheaded. 5 St Edmund. 6 Windsor Castle. 7 Henry V. 8 Miguel de Cervantes. 9 Royal Automobile Club. 10 St Peter.

Jackpot   Edward III.

Father's Day quiz answers

Round 1

1 June. 2 St Joseph's Day (23 March). 3 The child. 4 Cole Porter. 5 *The Tempest*. 6 Madonna. 7 The English Civil War. 8 Steve Martin. 9 Jazz. 10 Haiti.

Round 2

1 Hippocrates. 2 Computing. 3 Martin Sheen. 4 Scott Joplin. 5 John Logie Baird. 6 Izaak Walton. 7 Graham Hill. 8 Ernest Rutherford. 9 Igor Sikorsky. 10 Herodotus.

Half-time teaser   85.

Round 3

1 Ferrari. 2 Mackeson. 3 Status Quo. 4 He invented the Miss World competition. 5 Trevor (the name of the founder of the TVR sports car company, Trevor Wilkinson). 6 Neckties. 7 Liz Hurley. 8 Liquid crystal display. 9 Golf. 10 Manchester United.

Round 4

1 1908. 2 Richard Nixon. 3 The Mississippi (the child is the Missouri). 4 A scythe. 5 Private Frazer. 6 King Lear. 7 Gloucestershire. 8 *Mayflower*. 9 Father Ted (Crilly). 10 Idi Amin.

Jackpot   (the Venerable) Bede.

Hallowe'en quiz answers

....

Round 1

1 Trick or treat. 2 Ireland. 3 Samhain. 4 A coven. 5 Lancashire. 6 Hogwarts.
7 Edgar Allan Poe. 8 Abraham Lincoln. 9 A man-eating plant. 10 Matthew
Hopkins.

....

Round 2

1 *The Shining*. 2 Michael Myers. 3 Don't get them wet or feed them after
midnight. 4 *The Cat and the Canary*. 5 Lon Chaney (Senior). 6 *The Blair
Witch Project*. 7 Vincent Price. 8 *Night of the Living Dead*. 9 He is burned
to death. 10 *Carry On Screaming*.

....

Half-time teaser 70.

....

Round 3

1 Bram Stoker. 2 Vlad the Impaler. 3 Bela Lugosi. 4 Ray Reardon. 5 Sarah
Michelle Gellar. 6 *Nosferatu*. 7 Jonathan Harker. 8 Garlic. 9 Whitby.
10 True.

....

Round 4

1 Mary Shelley. 2 Spiders. 3 Narnia. 4 Boris Karloff. 5 *Most Haunted*.
6 Three. 7 Poltergeist. 8 The west. 9 The werewolf. 10 Because he had no
body to go with.

....

Jackpot Horace Walpole.

....

St Andrew's Day quiz answers

Round 1

1 30 November. 2 White. 3 The Order of the Thistle. 4 St Peter (otherwise called Simon Peter). 5 He was a fisherman. 6 Italy. 7 The tenth century. 8 St Andrews. 9 Fishmongers. 10 Edinburgh.

Round 2

1 In Edinburgh. 2 Orkney. 3 The Antonine Wall. 4 Jacobites. 5 Rockall. 6 True. 7 *Trainspotting*. 8 Prestwick. 9 James Boswell. 10 Thomas.

Half-time teaser 154.

Round 3

1 Julie Andrews. 2 Andy Murray. 3 Andrew Jackson. 4 Peter André. 5 Blue and white. 6 Dana Andrews. 7 Eamonn Andrews (in *This Is Your Life*). 8 False. 9 Andy Warhol. 10 Andy Kershaw.

Round 4

1 Saltire. 2 The Royal Navy. 3 Air Force One. 4 Menzies Campbell. 5 Henry Fielding. 6 Archie Andrews. 7 Holyroodhouse. 8 Hampden Park. 9 The M 8. 10 2006.

Jackpot HMS *Invincible*.

Christmas quiz answers

....

Round 1

1 Balthazar, Melchior and Caspar. 2 Turkey. 3 Jacob Marley. 4 St Stephen.
5 Norway. 6 Pauline Fowler's. 7 Advent. 8 1914. 9 Epiphany. 10 Raymond
Briggs.

....

Round 2

1 Irving Berlin. 2 Wenceslas. 3 'Mistletoe and wine'. 4 Thanksgiving.
5 364. 6 St Winifred's School Choir. 7 A blackbird. 8 A button.
9 Two front teeth. 10 Everybody.

....

Half-time teaser 1895.

....

Round 3

1 The Christmas card. 2 Mistletoe. 3 Christingle. 4 Prince Albert.
5 *Aladdin*. 6 Kevin. 7 Holly. 8 George V (in 1932). 9 The Christmas
cracker. 10 The yule log.

....

Round 4

1 A big, red india-rubber ball. 2 Lancer. 3 Bedford Falls. 4 Poinsettia.
5 Eat it (it was a spiced porridge once eaten at Christmas). 6 J. R. R. Tolkien.
7 Lapland (or the North Pole). 8 An invisibility cloak. 9 Macy's.
10 Bob Cratchit.

....

Jackpot 'The night before Christmas'.

....

Answer sheet

Team name

Round 1	Round 2
1	1
2	2
3	3
4	4
5	5
6	6
7	7
8	8
9	9
10	10

Half-time teaser

Round 3	Round 4
1	1
2	2
3	3
4	4
5	5
6	6
7	7
8	8
9	9
10	10

Jackpot

Total